# WRITING FOR THE TWENTY-FIRST CENTURY

## COMPUTERS AND RESEARCH WRITING

# Writing

## FOR THE TWENTY-FIRST CENTURY

### COMPUTERS AND RESEARCH WRITING

**William Wresch**　　**Donald Pattow**　　**James Gifford**

*University of Wisconsin–Stevens Point*

**McGRAW-HILL BOOK COMPANY**

New York　St. Louis　San Francisco　Auckland　Bogotá　Caracas
Colorado Springs　Hamburg　Lisbon　London　Madrid　Mexico　Milan
Montreal　New Delhi　Oklahoma City　Panama　Paris　San Juan
São Paulo　Singapore　Sydney　Tokyo　Toronto

### Writing for the Twenty-First Century: Computers and Research Writing

1234567890 DOCDOC 89321098

ISBN 0-07-072051-7

This book was set in Aster by the College
Composition Unit in cooperation with Better Graphics.
The editors were Emily Barrosse and David Dunham;
the designer was Joan Greenfield;
the production supervisor was Leroy A. Young.
The drawings were done by Wellington Studios, Ltd.
The cover photograph was provided by Orion Press/FPG.
R.R. Donnelley & Sons Company was printer and binder.

LIBRARY OF CONGRESS
Library of Congress Cataloging-in-Publication Data

Wresch, William, (date).
    Writing for the twenty-first century: computers and research
writing / William Wresch, Donald Pattow, James Gifford.
        p.     cm.
    Bibliography: p.
    Includes index.
    ISBN 0-07-072051-7
    1. English language—Rhetoric—Data processing. 2. Report
writing—Data processing.   3. Data base searching.   4. Word
processing in education.    I. Pattow, Donald.    II. Gifford, James.
III. Title
PE1408.W75  1988
808'.042'0285—dc19        87-27783
                        CIP

# ABOUT THE AUTHORS

**William Wresch** taught freshman composition for ten years. He is the author of two books on the role of computers in writing instruction: *The Computer in Composition Instruction* (NCTE), and *Practical Guide to Computer Uses in the English/Language Arts Classroom* (Prentice-Hall). His program "Writer's Helper" (Conduit) is being used in over 2,000 high schools and colleges to improve prewriting and revising. His television course, "Electric Language," has been shown throughout the country. He is currently the chair of the Department of Mathematics and Computing at the University of Wisconsin—Stevens Point, where he teaches courses in the educational use of computers.

**Donald Pattow** is Professor of English and Director of Freshman English at the University of Wisconsin—Stevens Point. He is also Coordinator of the Writing Emphasis Program, in which students take two writing-emphasis classes in other disciplines. He has conducted extensive in-service programs in interdisciplinary writing at high schools and colleges and has also presented papers on writing across the curriculum at regional and national conferences. He has published articles on composition, mystery literature, and adolescent literature and frequently serves as writing consultant to publishing, industrial, and service organizations.

**James Gifford** is Professor of English and Coordinator of Technical Writing at the University of Wisconsin—Stevens Point. He holds a joint appointment in the Department of Mathematics and Computing, where he teaches word processing, computer graphics, and systems documentation. He has presented papers at numerous conventions and is also writing a study of fantasy author Katherine Kurtz for Starmont Publishers.

# CONTENTS

# PREFACE

**W**riting, especially writing based on research, has changed dramatically in the last several years. This text recognizes that research isn't done the way it was ten years ago, or even five years ago. There are new tools, new skills, and a heavy reliance on computer storage and processing of data. Writers will have to learn how to use those new tools. They will either learn in a composition class or they will learn on their own.

This text tries to help writers learn to use the new computer-based tools while it helps them learn to do good research writing. The text is primarily intended for first-year composition courses involving research writing. Colleges that use a two-semester sequence will find this book appropriate for the second semester. Colleges that have only one composition course may want to supplement this book with a standard handbook. While this text is primarily intended for introductory writing courses, the concepts and approaches it presents may also be useful in more advanced writing courses where computer-aided writing is becoming commonplace.

The purpose of this text is to teach a method of research writing that makes full use of current writing and research tools. Such tools include online databases, word processors, outliners, spelling checkers, style checkers, spreadsheets, and graphics generators. Students are not required to use all these tools or to rely exclusively on them if others happen to be available on a given campus. But given the pervasive presence of such tools in professional writing, and given the increasing access to them on college campuses, it seems improper to pretend that such tools don't exist and to continue teaching writing as if nothing had changed in the last decade.

Besides describing the appropriate use of current technology, this text explores the manner in which the new tools change the process of writing itself. With a word processor, it is now easy to start writing at the end of a text rather than sequentially. With a spelling checker, spelling concerns can be left for later. With a graph generator, numeric information can be displayed in ways that not only clarify meaning for a reader, but help a writer analyze possible explanations or implications. With a style checker, writers have additional methods for matching writing to a given audience.

So these new tools not only change what writers use to write, but also how they approach a writing task. The first example of this occurs when writers begin to gather research materials. An online database makes vast quantities of information available instantly. The problem for users is not the old one of finding data—a process that could take days or weeks of digging. Rather, the problem is selecting which of thousands of sources are most useful. Finding appropriate combinations of key words and scanning numerous abstracts are required activities now. New tools, new skills, new approaches to writing.

To describe these new tools and new activities, this book devotes a chapter to each of six groups of activities. Here is a simple outline for the book:

Chapter 1 describes the general purposes and processes of research writing. It also contains an overview of the six categories of writing skills: gathering information, analyzing information, writing the first draft, revising, editing, and presentation of the research.

Chapter 2 reviews research writing situations and outlines the major forms they take.

Chapter 3 focuses on information gathering. It includes information on card catalog and index uses, online database retrieval, as well as other means of gathering information such as the personal database and the word processor.

Chapter 4 explains several means of analyzing numeric and non-numeric data. For numeric information it explains the uses of spreadsheets and graphics generators. For nonnumeric information it describes the use of personal databases and rhetorical questioning programs.

Chapter 5 reviews drafting approaches, from the transfer of outliner and database information to the efficient uses of word processors.

Chapter 6 describes the primary concerns of revising—for coherence, clarity, and sufficiency—and shows how revision can be aided by various tools. A special effort is made to describe how style checkers and a word processor's search and replace function can aid in matching writing to readers.

Chapter 7 covers editing. In this chapter students are shown a system of final checks for correctness using manual and computer-based tools appropriate to the discipline for which they are writing. One section of the chapter describes how certain conventions vary between APA, MLA, and CBE. Another section details the strengths and dangers of computer spelling checkers.

Chapter 8 describes the issue of presentation, including the appropriate use of graphics, abstracts, the value of explanatory footnotes, and the standard concern for footnote and bibliography forms.

Appendix A contains the final versions of the three reports used as examples throughout the text.

Appendix B contains a brief description of MLA and APA documentation formats.

Appendix C describes particular computer programs useful to writers.

To help clarify how research writing can best be done, the text uses three recurring examples. The first describes how certain classes of Southern officers were more likely to resign from the U.S. Navy and join the Confederate Navy. The second explores the current interpretations of evolution. The last follows the critical interpretations of Emily Dickinson's "I Heard a Fly Buzz When I Died." The examples were chosen to give a balance to the book—one humanist, one social science, one natural science—and to show the full range of sources and skills used in research writing. Actual data and early drafts of the reports are used throughout the book so students can follow the development of these examples in detail.

While the text describes numerous writing activities and shows how these activities work together in a total system, it does not demand a set sequence of activities. This is no "assembly line" text that assumes *one* writing process consisting of six steps ending in a research paper. The primary skills in research writing are described and grouped, but they are not ordered. The recursive nature of writing is recognized and described. Students are shown a set of activities and allowed to choose those appropriate to their task.

Teachers are also not forced into a specific computer or piece of software. In general, instructors will want a word processor with which they are comfortable. If their computer writing lab also has a simple spreadsheet and database, they may want to use them with selected students in certain writing situations. Any of the "integrated" programs currently available at substantial student discounts would work with this text. Other helpful software are computer prewriters, style checkers, and spelling checkers, all of which are optional and should be used only if students and instructors find them accessible and simple to use. One other source to seriously consider is the online database. While such services are still relatively expensive, these information sources will be a primary resource for students as they move into professional studies. Some discussion of these systems and at least a brief demonstration of their use seems appropriate even for first-year students.

A comment on time. If students use most of the computer programs described in this text, they may find that it takes them longer to write a report than it might have taken in the past. It should. The computer search will save them many hours in the library, but they will now have more data than usual to interpret and describe. Graphics programs may lead to more insightful analysis of data, but generating graphics is an additional step that may take novices half an hour per graph. Word processors may make revisions easier, but the style checker programs should make students more aware of revisions that need to be made. Efforts at improving presentation will make papers easier to read but will require additional time of writers. In sum, the computer will shorten the time necessary for some trivial tasks, but it will increase the number of higher-level tasks writers will perform. The result will be better papers but little time savings. Students should have no illusions that the procedures described in this text will somehow take the work out of writing. The focus of effort will change—not the quantity required.

We would like to express our thanks for the many useful comments and suggestions provided by colleagues who reviewed this text during the course of its development, especially to Judith Bechtel, Northern Kentucky University; Stephen Bernhardt, New Mexico State University; Dolores Burton, Boston University; Patricia Graves, Georgia State University; Barbara J. Griffin, University of Richmond; George Miller, University of Delaware; Donald Ross, University of Minnesota; and Edward Versluis, South Oregon State College. And we would also like to thank our colleague, Judy Peplinski, for testing the book with her students.

William Wresch
Donald Pattow
James Gifford

# WRITING FOR THE TWENTY-FIRST CENTURY

## COMPUTERS AND RESEARCH WRITING

# Chapter 1

# RESEARCH WRITING: THE PROBLEM, THE PURPOSE, AND THE PROCESS

## A NEW PROBLEM

Research writing is different now from what it was even a few years ago. Research is different because the information it is based on is different—there is simply more of it. According to one estimate, 6,000 to 7,000 scientific articles are written *every day* and "scientific and technical information now increases 13 percent per year, which means it doubles every 5.5 years" (Naisbitt 24). Furthermore, Naisbitt expects the rate of new information to increase because of better information systems and an increased number of scientists.

If there is twice as much information to learn, sort through, and synthesize now than there was five years ago, will it take twice as long to earn a college degree? Should we double the length of each semester? Have students take sixty credits per year?

Obviously, no matter how much information is suddenly available to process, there are still only twenty-four hours in a day and roughly seventy years in a lifetime. We will have to use more efficient ways of gathering, analyzing, and generating information.

## NEW TOOLS

Fortunately, new tools are available to help, new tools that are already in use by scientists, managers, technicians, reporters, and all other people who have to write reports for a living. These new tools include word processors, databases, spreadsheets, graphics generators, and spelling and style checkers, all of which use the increasing power of computers to help process complex information.

This is not to say that the old tools have disappeared. Libraries still have card catalogs and indexes. There are still valid uses for note

1

cards. And, of course, no computer will ever substitute for essential reading and writing skills. But the research writing process has definitely changed as a result of new information processing requirements and new information technologies.

## An Example

To see how these new research writing tools work with older tools to help meet the needs created by the information explosion, let's walk through one example paper. (We'll discuss this paper in much more detail in the following chapters.) For the last several years you have been interested in the Civil War. Lately you have been reading about the navies of both sides. In the course of some casual reading you discover that many Southern officers had formerly served with the North and resigned at the start of the war. In order to look more closely at this movement from North to South, you begin to do some additional research.

First stop, the library. Your college library has put its catalog online. So you sit down at a computer terminal and type in the title of your subject: "Civil War Navies." The terminal screen clears and then prints out the names of every relevant book in the library, their publication dates and locations, and whether they have already been checked out. You decide to check magazines also. Another computer terminal gives you abstracts of every article written on the subject in the last five years.

So much has been written about Civil War navies that you decide that the best way to keep track of your readings is to enter notes in a computer database of your own. The database records the source, the major and minor subjects, and pertinent quotes. Each entry roughly resembles a note card, but it is an electronic note card that allows you to insert and delete information easily. Also, since it is an electronic note card, you can have the computer group or sort your note cards automatically.

At one point you find a chart of resignations by Southern officers. The resignation rates differ considerably according to rank. To help determine whether any patterns exist, you enter the figures into a spreadsheet and have the program automatically draw several graphs for you. The graph clarifies what you had suspected: junior officers were much more likely to resign than senior officers.

To begin writing up your report, you create a rough draft on a word processor, inserting supporting figures and quotations automatically from your database of notes. The word processor lets you move paragraphs around as you reconsider how to present your ideas and lets you jump around and write some of the later sections of the report first so that you can clarify your conclusions before you begin your introductory comments.

Not a perfect speller, you next run both a spelling checker and a style checker to eliminate embarrassing spelling errors and to check for trite phrases and sexist terms. The style checker also generates a sentence outline of your report for you so that you can check for coherence and tells you your readability level to enable you to determine whether your writing matches the level of your audience.

After using the word processor to quickly rewrite several sections and correct a number of errors you found, you have the computer generate several graphs to help explain your conclusions. Now the computer prints out a final copy of your report with the graphs included. The report is now ready to give to several readers for their reactions.

## It's Still Work

Even with the help of a computer, a writer has to put in long hours to create a substantial report, and there is still no guarantee that the report will be good. The computer can create a list of all the available articles, but it can't say which ones are the best to read in detail. The database can collect all the notes and group them, but it can't say which groupings are most logical. The word processor makes it easy to make changes, but it doesn't say what should be changed. Even the style checker can point out only a few superficial errors; it can't find major errors in grammar or spot sentences that are false or frivolous.

What these new tools can do is collect large amounts of information from great distances and help you sort it, analyze information both numerically and graphically, write and rewrite and rewrite again without having to retype every letter every time, check for most common writing errors, and produce reports which communicate information in both words and pictures. For good writers, that's enough help to overcome the information explosion.

What about traditional research resources—the card catalog, journal indexes, and note cards? They still have their place. In some universities they may be the only resource available. For some shorter assignments they may be quicker to use. For some students, too much use of the computer may be a distraction; they may need to merge the old and new technologies at some level that they find comfortable. We have already pointed out that computer tools have limitations, too; they do some things well and some things very badly. Until they become much better than they are, there will remain plenty of room for a mix of the traditional and the new. Computer tools are improving and becoming much more common, however, so to ignore them totally is to do so at your own peril. Whether you see them as an aid or as a nuisance, you have to respect them as part of contemporary reality.

## ▰▰▰▰ *THE PURPOSE OF RESEARCH WRITING*

Clearly, there is more information for research than ever before and there are some exciting new tools to use for research, but is everything new? For example, is the purpose of research writing different now?

A number of people have looked at purposes for writing. One of the most popular views is that of James Kinneavy (1971), who divides writing into five categories: expressive (personal writing mainly to express feelings), formulaic (highly standardized writing such as business letters), imaginative (plays and stories), informative (providing information and giving evidence), and persuasive. These are five very different reasons for writing.

If we put research writing into these categories, it would seem most logically to fit as a type of informative writing, since the primary effort of most research is to inform. But isn't there also a persuasive element to research? Research about cigarette smoking not only informs people of the dangers but also may persuade them not to smoke. Research writing can also be formulaic. Isn't a laboratory report a highly formatted manner of reporting results? It may be informative, but it is also formulaic according to the standards listed above. So we can very quickly find three overlapping categories or purposes for research writing.

There may also be other reasons for writing. At least some professional writers feel that writing is a good method of learning. Janet Emig (1977, 122) describes how ideas "seem to develop most fully only with the support system of verbal language—particularly it seems, written language." Other writers also describe how writing is a discovery process for them. Take, for example, this classic quotation from playwright Edward Albee: "Writing has got to be an act of discovery.... I write to find out what I'm thinking about" (Murray).

Albee was primarily describing play writing, but much of research writing is also discovery. Whether it comes from taking an extra long look at evidence, trying to get initial ideas down on paper, or even some extra reading, most research writers end up with papers much different from what they had initially planned. Writing led them to discoveries.

While writing can be used to inform, to persuade, and even to discover, it has been given one more purpose—to create the entire world of science. David R. Olson of the Ontario Institute for Studies in Education has explored the cultural consequences of moving from oral to written communication. He sees one of the hidden consequences of writing as a drive toward logic:

> If one's mental resources are utilized in remembering a statement, there are no residual resources to reflect on the logical implications of those statements. Writing the statement down releases mental resources for other activities. But the use of writing not only has the consequence of making the logical implications of statements more detectable; it also has the effect of altering the statements themselves. The tendency to look at statements to see what could be deduced from them yields implications—implications which are often out of phase with experience. (Olson, 1976, 127)

Therefore, writing enables us to examine statements more carefully. This lets us find errors in the writing and thus causes readers to read more critically and forces writers to write more carefully. To quote Olson again, "The text had to stand on its own. Written material was now read in a manner in which it had not been read before—what is the text asserting and what are the necessary implications of that assertion?" (Olson 196) How important was writing in the development of science? According to Olson, "Modern science, like 'rationality' is an indirect consequence of the invention of a particular technology [writing]" (Olson 198).

So writing not only enables us to look at the world in a more logical way, it *forces* us to be more logical. Once ideas are on paper, they can be examined in great detail for accuracy and consistency. As a result, we are led to become more logical and more scientific as we write more. One consequence of writing is to train the writer and reader in careful thinking.

Clearly, writing serves many purposes; it informs, persuades, expresses, discovers, and objectifies. A typical research report contains most of these elements. Writers start out to inform but end up discovering and often persuading and finally creating a text which has to stand alone—which has to be sufficiently logical and accurate that readers can understand the report and use its facts, confident that they are using correct information.

It's no wonder that research reports are so hard to write. It's also no wonder that they are as valuable as they are.

## Readers and Purpose

One more way to look at the purposes of writing is to examine how it interacts with reading. A number of people have described writing as a triangle, with the writer at one corner, a reader at another, and the subject matter in the third.

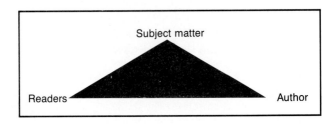

This helps to remind writers that readers are a crucial part of writing, but the triangle metaphor may be a little misleading, too. For instance, is the triangle equilateral? Are all three parts equally important? Or is the reader more or less important, depending on our purpose for writing?

Consider advertising. Do most advertising writers think as much about the content of their ads as they do about the people who will be seeing them? Or do they think most about their audience? Won't the ads have different subject matter for different audiences? On occasion it seems hard to find *any* subject matter in an ad, other than an appeal to an audience.

What about class notes? In this case there may be no reader other than the writer. The subject matter is much more important here, but there is no real audience. No effort is made by the writer to clarify information for a reader because there will be no outside reader. As long as the handwriting is legible, the audience has been served.

So the writing purpose will greatly affect how much we consider an audience. So will where we are in the course of our writing. In the quotation from Edward Albee above, it was clear that writing was helping him discover new ideas. A few of those ideas could come from considering who would later be reading his work, but he was concerned mostly with the subject matter and with his own ideas about it. This would be especially true early on, while he was beginning to write and to think about his subject. The same author would probably say that readers became very important later when he was well along with his writing and knew what he wanted to say.

How important are readers in research writing? When do we start thinking about them? One view is that readers don't matter at all. Why should they? If our goal is to report on research, our primary interest should be the subject we are researching. Our effort would be to give all the facts as accurately and logically as possible. Surely we would not choose which facts to include simply to create a certain impression in a reader. That's not ethical. For instance, if our research on groundwater pollution determined that much of nitrate pollution comes from farmers using fertilizers, we wouldn't choose to omit that fact for fear of offending farmers, any more than we would purposely include it in order to injure farmers. A report should be complete and honest, and its content cannot be altered to please a given audience. Advertising can be selective with facts; research reports cannot.

Besides the objectivity that is required of research reports, another influence away from readers is the internal consistency described by Olson. Remember, the text must stand on its own. Points raised in one part of the report should not be contradicted in another part. The writer must make sure that the whole report is logical. That effort at presenting all the evidence and explaining it coherently and consistently can be exhausting in itself. Making sense out of a body of data and presenting it in an entirely logical manner may leave less energy for concerns about readers' needs than with other kinds of writing.

Yet even research reports make some effort to reach readers. They can't do it by twisting or stifling the facts, but they can do it by making an effort to ease the burden of a reader. Remember that as difficult as it is to write a research report, it can be nearly as difficult to read one. Readers may not have as much background in a subject as the writer; they also have limited time, and they may be trying to scan (like you) dozens of reports before determining which ones are most relevant to them.

Research writers can and do help readers in a variety of ways. One of the most noticeable aids research writers include is an abstract. In 100 to 200 words they try to list the major points they discovered and the conclusions they reached. Such short summaries make it much easier for readers to decide whether they want to read the whole report. If they do read the report, the abstract becomes an "advance organizer," useful in helping them know which key points to watch for. In business the equivalent to the abstract is the "executive summary." It may be slightly longer, but the point is the same: give the major points in a page or two. If readers want to look more closely at your data, they can always read the rest of the report.

Other aids for readers are graphs, which help to clarify numeric information, and references and footnotes, which may supply additional clarifying or supporting information from the main text. Such footnotes are provided in case a reader needs them for clarity or wants them for additional data but can be ignored by readers who want to read for main points only. This speeds up the reading of the report and gives the reader some more control over how much detail to read.

Research writers may also do some of the standard tasks writers always do for readers—choose a level of vocabulary that matches a given audience and select examples that are clear to certain readers. Such efforts are expected of all writers. In general, however, the efforts research writers make for research readers are in the area of *presentation* rather than *content*. Readers influence how we present ideas, not what ideas we present.

# THE UNDERGRADUATE RESEARCH PAPER

So far we have considered the general purposes for research writing: to inform, persuade, and discover. We have seen the ways in which the purpose of reaching a reader can influence the contents of our writing. These purposes hold for all writing, and it is wise to remember them. When you begin to write, you participate in an activity that is both complicated and rich.

As a college student, however, you are being asked to write a research paper for several other reasons:

1 Practice for writing papers later in your collegiate or professional career
2 Development of reading and research skills
3 Further development of writing skills
4 Experience in independent learning
5 Development of higher-level thinking skills

Your instructor may have additional reasons for teaching you skills in research writing, but some or all of the five listed above are common. Taken as a group, they help to explain why universities put so much effort and so many resources into teaching those skills. Let's look a little more closely at each.

## Purpose 1: Research Writing as Practice

A major reason for learning to write a research paper as part of a composition class is to receive help as you learn the process. It is assumed that other professors will assign research papers and will expect you to be able to write the paper on your own. In a composition class you receive direct instruction in how to write such papers, and your instructor helps you as you work your way through the process.

An advantage of this system is that you receive the help you need; a disadvantage is that it may be tempting to regard a paper in a composition class as a "play" paper. It may seem that since you are writing a history or chemistry paper but no history or chemistry professor will mark it, you need not meet the usual standards for performance required in that class. After all, no expert in that field will read what you have written.

A better attitude to take is that the assignment will give you a unique opportunity—a chance to write about technical matters to an audience of people without specific training in the area. This means that you will have extra practice in responding to the needs of an audience—practice that is always valuable. So the writing of this paper will teach you the process of research writing *and* give you a chance to practice with a special audience.

## Purpose 2: Developing Reading and Research Skills

It's fairly obvious that doing a research paper will cause you to learn more about the resources of your library than you might learn otherwise. You will probably study periodical indexes that are new to you and find areas of your library's collection that are new. If you have access to online database searching or use a personal database to collect and manipulate notes, these may be new skills for you, too. Each paper you write will make you more adept as a researcher.

An area of growth you may think less about is reading. We tend to regard reading skills as something we learn in grade school. While we may not receive much formal instruction in how to read, reading skills are much more complicated than the sort of thing we studied as first-graders, and these skills take many years to fully develop. Writing a research paper is one more way to help develop those skills.

Think of the reading skills required during the creation of a research paper. First, there is skimming. The first step in finding sources to use for a paper is skimming over many articles that may or may not be useful. Those who are good at skimming can identify quickly and accurately which articles will be the most valuable. Those without such skills will either spend many extra hours separating useful articles from those which are irrelevant or will abandon articles that could have been useful to them.

Then there is summarizing. It is impossible to directly quote everything in every article you find. You will have to summarize the main points as best you can and limit direct quotations to those that are absolutely essential. But summarizing isn't easy. You must be able to identify the main points as you read them and accurately rephrase what you are reading. If you can't, your note cards or database records will be almost useless.

Inferences aren't easy to make, but as you read you will have to accurately determine what conclusions authors want you to make and bridge any gaps they leave. There will be no test to determine how accurately you read; if you err, you will end up misusing a source, and your error may be visible to anyone who reads your paper.

You will also have to develop skill in connecting sources. Using one source is not a paper; it is plagiarism. You may use dozens, and you will have to connect the various, and often contradictory, ideas they contain. There are some computer tools to help with these connections, but most of the connections will have to be made the old-fashioned way—through careful reading.

With practice, you should learn how to use one source as a springboard to further reading. You will follow the citations in one article like a trail of breadcrumbs to additional articles. At some point you should find that the most valuable piece of any article is the bibliography on which it was based. Now you are reading to prepare for future reading.

Your reading should carry you into uncomfortable reading situations—trying to make sense of highly technical reports for which you have little technical background. Learning to use abstracts and other aids to unlock difficult prose is a skill you will come to value, because there will always be difficult reading. Regardless of the class, whether it is English, history, art, or biology, the ideas will be complex and the reading for that class will reflect this complexity. Not all the important ideas of the world appear in each edition of *Newsweek.*

A final reading skill that writing a research paper will develop is judging authority. With textbooks, you assume that your instructors have chosen wisely and you are not being asked to read nonsense. With other sources, how do you know? You can obtain the help of your instructor and your librarian, but ultimately you will have to place a value on what you are reading. Do you trust this article or not? Do you believe article A or article B? Why? You are preparing for a life as an idea consumer. A research paper is excellent practice in learning good consumer skills.

So you may find that writing a research paper actually turns out to be a very useful reading activity. For the first time in years you may have an opportunity to let your reading skills grow.

## Further Development of Writing Skills

We know that good writing skills involve more than the ability to spell correctly and place a capital letter at the start of each sentence. We also know that these skills take many years to develop. There are several aspects of writing research papers that encourage the development of advanced writing skills.

The first skill that people think of in writing about research is the appropriate use of quotations. How many should there be, and how are footnotes or other forms of documentation handled? Actually, learning the conventions of documentation is one of the least demanding efforts required for research writing, but it is a useful skill that should be mastered.

A more difficult writing task comes from the length of typical research papers. It is one thing to organize a two- or three-page paper for coherence and clarity; keeping a ten-page paper on track is a very different organizational task. Writers who never saw the need for outlines before may suddenly find them valuable. Connecting multiple sections of a paper to achieve a logical development between them is a task that takes practice.

A related task is connecting the ideas from several sources into one coherent whole. It is difficult enough to keep your own ideas straight, but when you are trying to synthesize material from twenty or thirty sources, it may seem as though you are juggling in a tornado. Database programs and effective use of note cards can help in this area, but it is still a skill that has to be learned.

An additional writing skill that is emphasized in the research paper is writing for an audience. You are almost always explaining facts or events to people who know less about the subject than you do. After two or three weeks of researching a subject, you may know more about that subject than most of the professors on campus. So you will have to learn to write not to impress, but to explain. Your explanation must be complete, using the information you gathered during your research, but it must also be clear to people who haven't spent as long a time with the subject as you have.

A final writing skill you will acquire is a sense for the conventions of disciplines. You will quickly learn that there are no absolute rules about such things as bibliography form, or even for some matters of punctuation. There are only conventions, or agreements between people who work in the same area. Scientists like to have their bibliographies look one way, social workers another, and history professors another. No one way is "right"; they are all just accepted practice for people in that area. You won't need to learn in detail how each one differs, but you will develop an awareness of how much difference there is. Your writing perspectives should be broadened.

As a result, even if you are a very good writer, you should find that writing a research paper will improve your writing skills. That's one of the reasons they are assigned.

## Independent Learning

All colleges attempt to create some opportunities for students to learn independently. The hope is that if they develop the necessary skills and attitudes and have adequate experience in college, students will become lifelong learners—people able to adjust to the changes common to all professions—people who might even create some of those changes. Generally there aren't as many opportunities for independent learning as either the students or the college would like, but research papers have become a traditional way of fostering some independent learning.

Independent learning may be an admirable goal, but it is virtually impossible for people without the required skills. These are the skills we have been discussing over the last several pages: the ability to find library resources, read those resources with purpose and skill, and write about what we have read. These are all skills developed in research paper writing.

There is also a required attitude. You must have confidence in your abilities and a sense that what you are doing is enjoyable, even exciting. This attitude comes only from practice. Once you have written a major paper, you may be exhausted, but you will also be confident that you can do it. There may even be a sense of power. You learned so much about a subject that few people anywhere know as much about it as you do; you are now an expert. You will also remember that there was a great deal of surprise in what you found as you read. There may have been work or even drudgery in some parts of the research process, but you inevitably found new ideas. There were occasions for fun as you worked.

So the research paper does a good job of developing independent learning skills and attitudes. You learn how to learn and experience some of the pride and enjoyment that can bring.

## Developing High-Level Thinking Skills

You may be aware that there are levels of understanding. You may be able to name the capital of Wisconsin or New Jersey but not have any understanding of either city beyond its name. You don't understand either place in more than a superficial way.

In the early 1950s a group of educators tried to describe exactly what was meant by "understanding." The result was the *Taxonomy of Educational Objectives*, edited by Benjamin Bloom. This taxonomy divides understanding into these seven levels:

*Memory:* ability to recall or recognize information

*Translation:* ability to change information into a different symbolic form or language

*Interpretation:* ability to discover relationships among facts, generalizations, definitions, values, and skills

*Application:* ability to select and use appropriate generalizations and skills in a lifelike situation

*Analysis:* ability to solve a problem while conscious of the problem-solving process

*Synthesis:* ability to perform original creative thinking

*Evaluation:* ability to create standards for judgment (Sanders 3)

What is immediately striking about the levels described above is that writing a research paper involves *all* of them. You need to remember facts about the subject you are researching, you translate sections of articles into notes for cards or a database, you interpret the connections between the articles you are reading, you apply generalizations to your paper, you usually have to analyze a problem through your writing, you may need to create original solutions, and you certainly have to form some standards of judgment to select certain articles over others. In short, writing a research paper requires *total* understanding of your subject.

This level of understanding may be more remarkable than you realize. Ask yourself how completely you understand most of the things in your world. It is also probable that you don't understand most of what you study in classes in more than the most minimal sense. There may be nothing wrong with that. Given time constraints, can we really fully understand everything? We usually settle for whatever level is necessary to function.

In order to practice achieving these deeper levels of understanding, however, we do need to study some subjects fully from time to time. A research paper gives us just this opportunity. We pick a subject and closely examine it, practicing the higher skills of analysis, synthesis, and evaluation as we do. So we are learning about thinking while we are learning about our subject. We get to practice higher-level thinking skills.

For all these reasons the research paper has become a valuable experience for students. It can require a great deal of effort, but it is certainly worth it. Remember that the university has hired many instructors whose primary job is to teach you research writing skills. There must be some reason why the university is willing to go to all this expense.

## THE RESEARCH WRITING PROCESS

The process of writing a research paper is changing. As we pointed out at the beginning of the chapter, there is more information available now, as well as new tools for processing that information. This may change our writing process. Having a database available may mean that we are willing to look at more sources of information than before. Having a spelling checker program available may mean that we put off concerns about spelling until we use that program. Each of the new tools gives us a new way to write.

Here is an overview of the process people increasingly employ when writing research papers. Each step in that process is actually a set of new activities for writers.

## Gathering Information

A research project may start with a question ("Why did so many American writers live in Paris after the First World War?"), an opinion ("Groundwater pollution has got to stop"), or an assignment ("Determine the best site for the company's next expansion"). However research is originated, two early steps in the process are finding a reasonable scope for the research and gathering information about the subject. As a rule, the two steps are intertwined.

Let's say that you begin with a fairly general idea for a research subject: groundwater pollution. You are already used to looking for information in the card catalog or *Reader's Guide to Periodic Literature*. You may begin looking for information there, or you may look for the names of relevant articles in one of the specialized periodical indexes that university libraries have.

You may also be able to begin your search using an online database. Since so much information is available from so many sources, it has become common for universities, businesses, and the government to store information in computer databases. Specialized databases exist in larger computer centers around the country and can be accessed from your library by remote computers and telephone hookups. These databases hold an electronic image of magazine articles and other reports and can give you bibliographic information about their articles or even send a copy of entire articles to you electronically.

If you can get access to an online database, you will find that there are thousands of articles available on nearly any subject. As was already mentioned, there are so many articles being written in so many fields that there is almost always more information available than anyone could possibly ever read. Fortunately, computer databases let you narrow the focus of your research considerably and will generally tell you exactly how many articles are available on any subject you choose. For instance, the database might tell you that there were 5,437 articles on groundwater pollution. At that point you could see that the scope of your subject was simply too broad for reasonable research, so you might narrow your subject to nitrate pollution. The online database might respond that the number of sources for this subject is fifty-eight. If this seems sufficient to you, the database will then print out the abstracts of those articles so that you can choose which to read in full.

As you can see, an online database is one way to both gather information about your subject and determine an appropriate scope for your research.

There will still be a great deal of information to look through, categorize, and remember. Whether this information comes from your reading, your own laboratory, or interviews, it is easy to begin losing information. In the past you may have stored information on note cards. This method can still be used, but now you may also be able to choose a personal database. These databases are much more flexible and powerful than note card systems. With these smaller databases you can not only store your information but also have it grouped for you and later inserted in an appropriate place in a report.

Because of the new volumes of information available and the ease with which these databases can be used, information gathering could potentially be done totally by computer. You still have the older information-gathering tools available if you wish, but there are some handy new ones available for your use as well.

## Analyzing Data

People constantly draw conclusions without data. Listen to any normal dormitory debate. Sophomores aren't the only ones who often begin without facts. Scientists, too, can begin an investigation with a "hunch" and then look for data to prove or disprove what they had guessed. Whether you begin with a collection of data and no hypothesis or with a hypothesis which you hope data will prove or disprove, large amounts of data will probably mean that you won't just be able to read along and wait for the truth to jump out at you. There will be too much information and too many opportunities for alternative or erroneous conclusions.

Fortunately, there are analytical tools available. Databases are good ones, as we already mentioned. They help you group information, and the grouping process itself seems to help people make connections and form judgments about data.

If numbers are involved, a spreadsheet program can be a good way to begin looking for conclusions. All spreadsheet programs include basic statistical capabilities such as finding averages, and most can also sort information. They can also be used to project data, such as determining how much pollution might be left after five years, ten years, and so on.

One of the most powerful analytical tools that computers supply is graphics. Numerous programs are available which will pull a set of numbers from a spreadsheet and automatically create a bar graph, line graph, or pie chart. These graphs make it easier for you to see relationships within a set of numbers. For instance, a column of figures showing gross national products (GNPs) might be uninspiring to you until you generate a bar graph from them. Here's the same data in numeric form, which is presented in graphic form in Figure 1-1:

| | |
|---|---|
| Britain | 486.90 |
| Brazil | 261.00 |
| Korea | 77.40 |
| Japan | 1,091.60 |
| USSR | 1,768.60 |
| USA | 3,163.90 |

Some people wouldn't need the chart to see the major differences between GNPs, but for many of us, the bars would impress us much more than the numbers. The bars might give us ideas for writing or help us see connections we hadn't made before. In either case the graphic gives us a new tool to use when trying to make sense of numbers.

Here's another example of how graphics can help to clarify data.

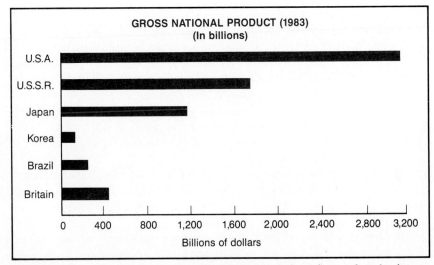

**Figure 1-1**. *A bar graph showing the gross national products of six leading nations in 1983.*

The following numbers show various levels of income for people with eight, twelve, and sixteen years of education. There is a great deal of overlap, with an equivalent percentage of grade school, high school, and college graduates at certain income levels. The minute the information is graphed, however, the major differences in income become obvious. Here is the numerical data, which is shown graphically in Figure 1-2:

Income by Years of Education (% at Each Income Level)

| Years | $5,000 | $15,000 | $25,000 | $50,000 |
|-------|--------|---------|---------|---------|
| 8 | 27.50 | 11.50 | 10.50 | 3.60 |
| 12 | 11.70 | 12.80 | 19.40 | 8.80 |
| 16 | 3.80 | 7.80 | 18.00 | 31.30 |

What is especially nice about such graphics programs is that not only do they help to clarify large block of numbers, but novices can learn to use many of them in an afternoon.

For nonnumeric research, there are questioner programs which will help writers to consider a topic from a variety of angles and check for alternative approaches. Their general function is to assist you in making

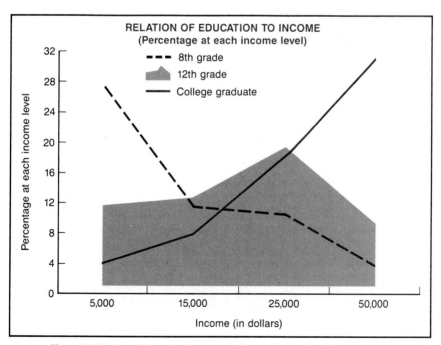

**Figure 1-2.** *The effect of educational attainment level on income.*

sure that you are being complete. Some of the questions they ask are based on rhetorical approaches over 2,000 years old, but they still are useful today.

Analyzing data still requires careful reading and time for insight and lots of experience, but at least now there are a few simple analysis tools to help.

## Drafting

Putting ideas down on paper can start at any time. Some people jot down a few ideas before they even begin their research, while others wait until they have completely finished their reading. In either case a variety of new tools are available to help you when you begin the initial drafts of your report. In general, the tools either help to supply organization or direction for your first draft or give you added flexibility in your writing.

Organizational assistance can come from templates, outliners, and your personal database. Templates are standard outlines created for such things as laboratory reports or forms. Once created, they are pulled in by the computer and can be used to help guide your writing. Outliners are programs that help you categorize information you have collected. This information can then be transferred to your word processor, where it serves as a framework that you can flesh out. The information in a personal database can be used the same way—it is transferred to a word processor and used as the basis for the first draft. In either case your rough draft doesn't begin with a blank page (or screen). An outline or template, or even whole blocks of notes, are ordered and waiting for you on the screen when you begin writing.

Other drafting tools are built into all word processors and make writing a rough draft much simpler. For instance, any word processor is flexible enough so that you can begin writing at the end of a report (if you prefer to) and write the beginning later. You can also change order easily with the block move function, which allows you to easily rearrange ideas. You don't have to be too concerned early on about the order of your presentation. You can write in the order that is easiest for you and later arrange paragraphs in the order that is best for your readers.

## Revising

Most writers never stop revising. As they read, they revise their ideas about a topic or the approach they want to take to their subject. Once they start writing, they may stop after each paragraph and reread for common errors. In addition to this continual, almost unconscious, revising, there is usually a time when writers stop writing and put a special effort into rereading and rewriting what they have written. When they do this, there is a whole set of programs available to help direct their efforts.

One group of programs helps you check for coherence. These programs will print an outline of your report and the first and last sentences of each paragraph and then graph out the length of each paragraph. The purpose is to help you determine whether you stayed on the subject, organized your ideas well, and fully explained yourself.

Other programs help you view your paper from a reader's perspective. These programs will determine the reading level of the report, check for the use of transitions, look for possible confusing references, and so on. The point is to help you see where your paper needs to be changed in order to make it more readable.

Another set of revising programs assist you in setting appropriate levels of diction and tone. They might look for trite expressions or slang or for stuffy prose. Their purpose is to help you see the impression your words give.

Such programs don't replace sound judgment. You still need to check for accuracy, emphasis, and clarity. However, these revising tools help you meet the additional expectations of readers—that your writing will be coherent, appropriate, and matched to your reader.

## Editing

Increasingly writers speak of "revising" as checking for major matters: completeness, coherence, and audience; "editing" is seen as a check for stylistic points: spelling, punctuation, and grammar. Elements such as spelling and grammar might not seem very minor, but they are less important than elements such as coherence—correctly spelled nonsense is still nonsense.

There are no computer tools to automatically find grammar errors yet (although there are people working on it), but there are programs to catch misspelled and misused words. Spelling checker programs automatically find many misspelled words. They are not completely accurate, but they are a start. Most such programs also compute word frequencies.

| A | 35 | ALREADY | 5 | APPROACHES | 1 |
|---|---|---|---|---|---|
| ABILITY | 1 | ALSO | 5 | ARBITRARY | 1 |
| ABOUT | 7 | AMERICAN | 1 | ARE | 12 |
| ABOVE | 1 | AN | 8 | AREA | 2 |
| ACCESS | 1 | ANALYSIS | 1 | AREAS | 1 |
| ACCOMPANY | 1 | ANALYZE | 1 | AROUND | 1 |
| ACTIVITIES | 2 | AND | 42 | ART | 1 |

Such listings make it easier to spot overused words.

Beyond spelling checkers there are words and phrase checks built into most style checker programs. Such checks look for common errors in usage (confusing "affect" and "effect"), trite or pompous phrasing, and gender-specific language. Using "fireman" when you mean "fire fighter" is not just sexist; it shows that you haven't been near a fire station lately. These programs are good at catching that kind of error.

Other programs will help to point out overuse of passive voice ("Taxes were raised" uses the passive voice to conceal the identity of the person who actually raised the taxes, while "Congressman Smith voted to raise taxes" uses the active voice to show responsibility), overuse of prepositions, and even the total percentage of nouns and verbs in a report.

Most such programs are helpful in editing but tend to be more useful to better writers than to those who are still struggling with the basics. A good writer might want help in reducing the passive voice and sexist language, while a poorer writer might be happy just to know that every sentence has a subject and a verb. In either case editing still requires a great deal of skill and experience, most of which cannot be replaced by even the best computer programs.

## Making Your Presentation

Once you have gathered the information, analyzed the data and written, revised, and edited the draft, you may think you'd be finished. After all, the paper should be accurate, coherent, and error-free at this point. But what about readers? Readers influence writing constantly. In research writing readers may not influence the facts we choose to include (What would be most impressive or most convincing?) but they may influence the order in which we present them (Do we start with what they know and build from there, or with what they don't know in order to get their attention?). Readers may also affect the vocabulary level we use to describe our ideas.

These are decisions we make the whole time we are writing. While we make them constantly, it is still advisable to make one final effort to check whether our writing matches an audience as well as it can.

As part of that final check, a natural step is to determine the need for presentation graphics. Earlier we described how graphics can help us to analyze data while we are writing. A second use for graphics is to communicate ideas to a reader. These may be the same graphics we used earlier, different versions of those graphics, or even a whole new set. In either case since computers create graphics so well, and graphics are so helpful in communicating information, a special effort should be made to determine what graphics should be created and where they should be located in the report.

Presentation still consists of the usual activities—creating an appropriate cover page, determining margin width and footnote form, writing an abstract, and adding clarifying references—but now it can also be used as one more opportunity to reconsider the needs of a reader and add graphics or text where helpful

# CONCLUSION

The activity of writing is more important than most people imagine. It clarifies ideas, objectifies meaning, and informs readers. However, writing—especially research writing—is changing. Because of the enormous increase in information being published now and the new computer-based tools available to process that information, the activity of writing is different from what it was even a few years ago. It is still an important activity, but now it is even more demanding; there is more information to sort through, an increased use of numeric and graphic information, and an increased expectation that writing will be matched to readers.

The new tools that enable research writers to meet these increased expectations can be classified into six groups: gathering information, analyzing data, drafting, revising, editing, and presenting your paper. These groups are discussed in detail in the next seven chapters of this book.

# EXERCISES

*1*. List the online resources available in your library.

*2*. Pick three articles from yesterday's newspaper. What efforts were made to meet the needs of readers?

*3*. Select one of the example papers at the back of this book. What efforts were made to meet the needs of readers? What more could have been done? What are some things the authors should *not* do to appeal to their readers?

*4*. David Olson says that writing forces people to be logical. What would he say about television? About using computers? Can you name some writing source that is *not* logical?

*5*. Make a list of assignments you have been given in other classes and determine which level of understanding they would require according to Bloom's taxonomy.

# Chapter 2

# RESEARCH SITUATIONS

As you might have already discovered, there is no one 'research paper." Rather, the research paper exists in many forms. The purpose of this chapter is to describe the most common research writing situations you are likely to find in an academic community.

In all disciplines, one of the writer's primary tasks is the transmission of knowledge to the readers. Whether a review of the literature or a laboratory report, research writing is designed to convey information. The student of wildlife records observations of feeding patterns of deer and reports them. The student of education visits a preschool and describes the learning activities of the children observed there. After reading certain material, the history student prepares a paper which summarizes that material. The English major conveys the content and nature of a literary work while simultaneously providing a personal analysis and interpretation of that work.

Regardless of your discipline, the ability to convey information clearly and concisely is indispensable. Whether your goal is the preparation of a forceful and convincing statement of your opinion on a controversial subject or an attempt to sway your audience to accept your stance on an issue and act accordingly, these opinions and positions must be carefully supported by facts. These facts are the informational components of your writing.

Obviously, the information you will transmit to your readers through your writing must have a source. As the preceding examples indicate, the sources of information are widely varied. Observation of the world around you, a laboratory experiment which you have carefully controlled, reading either a single article or a range of books and articles, or your own thoughts, all can and will be the subjects of your writing.

Your readers will want to know how you acquired your information. Your instructors will examine your methodology so that they can interpret the results and offer you assistance in case those results are unexpected. When you report your observations of the world around you, your readers will want to know the conditions under which you made your observations so that they can judge for themselves how accurate those observations might be. If you are reporting the results of reading, your readers have a right to expect an accurate citation of sources so that they can turn to those sources for further information.

In each case, you are responsible for providing information which will help your audience to evaluate your presentation. Usually, conventions will guide you in effectively presenting that information. For example, scientific papers are expected to follow a specific pattern of organization as they record and then analyze the writer's observation of natural phenomena. When you submit a book review to your history professor, the professor will expect to find certain items of information beyond your opinion of the book and will also expect this information to occur in specific portions of the review.

One source of information is, of course, your reading. Students convey the results of their reading experiences in many forms. While the formal research paper is perhaps the most familiar of the "reading reports," you will almost certainly be called on to deal with your reading experiences in other ways. The book review, the abstract, and the review of existing literature are characteristic methods of coming to grips with your reading and passing the knowledge you gained in that reading along to others. In so doing, you must acknowledge the sources of your information, as we discuss in Chapters 5 and 8, not so much to avoid the error of plagiarism, although that is important, but rather to give your own writing credibility and to provide your reader with a place to turn for additional information.

## TYPES OF RESEARCH WRITING

### The Book Review

Often instructors will ask you to demonstrate your understanding of both your reading and the principles and methodology of a discipline by preparing a review of a book in the field. While you may have written book *reports* in the past, the review is different. Unlike the book report, which generally provides little more than a summary, essential bibliographic information, and a statement of why you "liked" the work, the goal of the book review is to present your analysis of the purpose and effectiveness of the book. As you will see in Chapter 3, such analysis must be based on information about the work which you have provided your audience, and this information is usually presented as summary material. Remember, the review should be composed not simply to prove that you read the book (that is a minimum expectation) but also to demonstrate your grasp of the intellectual content of the work.

A thorough review covers not only the content of the work but also its relationship to other works in the field. Your review should consider the validity of the author's assertions and the degree to which such assertions are supported by fact and logic. Thus an effective review is one part summary, one part analysis, and one part demonstration of the reviewer's intellectual position.

## The Literature Review

As you write in a number of disciplines, you will find it necessary to summarize the range of current publication on a particular topic. While the literature review may be the sole purpose of a paper, more often it provides an introduction to your own research. This review of existing studies assures your readers that you are not duplicating the work of other researchers and establishes the context of the problem you are attempting to solve. Note how the following paragraph establishes parameters for the study which is to follow and defines those aspects of the problem which have already been investigated:

> Perhaps of equal importance is that low-crime-rate neighborhoods are more likely to be surrounded by neighborhoods whose residents are somewhat higher in socioeconomic status (Greenberg et al. 1982, 117). These findings suggest that what is important in producing high crime rates is the residential location of offenders relative to their victims, expecially for property (burglary and household larceny) and street crimes (robbery and auto theft). The attractiveness of communities to offenders, their awareness of criminal opportunities, and their ease of entry and egress are greatest for nearby neighborhoods. Offenders minimize the distance to their victims, especially for residential and street crimes (Boggs 1965; Schmid 1960; Smith 1972). (Reiss 47)

Note also how the review paragraph consolidates references to studies which reached similar conclusions. The goal here is not to provide an exhaustive summary of the work of others but to define the scope of previous work and to establish the relationship of the author's own work to this previous work.

## The Report of Observations and Experiments

As we have seen, one of the primary sources of information available to an author is the work of other writers. Students of history, for example, often must rely on the writing of others. Contemporary students were not direct observers of the Civil War, for instance, and thus are dependent on those who have already done primary research. It is also true that the investigations which lend themselves to direct research and observation are less obvious in the humanities than in the sciences. How many English majors anticipate prowling the paperback racks of a local newsstand to observe the reading habits of the indigenous fauna? How many music students would contemplate setting up a controlled experiment to determine the effects of Mozart's *Don Giovanni* on the social behavior of adolescent males? The answer to both questions is almost certainly "not many." However, students majoring in literature and the arts will generally be required to work in a variety of courses where the principal methods of gathering information are not reading but observation of the environment or controlled experiment.

While it is true that observations of the environment might be conducted differently from experiments, the reports are often presented in the same way. Whether you are presenting your observations of the world around you or writing about an experiment whose conditions you established and controlled, your writing must convince your readers of two things: (1) that you carefully recorded what you observed or the conditions of the experiment and (2) that you are a qualified observer under the conditions you reported and of the phenomena that you observed. You can create the necessary confidence in your readers by considering the manner of your presentation.

First, be accurate and precise in your use of language. Sloppy vocabulary choices can only lead the reader to doubt the accuracy of your information. The more precise your language, the more accurate your observations will be considered. The increasing level of specificity in the following sentences contributes to an increasing awareness on the part of the reader that the author is a careful and qualified recorder of information:

> The black-footed ferret is carnivorous.
> The black-footed ferret's principal food is small animals.
> The black-footed ferret's principal food is rodents.
> The black-footed ferret's principal food is prairie dogs (*Cynomys ludovicianus*).

While none of these versions are incorrect, and each is appropriate under the right conditions, clearly the last is the most specific and accurate presentation of the author's observation of the feeding habits of the black-footed ferret. If your writing consistently lacks the precision demanded by your instructors, you might pay special attention to Chapter 6, "Revising."

Note how the authors of the following passage enhance our confidence in their observations by the use of specific detail and careful word choice:

> Our 3-year study of the changes in U/C in Colorado wild bears began in the winter of 1981 and ended in the fall of 1983. The investigation was performed in the Black Mesa–Crystal area in west-central Colorado. The study area has three major vegetation associations in elevational bands. At the lower elevations (2235 to 2330 m), a mountain shrub community dominated by Gambel oak (*Quercus gambelii*) and serviceberry (*Amalanchier alnifolia*) is most common. Extensive stands of chokeberry (*Prunus virginianus*) can be found throughout the upper reaches of this association. Above the oakbrush, at elevations between 2330 and 3330 m, are large aspen (*Populus tremuloides*) forests. Chokeberry thickets are often found at a boundary of these lower associations. At higher elevations mixed Engelmann spruce (*Picea engelmanni*) and fir (*Abies concolor* and *A. lasiocarpa*) stands predominate. Mixed within the aspen and conifer forests are large meadows, once nearly pure Thurber fescue (*Festuca thurberi*), but now a mixture of seven to ten grasses, with significant number of geranium (*Geranium fremontii* and *G. viscossissimum*) and rabbit brush (*Chrysothamnus parryi*). (Nelson, Beck, Steiger 841)

Always remember that when you are reporting about some segment of the world around you, the quality of your information is dependent on a variety of conditions more or less beyond your control. The information provided by the field worker in wildlife is affected by the weather, the time of day, and the availability of subjects to observe. The goal of the physics laboratory report is to allow the reader to reproduce the experiment itself. Without an adequate description of the preparations for the experiment, the reader's results are quite likely to differ from yours, and your credibility will be severely damaged.

Readers will be better able to interpret and use your information if they know not only what you observed and how you conducted your experiment, but also the conditions under which you worked. Thus the most successful presentation can result only from thoughtful preparation. While gathering information and conducting experiments, you must be certain to record all details which could have affected your observations; you must be prepared to list and, depending on your audience, describe in detail any equipment that aided you in your observations and experiments. Finally, report any conditions which might have altered the quality of your observations and experiments and then discuss the expected effect of these conditions.

The following paragraph efficiently establishes in the reader's mind the essential details of the collection methodology of a study of the effects of moose on the plant life on which they feed:

> Actual use of foliage by Moose was measured by counting the number of leaves removed on stems within twenty-four 27-m$^2$ plots. Leaf removal by Moose was measured at 10-day intervals throughout the summer. To avoid recounting browse stems and to distinguish regrowth from primary foliage, each browsed stem was marked with plastic flagging. Although other North American ungulates are known to eat flagging, no evidence exists that Moose on Isle Royale reacted to it in any way. (Miquelle 18)

Note that the author tells us not only the methods used to collect the information but also the precautions taken to avoid error and the impact of experimental method on the results of the experiment. In its efficiency, clarity, and anticipation of possible questions, the writer provides us with a model of the effective presentation of observational methodology.

Remember, your goal in reporting observations and experiments is thoroughness and accuracy, not literary style. In reporting their experimental method, the authors of a study of the impact of diet on sparrows elected to present the details in parenthetical attachments. This choice effectively simplifies sentence structure and reduces overall length.

> We captured White-crowned Sparrows (Z. *gambelii*) during their migration through eastern Washington and kept them in an outdoor aviary where drinking water and chick-starter mash (20.7% protein, 74.7% carbohydrate, 3.1% fat, and 1.5% ash) were freely available. We undertook two series of experiments. About one month before the postnuptial molt started, we transferred the experimental birds from an outdoor aviary to constant-condition rooms (21° C, LD 16:8) and put them in individual cages (22 × 40 × 27 cm). (Murphy and King 165)

Finally, it is likely that your reports of physical research will be expected to adhere to the conventions of a national scientific organization, such as the American Psychological Association (APA) or the Council of Biological Editors (CBE); such organizations invariably include a section or sections dealing with experimental design, methods, subjects, and materials in their format for research reports. Be sure to find out which conventions are to be followed, and adhere to them.

## The Report of a Survey

Surveys are one way of collecting information. Some information is collected through interviews; some information is collected through questionnaires. You have probably been on the receiving end of a number of surveys, either on the street, over the telephone, or in the classroom. While some surveys are conducted as part of a research paper, faculty often require students to conduct surveys as an independent exercise.

If you worked for a large survey organization, such as Roper or Harris, you might only accumulate the information; someone else would evaluate it. However, in the university you will most likely have to conduct your own survey, whether in a sociology class, a psychology class, or even in a freshman English class, and you will most likely be asked to present the results of that survey.

There are two kinds of surveys: the in-depth, open-ended interview and the questionnaire. If you are asked to conduct an interview survey, you will collect information by choosing a small representative sample from a much larger population. If you are asked to conduct a questionnaire survey, you will collect information by asking people to respond to a series of questions.

Usually, your instructor will give you explicit instructions in how to construct questions, how to conduct an interview survey, and even how to report the results of the survey. The report itself is generally organized by topics, including at least one section describing the survey and another section analyzing the results of the survey. In a typical report, you might be expected to

1 State the purpose of the survey
2 Describe the sampling procedure
3 Indicate the type of survey design used
4 Define the major variables
5 Present the results
6 Analyze the results

*Important:* If you are doing research dealing with people, you should know that the Institutional Review Board for the Protection of Human Subjects is responsible for overseeing mandated federal requirments for all human research. The law specifies that you must protect the rights of the respondents. This is especially important when you are presenting the *results* of research. For example, rather than writing, "The police chief in Nineveh said that he had tried marijuana several times," you might write, "A law enforcement officer in Nineveh said that he had tried marijuana several times."

## The Clinical Report

The clinical report is based on direct observations of human behavior. A social worker interviews a client in order to gather information for a recommendation; a music therapist observes a disabled person in order to make a recommendation for treatment.

Although clinical observations are usually based on in-depth interviews, sometimes they are done solely through videotapes, and sometimes they use both methods. Regardless of the method used, the clinical studies demand exceptional skills of observation and analysis.

Clinical studies usually result in a written report that must be clear, precise, and above all unambiguous. If the study is done for a health-related discipline, such as clinical psychology, nursing, or communicative disorders, there may be a recommendation for therapy of some kind. Whatever the form, there must be no room for the possibility of misunderstanding. For example, if you are a speech therapist preparing a report on a client, there is a significant difference between recommending that "The client needs more testing" and "The client needs more lesion testing."

Regardless of the discipline or the purpose, clinical reports have two things in common: (1) each discipline has very specific procedures for making observations, diagnoses, and recommendations, and (2) there is often a form to be filled out outlining the procedures.

The most difficult part of writing up clinical studies is that they will usually be read by many different groups: the social worker's supervisor, the client, and the therapist, for instance. Each reader will have varying levels of education, interest, and specialized knowledge and different reasons for reading the report and will respond to the report in different ways. Your task is to choose words, sentences, and paragraphs that will allow each reader to understand what you are saying.

# THE PERSUASIVE AND ARGUMENTATIVE ESSAY

Although the primary purpose of much research is to inform, there is also a strong persuasive and argumentative element in many kinds of research. Some writers make a sharp distinction between argumentation and persuasion. To them "argumentation" refers to changing people's minds, and "persuasion" refers to moving people to action. While this is a legitimate distinction, it is also true that almost all argumentative writing has a strong persuasive component to it.

Much of what you will write will be argumentative in that you will take a position and try to convince readers to accept or believe that position. Similarly, much of what you will write will be persuasive in that you will try to convince your readers that they should not only believe you but also do something about it. Because the writing situations are so similar, we will define persuasive writing and argumentative writing as any writing whose purpose is to influence people's beliefs or actions.

Not all topics, of course, are arguable. The topics that are not arguable are those that can be answered with facts, those that are matters of taste, and those that demand a belief in faith. Because facts are easily verifiable, it is simply not worthwhile to argue about which city is the most heavily populated, who is credited with first discovering penicillin, or what famous actor's real name is Bernard Schwartz. Similarly, it is not worthwhile to argue matters of taste; a preference for liver and onions is a matter of personal preference and is not debatable. And if you have ever heard a religionist and an atheist debating the existence of God, you will understand the futility of arguing matters of faith.

What is arguable, however, are topics about which there is disagreement *and* about which reasonable and logical evidence can be found. Those topics can range from the issue of retaining the designated-hitter rule in baseball to the issue of using forced busing to achieve racial integration to the issue of saving the California condor from extinction. The opinions or stands we take on those topics are conclusions we have reached from the information we have gathered.

There are two types of persuasive and argumentative essays; the defensive argument and the offensive argument. A defensive argument is written in response to an already existing argument; an offensive argument initiates an argument.

Because it is usually responding not so much to the details of an argument as to the conclusions reached in an argument, the *defensive argument* frequently begins with a differing conclusion and offers evidence and opinions to support that conclusion. Here are the first four paragraphs of a paper on school desegregation. Notice the attempt to offer both sides of an issue, even though the writer is clearly opposed to mandatory busing.

> In 1954, the Supreme Court ruling in *Brown v. Board of Education* was the first step in the long road to ending racial segregation. In 1970, the Supreme Court ruling in *Swann v. Charlotte–Mecklenburg Board of Education* began the program of forced busing (Wilkinson 146). Mandatory busing does indeed create racially balanced school systems, but the negative economic and social aspects of this program far outweigh its benefits. Mandatory busing is unnecessarily expensive, increases racial tensions, and disrupts neighborhood school systems (McClendon 63).
>
> Let us look at the cost factor involved in mandatory busing programs. The implementation of a mandatory school busing program requires mon-

ey. Buses must be repaired, drivers must receive a salary, and gasoline must be purchased (Wilkinson 166). Funding a bus program can be a debilitating factor to many school systems that must follow strict budget plans.

Proponents of busing might reply that the amount of money needed to operate a mandatory busing program often is only a small amount of a school board's total budget (Wilkinson 166). In fact, they might say, the cost of busing after desegregation has started is not as high as the public believes (Orfield 119).

In reply to the above statements, it should be known that the federal government will not give financial aid to school districts that would use the money to help fund busing programs (Wilkinson 166). Now what can financially handicapped schools do? In order to meet the cost of busing, many schools simply cut out educational programs (Wilkinson 167). The quality of education suffers just because every school is required to have a certain percentage of blacks and whites.

In these paragraphs, notice the phrasing that often denotes a defensive argument: the complaining tone of the second paragraph, the phrases "might reply" and "might say" of the third paragraph, and the phrase "it should be known that" of the fourth paragraph.

The *offensive argument,* because it is not responding *to* an argument, frequently just piles evidence upon evidence until the conclusion or generalization is reached. Here is the conclusion of an offensive argument. The tone is objective; the approach is even-handed, not protective, and the conclusion seems so reasonable.

Which of the theories are we to accept as the most likely mechanism for evolution? As we have seen earlier, the Lamarckian theory of adaptive evolution appears to be refuted by everything we know of the hereditary process, so we must choose between Darwinian gradualism and the concept of abrupt steps. Logically, we must believe that the large steps which must occur for the latter theory to operate must be few and far between. To expect such leaps to be accompanied by the isolation required for the fixation of a new species is to expect a very unlikely series of events. It has also been pointed out by a series of computer simulations that the complexity of the step theory is not required to explain the development of current life forms (Mednikov 35).

Thus, applying Occam's razor, the explanation of the evolutionary process offered by the "modern synthesis" of Charles Darwin's views and modern genetics, the process of gradual change over vast periods of time, seems most satisfactory.

There is no harshness or shrillness to the conclusion. There is no sense of "I told you so." The writer is almost apologetic. There is even some doubt left; note the use of phrases such as "appears to be refuted" and "seems most satisfactory." The writer knows that scientific inquiry and the scientific method are never-ending, and as new information is gathered new conclusions will be reached.

Much of the success of your argument depends on the effectiveness of your appeal to the reader. Some arguments use only one kind of appeal; many arguments use more than one kind of appeal. In the following section we will discuss the two basic appeals: logical and ethical.

## Logical Appeal

To appeal to logic means to appeal to the intellect, to convince a reader or listener to believe something because of sound reasoning. While all writing must be well organized in order to be effective, persuasive and argumentative writing demands an exceptionally clear line of reasoning. Generally we present arguments in one of two ways, inductively or deductively.

An *inductive argument* begins with particular bits of information (usually facts, interpretations of facts, and authoritative opinions) and arrives at a conclusion based on that information. The conclusion (or generalization) is rarely perfect because it is almost always based on a limited sample of all available information. Some conclusions appear obvious to us because of our experience; we accept them unhesitatingly ("How many of us doubt that the sun will rise tomorrow?"). Other conclusions, however, often demand substantial evidence before we will accept them ("Do you believe that socialized medicine will increase health care and reduce medical costs?"). The more evidence we offer, the better our conclusions will be. The better our evidence, the more likely we will be to convince our readers.

A *deductive argument* begins with a general statement ("It has been scientifically established that alcohol consumption during pregnancy has adverse effects on offspring.") and then derives specific statements from that generalization ("Pregnant mothers shouldn't drink alcoholic beverages"; "All alcoholic beverages should contain a warning that alcohol can adversely effect newborn children.").

Just because you have logic on your side does not mean that your audience will automatically be convinced and accept your argument. You must be sensitive to your audience, which means that you must have some idea about how strongly your readers feel toward the subject and how best they might be moved, what tone of voice to adopt, and what level of vocabulary to use. To be sensitive to your audience means that you don't call people names or threaten them or their friends or their family or their livelihood. It also means that you avoid phrases that will demean your reader (e.g., "of course, it follows that...;" "anyone but a fool can see that...."). Instead, use phrases that neither intimidate nor anger ("it seems that...;" "thus the facts appear to support the view that...;" "because of this, we believe that ... "). If you find yourself consistently using phrases that might be demeaning, refer to Chapter 7, "Editing," which offers several suggestions that could help you avoid these errors.

We are not suggesting that you be wishy-washy or that you curb your opinions, only that you become more sensitive to your ultimate purpose, which in persuasive and argumentative writing is to convince your readers and get them to agree with you, or at least to look at something in a different way.

## Ethical Appeal

An ethical argument appeals to a reader's sense of right and wrong by assuming a set of values shared by the reader. For example, arguments against advertising by physicians often appeal to the traditional injunction against advertising that most physicians have adhered to since Hippocrates [or at least since the formation of the American Medical Association (AMA)]. Ethical arguments against capital punishment usually appeal to the Judeo-Christian commandment, "Thou shalt not kill." Much of the effectiveness of ethical appeals depend on the respect and trust the reader has for the writer or for the authorities cited by the writer. Appeals that are primarily ethical may also use logic, as in many arguments for and against capital punishment.

Good *writers* limit their appeal to the most effective and the most responsible appeal. Good *readers* recognize the kind of appeal being used. As you read the writings in this book, assignments for classes, and recreational reading, see if you can determine the kind of appeal being used.

## ▰▰▰▰▰EXERCISES

*1*. In many persuasive and argumentative essays, writers either do not present both sides of an issue or do not present both sides evenly. Here, for example, is a typical letter to the editor (maybe a little better written than the typical letter). The immediate purpose of the letter is to convince readers that a student union ban on *Playboy*, *Playgirl*, and *Penthouse* magazines should not be rescinded; the ultimate purpose is to convince readers that pornography in general is harmful to everyone.

> A recent journal editorial noted the decision by the Board of Regents that the student union ought to rescind a ban on the sale of *Playboy*, *Playgirl*, and *Penthouse* magazines.
>
> "It's an ironic situation," the editorial commented. "Among the

leading opponents of *Playboy*-type magazines are members of the feminist movement, who generally are liberal types. But here they were taking what could be considered a reactionary position on freedom of expression."

As a feminist and also a liberal on many (but not all) issues, I think I can clarify the apparent contradiction.

I believe pornography—even the so-called "soft-core" pornography found in *Penthouse* and *Playboy*—is harmful for the following reasons: First, it dehumanizes the human being (generally a woman) to the status of an object, a "thing." "The pornographic camera performs a miracle in reverse," writes Susan Griffin in *Pornography and Silence*. "Looking on a living being, a person with a soul, it produces an image of a thing.... In pornography, even when a real woman poses for the camera, she does not pose as herself. Rather, she performs. She plays the part of an object."

Second, so-called soft-core pornography rather quickly degenerates into the hard-core variety. Hard-core pornography is a $4 billion a year industry that glorifies violence against women. Magazine photos and videos show women being bound, raped, tortured, killed, or degraded for sexual stimulation or pleasure.

Third, this brutally affects the lives of all women. The FBI states in its annual publication that a woman is raped every eight minutes. A San Francisco policeman says that the sex crimes division is seeing fewer "clean" rapes and more rapes in which women are brutalized, blatantly humiliated, and tortured as well as sexually assaulted.

Fourth, what is done to women is—sooner or later—also done to children. Our society now faces the hideous phenomenon known as "kiddie porn," and chilling stories of systematic child abduction and child molestation are coming to light with ever increasing frequency.

I have as great an aversion to narrow, hysterical censorship and a bookburning mentality as anyone. But where, I wonder, does censorship end and legislating against blatant violation of the rights and the dignity of the human person begin?

I think this needs to be the subject of continuous public scrutiny, dialogue, and decision-making—with women's voices and women's opinions very much in evidence.

I also believe the consequences for women and children of a society in which "anything goes" should deeply disturb us all.

Whenever a fellow human being is treated as less than human we are all, somehow, less whole.

The writer has used a traditional form to present her argument. She states the thesis early (in paragraph 3) and then supports her thesis with what she hopes is enough evidence to convince her readers. Are you convinced? Do you agree with the logic, especially the argument that pornography has certain effects on women and children? What do you think about the relationship between the thesis and the statistics the writer offers? How does the the quotation from Susan Griffin help the argument? Has the writer addressed the issue of censorship and freedom of expression in a democratic society sufficiently for you? Do you like the way the letter is organized? Can you think of a more effective organization?

2. Write a book review of one of the chapters in this book.

3. Buy a plant (preferably not a cactus), and for at least one week record your observations of the plant and your observations of the attitude of others toward the plant.

4. Find, and bring to class, an example of each of the following:

   a. An argument presented inductively
   b. An argument presented deductively

# Chapter 3

# GATHERING INFORMATION

**Y**ou are about to embark on the most academic of activities, one which is essential to the university experience: the gathering of information from a variety of sources to answer a question or resolve a conflict. One major benefit of a college or university education is the breadth of knowledge you acquire as a result of a range of classes in a variety of academic areas rather than the information you obtain from a specialized, career-oriented area of study. When you complete your college work, you will know the value of acquiring knowledge for its own sake. The freshman research paper is the first step in that process.

This book stresses the role of a range of computer aids in the research process; however, you can produce successful research even if you do not have access to a computer. You can, in fact, apply most of the principles that contribute to the success of computer-assisted information gathering regardless of the method you are able to use. What really matters is not the method used to produce the paper but the final paper itself.

The successful paper begins with the selection of a topic. The degree of freedom you have in this selection depends on the nature of the assignment your instructor provides. Some assignments clearly and specifically require a specific topic, often by asking a question to which you must respond. Others provide a general topic area, such as nineteenth-century American poetry, and allow you to narrow your paper to a specific topic within that field. Still others—and these are by far the most difficult to respond to—give you full rein to select a topic that interests you. Our three sample papers illustrate three different assignments, each requiring a different level of topic selection by the student.

In Jonathan's American literature class, the instructor made a very specific assignment: "Review the critical interpretations of Emily Dickinson's poem 'I Heard a Fly Buzz When I Died'." Jonathan does not need to select a topic; the direction of his research is clear. He can move directly to locating information for his paper.

Jennifer's history instructor asked the class to investigate some aspect of Civil War military history. Jennifer is faced with greater latitude in topic selection than Jonathan. For example, she could research the role of railroads in Northern campaign strategy, the role of conscription on the Northern war effort, or the impact of some weapon on the course of the war (a topic which would clearly need further limitation and refinement as her research progressed). Given her instructor's assignment, she should not, however, research the factors which led to Lincoln's reelection in 1864 as this is not a *military* issue.

In her introductory biology class, Kris is faced with a greater need to determine a topic than either Jonathan or Jennifer. Her instructor required only "a research paper on some aspect of evolution." Clearly, Kris must quickly limit her research. Her first thought is to examine the available evidence on the validity of evolution. She rejects this almost at once; there is simply too much written on this issue, most of it controversial, and she realizes that she would be able to neither read nor evaluate a significant portion of the resources available within the time allowed for the assignment. Remembering that her instructor's class lectures had assumed the validity of evolution but had indicated debate existed on the mechanism by which the process operates, she decides to investigate the latter issue.

While each of the three assignments offered *some* guidance in helping to formulate a topic and thesis, you should be aware that lurking in the jungles of academe is the possibility of the dreaded assignment to "write a ten-page research paper; you pick the topic." This is the most difficult of all paper assignments because it is the most general. Here the need for careful preresearch activity to even begin to formulate an area of investigation is of paramount importance. If you are faced with such an assignment, use the prewriting tools described in Chapter 4 to select your topic area. At this stage you are analyzing not information you have collected but your own interests and prior knowledge—a necessary step in working with the general assignment.

Of course, even though Jennifer and Kris have limited their topics and quickly formed a working thesis, they are not surprised when they find it necessary to further modify their topics. Work in the library often leads to further refinement of topic and thesis; this refinement will give new direction to analysis and require further research.

This circularity of process is especially significant because it illustrates the proper attitude toward writing a research paper. Gathering information is not simply locating and recording information that supports your current point of view. You must approach your subject with an open mind; this does not mean that you should not begin with a tentative thesis, but rather that you should always be willing to move your thesis in whatever direction a fair and objective review of the evidence thus far dictates. No matter how strongly you *feel* that punctuated equilibrium is the best explanation of the mechanism of evolution or that vitamin C is effective in preventing the common cold, you are obliged to gather information impartially. You must collect and consider both factual data and the responsible, informed opinion of experts which indicates that Darwinian gradualism presents a better model or that vitamin C has little effect on the incidence of colds. If you do your research well, your opinions will often change as you encounter additional information and new viewpoints.

Do not approach your research paper with the idea that you must begin with a point to "prove." Too often, when students begin their research projects intending to demonstrate the truth of a position they already *know* to be true, they act as if "proof" consists of excluding facts and opinions which support a contrary view. This attitude may extend to the failure to examine resources which, because of title, author, or source, are believed to be in opposition to the predetermined thesis.

What is important is that you conscientiously and efficiently collect and record information pertaining to your continuously evolving topic and thesis.

# TOOLS FOR GATHERING INFORMATION

This book emphasizes the use of computerized tools as aids in the research process, but, of course, electronic tools are not necessary in preparing a college-level research paper. After all, such papers were being assigned to students long before the birth of ENIAC in 1946. While access to a computer and various software packages can make the research process easier and, what is more important, more successful, an understanding of the basic techniques of manual information gathering provides both a necessary background to computerized methods and an alternative method when electronic aids are not available. Just keep in mind that this book covers a range of tools; select those that are available and appropriate in a given research situation.

## Conventional Methods

Of course, you can collect the information you need to complete your research paper by using a pen or pencil to record each item of relevant information clearly on a 3 by 5 card. We emphasize cards, each containing a single entry, to facilitate the sorting and selection that is an integral part of the analysis and drafting process. There are many advantages in using individual cards that can be sorted into order and then copied one after the other into your paper rather than working from a sheet of paper containing a multitude of entries. One important advantage is in alphabetizing the items for your final bibliography. Invariably, working from items scattered through two or three sheets and scraps of paper, you will find yourself typing in a work by John Watson, only to discover that you have omitted a work by Arthur Doyle. Sorting notes by subject is even more cumbersome if those notes are on sheets of paper; you may find yourself tearing those sheets into pieces so that you can collect, for example, all notes discussing the effect of cocaine on the creative process.

When working with note cards, it is most important to establish a systematic procedure. The greatest danger in any information-gathering system is that you may omit some important item of information: the date of a periodical article, the pages in your source from which you took a note. When working with one of the computerized information-gathering systems, you will be prompted to fill in all essential blanks by a to-be-completed word processor template or database entry screen. No such prompting is offered by a blank note card. To assure complete, accurate information collection, establish a routine and follow it precisely for each card, thus minimizing the danger of omission. For example, when taking notes, put the source in the upper left corner of the card, complete your quotation, paraphrase or summary in the midsection of the card, add the page reference in the lower right corner, and then place any key words in the upper right corner. Even if you are taking several notes from the same source, complete each step in sequence; don't plan to return to add the source name later so as not to interrupt your note-taking train of thought. To do so virtually ensures that the sources will not be indicated in some notes and that these notes will thus be useless to the overall project. The sample card in Figure 3-1 was prepared in exactly this way: each item was recorded in turn, in the same relative location as all similar items on other cards.

## The Xerox Machine as a Research Tool

There are times when you need to record complex, heavily detailed information, information that you simply cannot summarize effec-

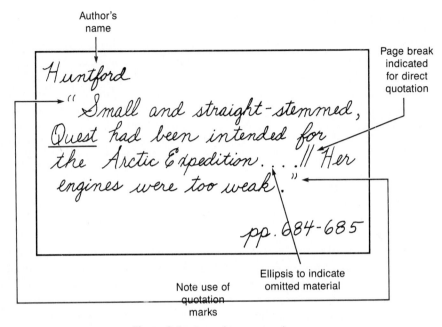

**Figure 3-1**. *Sample note card.*

tively, at least at the note-taking stage. Perhaps you have not yet explored your topic sufficiently to analyze an important passage so as to avoid misrepresentation and error in your note taking. Should you devote precious time to copying a page or two onto cards or into your database? How can you record a graphic or table which you wish to incorporate in your text in its original form? Does reading microfilm give you a headache?

Enter the student's friend: the library photocopying machine. There are times like those just described when judicious use of a photocopy is the most appropriate course of action. When you do elect this option, you must, however, keep some rules and restrictions in mind.

Make certain that you get a clear, properly contrasted copy, especially if you plan to incorporate a photocopied graphic in your final presentation. Remember that images with a heavy concentration of black tend to produce unsatisfactory copies.

Position the original so that all the material you wish to preserve is exposed. Align the copy using the guidelines on the machine and be careful to get as much of the inner edges of tightly bound volumes as you can without damaging the spine of the volume. Also check to see if you need to turn to the end of an article or book to record the text of references noted in the material you are copying.

Be certain to record all bibliographic information—author, title, source, date, and pages—on the copy. All too often students assume that the name of the periodical will be on every page, only to discover the error when it's too late.

Be aware that, if you are using one of the computer tools for note taking, you will want to incorporate some of the photocopied material in your database or word processor file. Unless you do this, that material will not be involved in the search, selection, and organization techniques that make the computer so important to the process.

## The Word Processor

Of all the computer tools discussed in this book, the word processor will probably effect the greatest, immediate change in your writing. However, don't think that its uses are limited to the obvious: the drafting, revision, and editing of your writing. The word processor can also serve as an electronic notebook, automating your note cards and bibliography, and as outliner in both the planning and revision stages.

Before any words appear on paper, they appear on the monitor of the computer. Therein lies both the magic and the danger of the word processor. Remember, the screen image is just that: an image. Nothing is permanent until you make it so by saving your text on a disk (and even then, it can be changed by reediting) or by printing it. You don't like a certain word or a phrase? With just a few keystrokes you can replace it. Want your third paragraph as your introduction? Again, change is just a key press away. Those patterns of light on the screen are your guides as you move through drafting and revision, so before examining more specifically what the word processor offers, let's look at a typical word processor screen (see Figure 3-2) and develop a little vocabulary.

This screen illustrates screen features common to most full-featured programs; although screens are arranged differently for different programs, the same three basic areas of information are usually found somewhere on the screen.

1. *Current status.* This includes the name of the document being entered or edited, the location (page, line, and column) where you are currently working, and any special settings controlling the program operation, such as line spacing and whether new letters will replace existing characters or will be inserted. As on this screen, many word processors add to the status information by including a "ruler line" which shows you the current right and left margins and the location of any tabulator stops (on the sample screen, the tabs are indicated by a "!").

**2.** *An Operation Control panel.* To perform operations other than simple typing, you must give instructions to the word processor program. This information is conveyed in one of two ways: by issuing "commands" (keystrokes that have a special meaning to the program) or making a selection from a "menu" of available activities. The sample screen is taken from a command-driven word processor: the Main Menu is actually just a list of useful commands to help you remember what keys to press to carry out a particular activity. On the sample screen, the "` "` before a letter in the menu indicates that both the Control key and a letter key are pressed at the same time to perform a particular operation. For example, if the Control key and the Y key are pressed at the same time with the cursor on the last line as shown, that line will be removed. In a menu system, an area similar to the illustrated Main Menu will appear; you perform an activity by making a choice from the menu (often by pointing to it with a secondary cursor and pressing Return).

**3.** *The document.* This area contains the words you are entering and editing. Of course, only a portion of your writing can appear on screen at a time, but you can move freely back and forth through the paper using the appropriate cursor control key combinations.

You are probably wondering what the "cursor" is. It is the indicator, in the text, of your current position. It may be either a small rectangle or an underline, "_____", often flashing to attract your attention. When you type a letter or begin to mark a block for

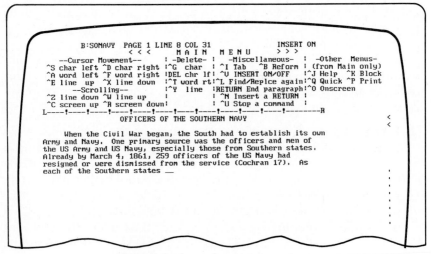

**Figure 3-2.** *A word processor screen.*

deletion, the change will occur at the current location of the cursor.

Word processors are available in a wide variety of levels of sophistication, from basic models that offer little more than automated typing to full-featured versions that allow the user to view several documents at the same time and automatically adjust footnotes and bibliography within any of several professional formats. Regardless of its level of complexity, the word processor you use will certainly contain several basic capabilities.

Using a word processor, you can *add text* at any point in your document. Such additions can take the form of *insertions* or *replacements*. In insertion, the added material simply pushes the existing words to the right and, thus, new words are added to the old. In replacement, the new material is typed *over* existing material and removes it by taking its place. Most beginning users rely more heavily on insertion. This ensures that you won't eliminate anything by mistake; when you have finished making your additions, you simply delete the now unnecessary words and characters.

The word processor allows you to *delete text* quickly and easily. Basic word processors allow you to delete single characters or larger sections which you select and mark off as a "block." More advanced versions will automatically select other lexical units; you can delete a word, sentence, or paragraph. Some will allow you to recover ("undo") your last deletion.

You can also *move* blocks of text from any point in your document to any other point. The concept of the *block* is central to most word processing systems. A block is a portion of text, from a single letter to several pages of material, that will be operated on as a unit. You can mark a block manually by placing the cursor at the start of the material you wish to delete, move, or copy and then "dragging" the block, usually marked by highlighting, along behind the cursor as you move it to the point at which you wish to end the block. Many word processors will automate the marking of blocks which fall into certain categories (e.g., words, sentences, and paragraphs) to spare the user the time and trouble of moving the cursor to mark the block.

Few writing sessions move directly from the opening of a first draft through revising and editing to printing of the final presentation copy of the paper. You will return to the computer to work on a paper several times. It is therefore necessary for the word processor to *save* your work to a disk and *reload* work from the disk at a later time so that you can make additions and alterations. Saved papers are referred to as *files*. When you save a paper to a file for the first time, you will be asked to give the file a name. Two factors in the naming of files are crucial:

1. You cannot give two files the same name. If you do this, the newly created file will simply replace the older one. This is fine when the new file is an updated version of the older but a disaster if the two are different since the older file will be irretrievably lost.

2. You should give some thought to naming your files within the naming constraints imposed by your computer system. Typically, file names can be up to eight characters long and should begin with a letter; they should contain neither spaces nor special punctuation characters such as a period. Thus EVOLVE and CIVILWAR are acceptable file names; EVOLUTION (too long) and FLY BUZZ (containing a space) are not. Try to give your files descriptive names; you will reload the file by name, and as your disk contains an ever-increasing number of files, well-chosen names will help you select the file you want. A week from now, EVOLVE or DICKENS will mean more than NUM1 or PAPER ever can.

In addition to saving and reloading whole files, most word processors allow you to add another file from the disk to the paper you are currently working on. This process, called *merging*, does not alter the state of the file being added and is central to the effective use of word processor templates as an aid to the information-gathering process.

In order to submit your paper, you must *print* it. It is here, in determining the appearance of the printed page (often called *formatting*), that word processors show the greatest variation. At a minimum, your word processor will allow you to set the right and left margins for the printed page and the spacing between lines; when asked, it will then produce as many printed copies as you desire. Most word processors allow you to print portions of your text with underlining and a darker print called *boldface;* some even allow you to print in italics. Additionally, you can usually print any portion of the text, useful if you need to make a short correction on a single page and don't wish to reprint the entire paper. Finally, many word processors will automatically number your pages and place a text passage, such as your name and class number, at the top (called a *heading*) or bottom (a *footing*) of every page.

The word processor really begins to show its usefulness for the research process when we use it to *integrate* material from several areas. Using the merge capability we discussed earlier, you can combine several files and then edit them as a unit. For example, you can add your note card file to the end (or, for that matter, the beginning) of the first draft of your paper; then, using the block move capability, position the notes you wish to incorporate in the paper, and, using the block delete capability, remove notes you have decided not to incorporate. When you have completed the paper, you can follow the same procedure to append your working bibliography and then delete works which are not referenced.

Merging files is, however, limited to adding complete files to the draft. If the merged files contain substantial material you don't wish to use, deletion activities can take quite some time. (Also, if you are not careful, a passage or two that you meant to remove will find its way into your final draft.)

If your word processor supports *windows*, integration is even easier. Windowing allows you to view two different files at the same time and to move the cursor between them to edit each. You can also move or copy a block material from one window to the other and thus move it between the files. A window can also display your outline so that you can reference your plan of organization as you develop your draft; if you elect this procedure, you can copy outline headings from one window to the other to serve as section headings for the paper (see Figure 3-3).

This screen demonstrates the use of windows to keep an outline in view during drafting. The upper window (window 1) contains the outline; the lower (window 2), the draft. The cursor appears only in window 2 since that is the file currently being edited.

Incidentally, this screen, taken from a different word processor than Figure 3-2, displays a different method of implementing commands. Below window 2 lies the Command Menu; the line "Select option or type command letter" and the presence of the highlighted

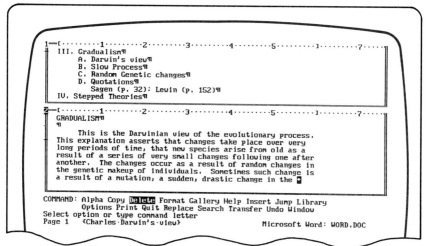

**Figure 3-3**. *Word processor screen with windows.*

block in the menu indicates that the program is ready to receive an operational command rather than to simply add more text to the draft. Note the position of the highlighting. If Return were pressed, a deletion would be made at the current cursor location. The status line at the bottom of the screen has another feature we have not previously seen: it displays the last block deleted. Since this word processor has *undelete* capability, we could restore that last (but only the last) deletion, in this case Charles Darwin's view, with a single command.

Suppose that you are using a data management program to collect information. It almost certainly will allow you to create a file based on the database which can be read by your word processor for merging. This makes integration even easier because the sorting and selection capabilities of the data management program can eliminate extraneous material before it goes to the word processor, thus minimizing block deletion activity.

The word processor will also perform elementary selection activities using its *find* functions. When you select this option, you will be asked for the text you wish to locate. After indicating this choice, you may be asked about other options such as direction (whether you wish to search from the current location of the cursor to the end or to the beginning of the file), the importance of case (whether you wish to locate "Fly" as well as "fly"), and whether you wish to include words which contain your text ("Darwinian" as well as "Darwin"). By repeating the same find function you can move through the entire file locating each occurrence of the selected text. As they are located, you can move them so that they appear together or copy them to another file using windows.

Putting several of these functions together demonstrates the great value the word processor can have for the research process. To facilitate the recording of information in a standard form, you make use of a *template*. A template is a file you created which serves as a guide to filling in necessary information. The template file consists of *prompts;* a prompt is simply a word or a phrase to remind you of the information to be recorded, followed by enough blank space to contain the information you will enter. For example, a template file for collecting bibliography information on a periodical source is shown in Figure 3-4. Notice how the file allows more space for items likely to need it (such as "title" and "comments") and contains a line of special characters ("**********************************") which visually separate individual entries when several copies of the template have been added, and filled in, consecutively.

To use the template to build a working bibliography, follow the following steps:

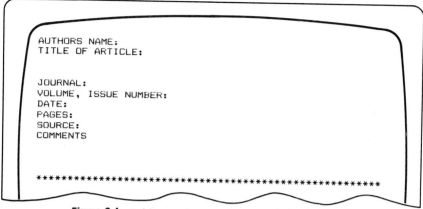

```
AUTHORS NAME:
TITLE OF ARTICLE:

JOURNAL:
VOLUME, ISSUE NUMBER:
DATE:
PAGES:
SOURCE:
COMMENTS

**************************************************
```

**Figure 3-4**. *Bibliography template—periodical source.*

1. Create the template file, just like any other text file, placing the prompts (e.g., "AUTHOR'S NAME") as you wish. Put the prompts in all uppercase so that they stand out from your entries. Use the space bar to add as many spaces as you feel each item will require.

2. Save the template file with a descriptive name such as BIBTEMP (for "bibliography template").

3. Open a new file called BIBLIO and begin the working bibliography file by merging (or, for some word processors, "reading") the file BIBTEMP. This will place a single copy of the blank form in the bibliography file.

4. Add information for the current entry. Turn your word processor's insert feature off; if the insert remains on, the benefits of restricting entry length will be defeated. Move the cursor to each entry line and fill in the information.

5. To add another source to your working bibliography, move the cursor to the end of the existing bibliography file and merge in another copy of BIBLIO.

6. When you have finished entering new bibliography items, don't forget to save the BIBLIO file.

Through all this, the BIBTEMP template file remains unchanged and can be used as many times as you wish. It can be used to create different working bibliography files, as long as each file has a different name.

Useful as it may be, the word processor has certain disadvantages as an information-gathering tool. While these limitations are not apparent when you are gathering information, they become obvious when you begin to analyze your research material. Unlike the database, most word processors have a limited sorting capability. As a result, alphabetizing your working bibliography in order to see how many works have been published by a given author, for example, is inconvenient at best. Moreover, the word processor is limited in its ability to select notes containing specific information; again, this task is more suited to the database. The word processor can search for keywords or key phrases, but once you have located the search item, you must manually copy the information to a separate file if you wish to isolate material for analysis. Additionally, searches for items that meet multiple criteria (for example, a single search which locates all notes from articles containing the words "evolution" *and* "gradualism" anywhere in their titles) is impossible with a word processor.

## The Database

A database is, simply stated, a systematic method for storing a body of information structured so that individual items of information can be selected and retrieved on the basis of questions asked by the user.

You might have worked with nonelectronic versions of the database concept countless times in the past. The card catalog in your library is a database; each card in the catalog contains a collection of similar facts arranged according to a set of rules. Actually, in most libraries the card catalog consists of two databases: the author-title catalog and the subject catalog; these are different databases since the cards contain somewhat different items of information, and they are arranged according to different principles. Another familiar example of the database concept is the timetable of your university. Each entry in the timetable contains the identification number of a course, the title of the course, the days and the hour at which the class meets, the room where it meets, and the instructor's name. To find a particular course, we need to know the identification number (usually a combination of department and course number) since this is the guiding principle of organization.

While nonelectronic databases are both familiar and useful, there are significant advantages to manipulating the information by means of a computer. In a conventional timetable it is not difficult to obtain information on Section 7 of English 244 and not really much more trouble to see how many sections of Biology 150 are being offered next semester; after all, both these selections make use of the fact that the information is organized by course name and section number. Consider how much trouble it would be to determine which classes meet at 9 o'clock on either Wednesday or Friday mornings. This would require your scanning the entire timetable, looking at the time and day(s) of class meetings and copying those which meet at the specified times into a separate list. That is exactly what an electronic database does; it does nothing that you couldn't do with the timetable, a pencil, and some paper. Its advantage is that it can scan a large body of information with much greater speed and accuracy than you could ever hope to achieve. All you need to do is formulate a question which will guide the selection of information items.

Using a database allows you to make use of a far wider range of sources than would be possible with purely manual methods. The database can sort a bibliography of fifty items into alphabetical order in seconds. In a minute or so, it can search a collection of 250 notes and find all those which are taken from works by a given author and contain a particular word or phrase. It allows you to try several different analytical strategies and arrangements of information quickly and easily.

Three terms are important to understanding the construction and use of database files: file, records, and fields.

The first of these terms, *file*, should be familiar to you from our discussion of the word processor. A database file, like a word processor file, is a collection of related items of information stored together so that they can be retrieved and manipulated together. In the database, this means that a file contains the same pieces of information for a set of related items. For example, the subject catalog of your library can be considered as a database file. It contains the same information (a subject classification, author's name, title of the book, etc.) for a group of similar items (books in the library). Within far broader limits than you are likely to reach, a file can hold information on any number of items, but the information stored must be of the same type for each item.

The individual items stored in a database file are called *records*. As noted above, a file can contain a very large number of records, but each record must be able to hold exactly the same kind of information as every other record in the file. For example, consider the employment forms workers fill out when they join a company. When all the forms are collected in a single folder, that folder is a file and each of the forms is a record. Each form has the same number and type of possible blanks to be filled in. For each employee, the employer can record Social Security number, name, address, age, and so on. If the employer wishes to include the spouse's name for a married employee, all forms must include a blank for that information. Thus all records *can* contain the same information, even if, for some records, not all information is entered.

The slots that hold the individual pieces of information within each record are called *fields*. In the personnel file, each blank that an employee might fill in is a field. Fields have length; that is, each field is limited in the quantity of information it can hold, although different fields in the same record can have different lengths. In the same file, all records must contain the same fields, and from record to record the fields must match in type (whether they are to contain text or numbers) and size.

In the sample screen illustrated in Figure 3-5, you can see a single record from a database file, BIBLIO, containing a working bibliography. As the status line indicates, this is record 13 of a total of 42 records in the file. Each field is identified by name (e.g., "Lname," "Title," "Publisher"). Following the field name, the content of the field is displayed. Since this is a record for a periodical article, the place and publisher fields are unfilled.

The field is the controlling unit of the database. If you are using a personal database program to construct your own database, you should spend some time deciding what information you may wish to use and be certain to allow a field for each different item of information. Also, be certain that you create your fields with adequate length to hold the largest possible response you may wish to store in a field; for example, if you try to record a book by Jacob Bronowski you will quickly see that a field length of seven letters for the last name field of a bibliography database is inadequate. These determinations must be made at the conception stage; once you've begun to fill in records, it's really quite cumbersome to go back and add fields or change their size.

In this book we shall consider two kinds of databases: the personal database and the online database.

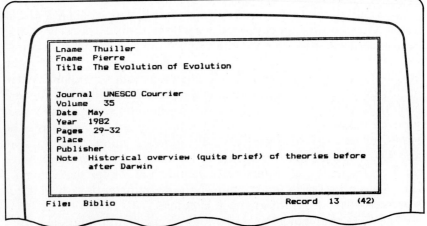

**Figure 3-5**. *Data management screen—bibliography.*

**Personal Databases** Personal databases are created by a database management program according to specifications that you (or your instructor) establish; they contain only the information you have selected for inclusion. When you decide to collect your notes using a personal database, you must decide what information you wish to record for each note, set up the structure (the number, size, and type of the fields) of your electronic "note cards," and enter each note into the database you have created.

A personal database is limited only by the management program you use to create it. Typically, it can contain several thousand records, each with 100 or more fields. Most programs allow fields of 250 or more characters. What all this means is that a personal database created with a personal computer data management program has limitations which far exceed any demand you are likely to make. In addition, since you decide what to place in each of the fields, any information you acquire can be stored and manipulated by a personal database.

Once you have entered information in a personal database, you can sort and select records based on the information in any field or combination of fields. For example, you can search a working bibliography database to isolate all the articles from issues of *Science* published between the years 1970 and 1980 which contain "DNA" in their titles.

A personal database with hundreds of records can be processed in seconds. Performing the same search through material written on 3 by 5 cards might take hours—so long, in fact, that you are likely to limit the number of cards. Thus the personal database allows you to use a far larger number of items of information from a far wider range of sources than is realistically possible with manual methods.

Once you have selected a subset of your database, you can export it to a standard text file for later incorporation in your paper, thus avoiding the need for retyping and eliminating the typing errors which always seem to creep in.

The personal database also provides great assistance in organizing material. It can arrange your bibliography alphabetically by author for final printing. If you would like to see the spread in time covered by your research, the database will arrange your bibliography chronologically; this organization might also reveal a gap in coverage. Arranging your notes according to their source could reveal a bias for a single source.

**Online Databases** The online database is a collection of information you can search with a personal computer or terminal. This information was selected and prepared by a third party. This has both advantages and disadvantages: there is far more information available than you could ever hope to collect on your own, but it may not always be in the precise form you wish.

The online card catalogs which are beginning to appear in all universities, large and small, are examples of online databases. Information-retrieval services such as Dialog and BRS provide remote access through telephone lines to a range of online databases. After connecting to Dialog, for example, you can access over 220 different databases containing more than 110 million separate information records. Dialog's databases cover a wide range of fields, including the physical and biological sciences, engineering, the social sciences, education, history, language and literature, and business and economics. The great advantage to this is that, using essentially the same search strategies you would employ using manual reference materials, you can locate a wealth of precisely focused information with great speed. Like all things in life, however, there is a cost for such convenience. Such services are offered on a charge basis; you pay for the time you use them. However, when search patterns are thought out in advance, the speed of electronic data manipulation means that actual connect time can be quite short and relatively inexpensive. As a result, many university libraries offer connection to such services to students at no or reduced cost. It is an investment well worth considering for major research projects.

## Mental Tools for Information Gathering

Whether you are using the latest electronic aids or 3 by 5 cards to collect material, you have another information-gathering tool at your disposal: your imagination. Whether you are using the periodical indexes in the reference room, accessing an online bibliographic database such as the *Book Review Index* on Dialog, or working with the card catalog, you must exercise your imagination.

Most of your research will involve using some form of subject search. For this type of search to be successful, you must continually ask yourself what categories could possibly contain information on your subject. Remember, indexes and catalogs are created by human beings just like yourself; each item is assigned to a location, or provided with cross-references, by someone who asked a similar question: "What is the most appropriate classification for this material?" Try to think like the person who created the index. If your first inquiry doesn't turn up anything useful, don't assume there's nothing available and give up; try again with a different approach. Try different possible subject areas.

Suppose you are writing a paper on the sources of the imaginary creatures in J. R. Tolkien's *The Hobbit* and *The Lord of the Rings*.Obviously, you've located sources indexed under "Tolkien, J. R." and the titles of the works in question, but when you turn to the subject heads "Hobbit" and "Orc," you find nothing. If you stop now, you've left much of your job undone. Not until you've looked at the sections "Fantasy" (or "Fantasy literature"), "Children's literature" (where much of the best criticism on *The Hobbit* is listed), and "mythical beasts" can you begin to be confident that you've collected the available resources.

If you have trouble imagining possible alternative subject headings, you can turn to the same tool that library catalogers use: the *Library of Congress Subject Headings*. This two-volume work contains the subject categories, cross-references, and "See also" references used by the Library of Congress in preparing its card catalog. Useful, of course, in searching the card catalog of your own library, this work can also help you in the various subject-oriented periodical indexes.

This technique of imaginative subject searching is, perhaps, even more important in online searching. The problem here lies not so much in locating material as in selectively limiting the scope of your research. The computer can help you by gradually narrowing the list of sources as you provide increasingly specific search criteria. For example, if you are researching the role of the paper industry in environmental pollution and you ask an online source such as *Environmental Bibliography* (which contains over 275,000 individual records extending back to 1973) to search for items dealing with "pollution," you are going to be faced with literally thousands of possible sources. By applying increasingly restrictive limits to the results of each search, you can swiftly narrow the list of sources to a manageable level. After the search for "pollution," narrow the list to include only those works dealing with water. Further narrow the scope of potential sources by asking for only those items in the most recent list which relate to paper industry or paper production. The resulting list may still contain more than you can deal with, so you limit your search by asking only for those items which relate to heavy metals. Now the list of sources has been narrowed to the point where you can order a printout and begin your reading.

## Limiting Your Search

As you begin to acquire more and more sources of information and investigate these sources and collect notes, you will certainly reach the point of asking "Can I stop now? Haven't I collected enough information?" If you are using electronic information location and retrieval tools, the question becomes even more pressing since these resources provide access to even greater numbers of sources. Realistically, it is impossible to use every available item of information. How then can you limit your research and still do an adequate job?

First, realize that some of the reasons students often use for abandoning further research are simply unacceptable; for instance, "I've seen some of the same information now several times." Granted, the sources you've looked at *so far* have demonstrated some repetition, but it's entirely possible that the next source may present an entirely new perspective. Keep on searching.

"I've gathered enough information to fill up five pages, and that's what the assignment requires." Remember, your goal in carrying out a research project is to collect information to answer a question or solve a problem, not just to fill up a predetermined number of pages.

"I'm finding information that contradicts the thesis I've selected." Research should be a process of discovery, a search for the *best* answer. If information begins to demonstrate that your thesis needs to be changed, let that information take you where it will and change the thesis if such a change is dictated by your research.

## Filtering Your Sources

If the reasons above are not adequate to terminate your research, how can you effectively limit your inquiry? By "filtering" potential sources, you can focus your attention on those sources most likely to prove valuable and can effectively limit the amount of reading you will need to do. Three filters can be applied to the library research process: chronological, citation, and source.

For most projects, especially for those in the sciences, the chronological filter is most effective. Simply stated, this filter operates on the premise that more recently published works offer the most complete and accurate information. This means that newer works should be read first; often they will indicate the distance into the past your research must travel. When you must curtail your research, forgo consideration of older material *unless* your reading has indicated it to be of great importance. For example, research into the role of DNA must consider the crucial articles published in *Nature* by Crick and Watson, even though they appeared over thirty years ago. The chronological filter is also important for it offers information that can be applied to the other two filters. For example, the documentation included in recent material can indicate which authors should be retained by citation filtering.

You should keep in mind, however, that not all subjects lend themselves to chronological filtering. Certain subjects require an historical perspective. For example, Jennifer's paper on naval enlistment patterns in the Confederate Navy during the Civil War gains much from the use of contemporary letters, material garnered from an 1880 volume which would have been neglected had recent publication been the sole guide to resources.

Authors and articles which are widely cited (referred to) by writers in the field are likely to prove valuable resources to student researchers as well. As you examine recent sources, take note of their lists of references. As you see the same authors appear again and again, be certain to examine their writings.

Finally, consider location. Within any field some journals have greater credibility than others. As you begin to filter out material, be certain to examine articles located in these respected journals. Journals aimed at sophisticated readers such as *Nature* and *Science,* are far more likely to produce information for college-level research than are general-interest periodicals like *Time, Seventeen,* and *The Readers' Digest.*

## ▰▰▰▰LOCATING AND RETRIEVING INFORMATION

As a research writer, your principal goal is to formulate, refine, and ultimately support a thesis. While other forms of writing have the same goals, your research paper is based on knowledge you have gained from sources outside your own immediate experience and goes beyond common knowledge of the general readership. However, before you incorporate such information in your work you must locate, read, and understand material from a substantial number of sources.

Probably you will first think of moving at once to the card catalog to begin the information-collection process. After all, you've been locating books with card catalogs ever since you first went to the children's library back home to check out a copy of *The Island Stallion.* Certainly the card catalog will be part of your research strategy in some instances, but you are more likely to find greater value in materials not indexed in the card catalog; it is to those sources that you should first direct your attention.

Remember that books are not the most current of sources. Once an author has completed the writing of the book and submitted the manuscript to the publisher for production, it generally takes a year for a book to reach your library. When you add to that the time it took the author to write the book, you can see that information located in any volume found in the card catalog is probably two or more years old. If you are researching the causes of British involvement in the Crimean War or early twentieth-century attitudes toward drug use, for instance, such a lapse in time may not be important, but for most topics, especially those involving the sciences, current information is vitally important. To effectively research such subjects, you must turn to periodicals, works published at regular intervals (usually four or more times per year).

## Indexes

Periodical sources are usually shorter and more focused than those found in books, enabling you to concentrate your research on directly relevant information. To locate these items of information, you will use general and specialized indexes found either in your library's reference room or in an online database.

**General Indexes**   If you draw on your high-school experience, you will probably go immediately to the *Readers' Guide to Periodical Literature,* but before you do, consider the difference between high-school and college-level work and how the purpose of a general-interest index such as the *Readers' Guide* may affect its utility for your current project. High-school papers frequently focus on gathering and reporting information; college papers attempt to bring new information *and their author's analysis of that information* to their readers. For the high-school paper, magazines such as *Newsweek* and *Popular Science* may provide an adequate source of material but usually contain little information not already familiar to the college reader. The general readership magazine commonly fails to report in any detail the work and interpretations of acknowledged experts in disciplines studied at the university level. If you are interested in the opinions of the person on the street concerning the 55 mile per hour speed limit, locate sources in the *Readers' Guide;* if you are researching the impact of reduced speed on the American economy, look elsewhere.

The *Readers' Guide* can, of course, prove valuable in providing background information in some areas. If you know nothing at all about the cause of the extinction of the dinosaurs, you can get started by a quick look at some of the recent popular writing on this complex subject. But you will soon wish to examine the writings of respected paleontologists rather than read summaries of their work in *Time* and *Analog.*

If you do use the *Readers' Guide,* you must understand its rather individualistic method of presentation (see Figure 3-6). It lists most entries twice: once under a subject heading and again under the author's name; you will generally find the subject categories most useful. Most subject headings contain subheadings to aid your search, as well as cross-references to related subject areas. Unlike most other

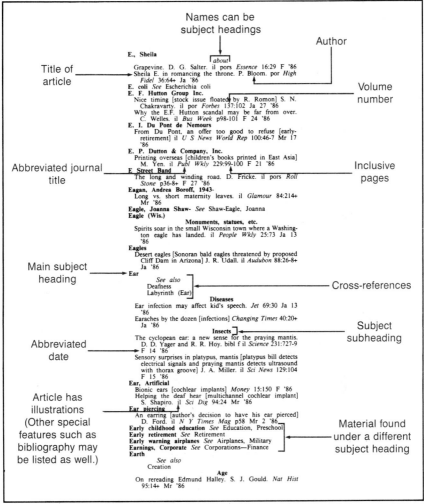

**Figure 3-6**. *Typical entries from the Readers' Guide..*

references, the *Readers' Guide* provides the titles of indexed articles *before* the name of their authors. In addition, the work uses a very concise (and often cryptic) system of abbreviations; be sure to check the details of the system printed in the front of each volume. Be especially careful to check the list of abbreviated periodical titles if you are not absolutely certain of the title of a magazine which contains an article you wish to read; failure to do so may lead you to believe that your library does not subscribe to the periodical you require.

A final word of caution: the *Readers' Guide* system of describing entries is *in no way* an acceptable form of documentation for your final paper. *Do not* simply copy a *Readers' Guide* entry into your final bibliography.

**Specialized Indexes** The *Readers' Guide* might be your first stop in a search for current information on your topic, especially if you need basic background information, but you must recognize that drafting an effective paper will require you to move beyond the general level of information provided by the sources indexed there. As you refine and narrow your topic, you become something of an expert on a limited subject area; as a result, material which is needed by the inexperienced reader—material that you once found useful because of your own lack of knowledge—is now too elementary. As you acquire basic information on your subject, you will need to refer to increasingly sophisticated sources of information, information that you will assimilate and pass along to your readers. To locate this material, you must turn to more advanced sources: the professional journals in the field you are researching. Just as there are specialized professional journals, there are specialized indexes to those journals.

Your first step into more specialized research may bring you to either the *Humanities Index* or the *Social Sciences Index*. Each of these indexes reviews scholarly journals rather than magazines for the general readership. The *Social Sciences Index* covers journals in

| | |
|---|---|
| Anthropology | Medicine |
| Economics | Political science |
| Education | Psychology |
| Law | Sociology |

The *Humanities Index* treats journals of similar scope in

| | |
|---|---|
| Archaeology | Literature and language |
| Classics | Performing arts |
| History | Philosophy |
| | Religious studies |

The *Humanities Index* and the *Social Sciences Index* often provide an adequate range of material for a freshman research paper. You should remember, however, that, like the *Readers' Guide*, they are relatively broad in scope and cannot possibly cover all the scholarly and professional publications in each field they index. In almost every field and subfield studied at our universities, dozens of specialized publications appear on a regular basis. As a result, field-specific indexes attempt to list all pertinent publication on their area of focus.

Admittedly, the material found in these specialized indexes often has drawbacks for the average undergraduate. Many college libraries will have a limited selection of the journals indexed in these resources; you may often find that an article that sounds like just what is needed to cap off your research was published in a journal your library does not receive. While interlibrary loan or use of an online retrieval service may provide access to the material, time or cost factors may preclude these approaches.

Also, many of the articles located in these indexes are too specialized and difficult for the average undergraduate paper. Nevertheless, a thorough job of research demands that you consider such sources. Often, your preliminary research reading in less specialized journals will provide you with the background to understand more complex writing. Most of the journals indexed here provide abstracts to accompany their articles; these will often provide valuable assistance to understanding complex reading material. In many fields, such as the physical and biological sciences, you can make your reading more productive by keeping a specialized scientific dictionary at hand. What is most important is that you make an effort to work with such material; more quickly than you might believe, your research will begin to bring complex material into focus and you will begin to select useful information from these expert-oriented sources and to paraphrase and summarize it so that the reader of your paper can understand and make use of it. A selected list of indexes to specialized professional periodicals in major fields follows. Additional bibliographies are cataloged in the *Bibliographic Index,* a monthly publication listing, by subject, bibliographies containing more than fifty entries either published as separate works or included in books and articles during the reporting period. An additional resource, the *Guide to Reference Books* by Eugene P. Sheehy, lists a wide range of reference tools, including bibliographies such as *The New Cambridge Bibliography of English Literature,* which are not published on an annual basis.

ART

*The Art Index: A Cumulative Author and Subject Index to a Selected List of Fine Art Periodicals*

BIOLOGY

*Biological Abstracts*
*Biological and Agricultural Index*

BUSINESS AND ECONOMICS

*Business Periodicals Index*
*International Bibliography of Economics*

CHEMISTRY

*Chemical Abstracts*
*Current Abstracts of Chemistry and Index Cemicus*

EDUCATION

*Current Index to Journals in Education*
*Education Index*

ENGINEERING, SCIENCE, AND TECHNOLOGY

*Applied Science and Technology Index*
*Engineering Index*
*General Science Index*
*Science Citation Index*

ENVIRONMENTAL SCIENCES

*Pollution Abstracts*

FILM

*Film Literature Index*

HISTORY

*Historical Abstracts: Bibliography of the World's Periodical Literature*
*International Bibliography of Historical Sciences*

LAW

*Index to Legal Periodicals*

LITERATURE AND LANGUAGE

*Abstracts of English Studies*
*MLA International Bibliography of Books and Articles on the Modern Languages and Literatures*

MUSIC

*Music Index: The Key to Current Music Periodical Literature*

PHILOSOPHY

*The Philosopher's Index: An International Index to Philosophical Periodicals*

PHYSICS

*Physics Abstracts*
*Science Abstracts*

POLITICAL SCIENCE

*Political Science: A Bibliographic Guide to the Literature*

PSYCHOLOGY

*Psychological Abstracts*

RELIGIOUS STUDIES

*Religion Index One: Periodicals*
*Religious and Theological Abstracts*

SOCIOLOGY

*Sociological Abstracts*
*Sociological Index*

WOMEN'S STUDIES

*Women Studies Abstracts.*

**Computerized Indexes**  The computer can aid you in your search for sources of information. Many libraries subscribe to computerized periodical indexes. Like its printed cousins, a computerized index covers a broad, but still limited, selection of periodicals; it does have the significant advantage of speeding up the selection process. Using the indexes' database features, you can use author, title, subject, and keyword search strategies to quickly obtain a list of articles related to your topic in a fraction of the time it would take to locate the same material manually. Computerized indexes are not, however, suited to all research projects; their utility is diminished by their limited time span. The *Readers' Guide* indexes periodicals beginning in 1890 (its predecessor, *Poole's Index to Periodical Literature*, was first issued in 1802); the computerized indexes cover a far shorter time span. Because of space limitations (the indexes generally rely on a storage device linked to a personal computer) and the considerable cost of going back to enter material published before the initiation of the service, these indexes generally allow you to search only a few years prior to the current year. If your topic is contemporary, this is no hindrance; remember, currency is often a test of a source's usefulness. If, however, you need to consult older material, you will need to work with conventional, printed indexes.

*InfoTrak*, produced by the Information Access Corporation, is a typical computerized index. It covers over 900 periodicals, including titles in business (e.g., *Econometrica, The Journal of Business Research*), science and technology (*Science, Natural History*), as well as general-interest periodicals such as *U.S. News and World Report, Sports Illustrated*, and *Popular Mechanics*. Admittedly, many of the journals indexed here will not be available in your library. (Does your library subscribe to *Candy and Snack Industry?*) Updated monthly, the *InfoTrak* index covers the current year and three previous years. In addition, it indexes the last six months of *The Wall Street Journal* (and includes the full text of articles from that publication) as well as the last sixty daily issues of *The New York Times*. Other computerized indexes include the *Legaltrac Database*, covering 750 legal publication beginning with 1980, and the *Government Publications Index*, which allows subject, author, and issuing agency searches of material from the *Monthly Catalog* of the U.S. Government Printing Office.

## Online Databases

This is the ultimate in computer-assisted research. The use of an online database puts you in contact with a large computer which holds a wide range of specialized information resources. For example, the Dialog system can put you in touch with over 200 different resources, ranging from full encyclopedias, through bibliographies in most scientific and technical fields, to the files of national news services such as the Associated Press. Once you have located a source of information, in many cases the online database can provide you with the full text of the source (at an additional charge, of course), a useful feature for those with limited library facilities in their special areas of research. Information transmitted from the database can be saved on a floppy disk and later merged with a word processor into a draft of your paper.

Effective use of the online search requires the same search strategies as the use of any subject-oriented resource we have already discussed.

## The Card Catalog

Important as periodical resources are, your search should still consider the possibility of book-length resources. For certain topics with a historical focus, books may be your most complete source of information. Additionally, books often contain extensive bibliographies which will help you to expand your search. As we mentioned above, we locate books by referring to the card catalog.

In effect, any card catalog, whether it is the familiar box structure with lots of funny little drawers (where the tray you want is always

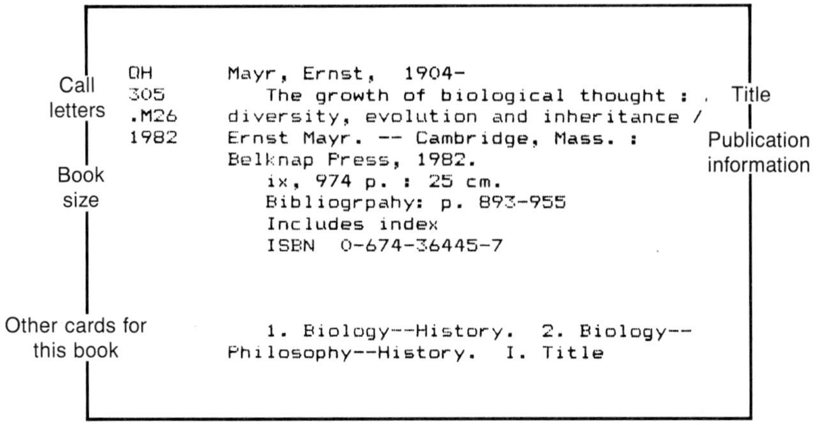

QH
305
.M26
1982

Mayr, Ernst, 1904-
The growth of biological thought : diversity, evolution and inheritance / Ernst Mayr. -- Cambridge, Mass. : Belknap Press, 1982.
ix, 974 p. : 25 cm.
Bibliogrpahy: p. 893-955
Includes index
ISBN 0-674-36445-7

1. Biology--History. 2. Biology--Philosophy--History. I. Title



**Figure 3-7**. *Author entry from card catalog.*

in the bottom row) or a computerized system with database searching capabilities, is used with the same "put yourself in the cataloger's place" method as any other index. Only it often seems that card catalogs require more imagination to get at the material you desire.

While we have all used card catalogs and almost certainly don't require instruction in mechanical details of their use, a quick, visual review of the three principal kinds of card you are likely to encounter may be in order (see Figures 3-7, 3-8, and 3-9).

Increasingly, university libraries are converting to *online card catalogs*. These electronic versions of the manual catalog have the distinct advantage that the same electronic database search procedures dis-

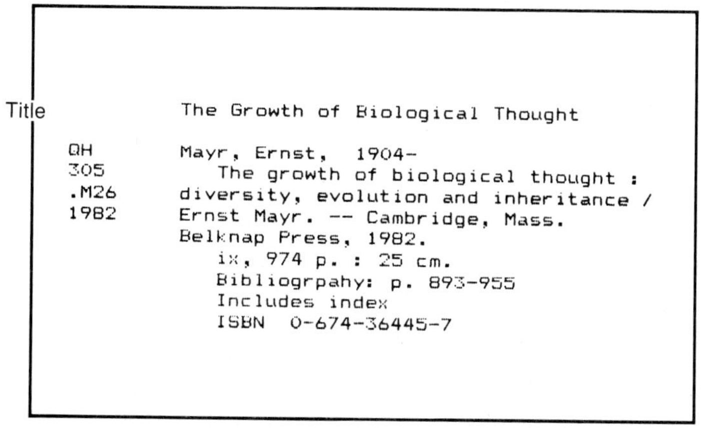

The Growth of Biological Thought

QH
305
.M26
1982

Mayr, Ernst, 1904-
The growth of biological thought : diversity, evolution and inheritance / Ernst Mayr. -- Cambridge, Mass. Belknap Press, 1982.
ix, 974 p. : 25 cm.
Bibliogrpahy: p. 893-955
Includes index
ISBN 0-674-36445-7



**Figure 3-8**. *Title entry from card catalog.*

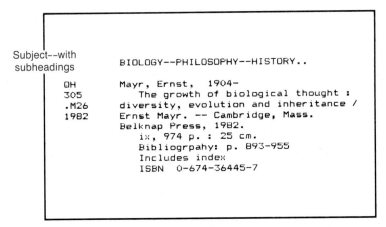

**Figure 3-9**. *Subject entry from card catalog.*

cussed above work quite well. Rather than searching a personal database, however, you use selective retrieval methods to quickly extract only the books you want from the catalog. Normally, the most effective initial searches incorporate subject and keyword in title searching.

Some online catalog systems use a technique of gradual limitation for searching. To use this system, you ask it to provide you with all works which meet a certain criterion—for example, all works in the subject category "Evolution." Almost certainly, this list will contain far too many titles to be useful, so you ask the system to use another criterion, say, works with "History" in their title—but this criterion is applied *not to the entire catalog* but only to the subset created by the previous query. By thoughtful limitation through several linked requests, you will soon reduce the response to a quite workable selection of titles.

You should be aware of one problem currently plaguing many online catalogs. Transferring the existing holdings of a university library from the manual catalog to an online system is a time-consuming and costly process. Thus, only a portion of the holdings of many libraries are recorded online. This means an effective search strategy in this situation will require you to examine both the online and manual card catalogs.

Once you have located several titles in the card catalog, either manually or online, and recorded them in your working bibliography, you may wish to do a little browsing in your library's stack area. While not the most systematic of approaches to the research process, this activity often yields good results. Take note of the call letters of books you have already identified as possible sources. You will soon notice that titles which may be of use fall within certain call letter categories. This means that they will be shelved in the same area of the library. Spend some time in this area looking at titles on the shelves and leafing through those titles that sound promising. You will be surprised at the number of excellent sources you may obtain in this way.

You can further expand the scope of your research by examining the bibliographies found in the books you gathered using the card catalog's subject cards. This is referred to as "chaining" bibliographies. Even if a book contains little useful information itself, it will be helpful to you to examine its bibliography. When these bibliographies yield interesting possibilities, turn to the author-title catalog, or an on-line search by author, to discover which volumes your library holds.

# ▬▬▬ RECORDING INFORMATION

Locating information is a pointless exercise unless, in some way, we record it for future use. Whether you record the information on a computer disk or on cards, the information you collect should be in a form that will help rather than hinder in the preparation of your paper. This means taking care to observe a few simple procedures as you move through the information-gathering process.

Above all, be consistent in recording information. Get into the habit of recording the same information in the same way; it will save trouble later. No one wants to be polishing the final draft of an important assignment only to discover that a page reference has been omitted from a note and the library is closed. A consistent approach to the process will eliminate most such disasters.

## Recording Bibliographic Information: The Working Bibliography

Each time you locate a potential source of information, record as much information as you can immediately. We cannot overemphasize the importance of developing the habit of prompt recording of this information. If you fail to do so, you have virtually guaranteed yourself extra work and frustration.

The process of recording bibliographic information is essentially the same regardless of whether you are using 3 by 5 cards, a word processor, or a personal database. The electronic tools are useful in the way they prompt you to provide information by, essentially, providing you with a form to fill out, but to best understand the logic of bibliography recording, let's begin with the manual method.

**Using Note Cards** As we noted in our earlier introduction to the information-gathering process, each card should contain a single entry to facilitate the sorting and selection which will take place later in the research process.

Too often students jot down just enough information to get their hands on a potential source and wait to see if the source is useful before filling out the bibliography entry. "After all," they say, "why take the time to record all that information for a lead that didn't pan out?" This runs contrary to the concept of developing a *working* bibliography, a list of all *possible* sources. By recording the information at once, you are creating a permanent record of all sources, good, bad, and indifferent. In a research project of some duration this will prove to be of great benefit. Do you really think you will remember an apparently promising source you skimmed and rejected, when you encounter another reference to this same source five weeks later? Its title is likely to appear just as promising as it did weeks ago, so off you go to the stacks, only to discover it's the same disappointing volume all over again. If you had created a bibliography entry at your first encounter, with a note indicating the lack of relevance of the source, you would have been saved time and effort.

An effective working bibliography entry contains two kinds of information: required and optional. Each entry *must* contain the bibliographic information required to identify the source and to prepare a final bibliography entry in case that source is referenced in the final development of the paper. For periodicals, your bibliography entry must include:

Author's full name

Title of the periodical artinle

Name of the journal in full (use of index-specific abbreviations are likely to prove confusing when the time comes to prepare the final bibliography, so record the unabbreviated title now)

The volume, issue numbᴗ., and date

The pages covered by the article

Not all this information will be required in every case to prepare the final bibliography. For example, it's almost certain that you won't need to know both the issue number and the date; in fact, often you won't need either. But since it will take practically no time at all to record this information, it is wise to do so, just in case you have misunderstood some detail of bibliographic convention and suddenly discover that you need information you haven't been recording. Not every reference source will provide all the above, so record whatever is available and complete the information as soon as you physically locate the article.

Examine the sample card for a periodical article in Figure 3-10.

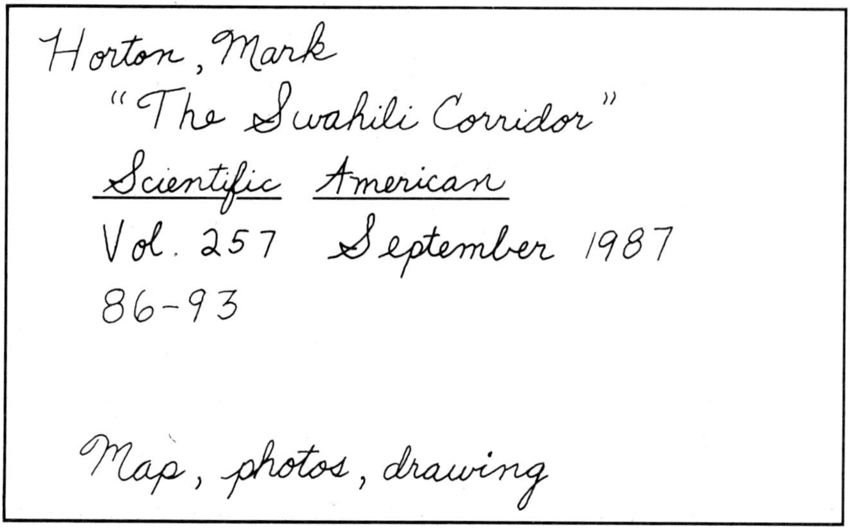

*Horton, Mark*
*"The Swahili Corridor"*
<u>*Scientific American*</u>
*Vol. 257 September 1987*
*86-93*

*Map, photos, drawing*

**Figure 3-10**. *Bibliography card—periodical source.*

Note that it isolates each item of information for clarity and that it does not use abbreviations.

The bibliography entry for a book requires far less information, and your card catalog is certain to record everything you need—so get it down in that bibliography at once! The essentials are:

Author's name
Title of the book, including edition
Place of publication and publisher
Date of publication

Many students copy most, or all, of the card catalog information into the bibliography, including such details as the total number of pages and the presence or absence of illustrations. It is best to omit such details as they take time to complete and may prove confusing when you prepare the final bibliography, where their inclusion is inappropriate.

Your bibliography entry can also contain additional, optional information which will help to save time and effort. It is wise, for example, to record your library's call letters for a book. Additionally, if you examine a source and find it to be of no value, record that as well to avoid a repeat examination. The presence of certain special features, such as an extensive bibliography, also deserves mention. Finally, as an aid to the analysis process, it is wise to record the source, such as the name of the index where you first learned of the item. Remember, however, that this information serves only to assist you in the information-gathering process; it should not find its way into your final bibliography entry.

The sample card in Figure 3-11 illustrates a bibliography card for a book-length source. Notice that in addition to the essential information, it includes the call letters, an observation of a special feature ("Many Drawings"), and a brief notation on the book's usefulness.

While your bibliography card can contain optional information, it should focus on bibliographical matters. Do not enter notes which summarize or quote content. Such notes, which will guide the analysis and drafting stages of your project, are the province of note cards. Trying to combine notes and bibliography on the same card is an invitation to frustration. Sooner or later you will want to use that card in two different plans of organization as the notes and bibliography will be separated and sorted in quite different ways.

**Recording Bibliography on the Word Processor** If you have access to a word processor when collecting your working bibliography, by all means make use of it. Properly used, the word processor will remind you to record all the necessary information, and having this information already on disk when the time comes to prepare your final bibliography will save you time and eliminate errors.

To use the word processor for this purpose, using the process described when we first introduced the template concept earlier in this chapter, set up a template file with prompts for each of the

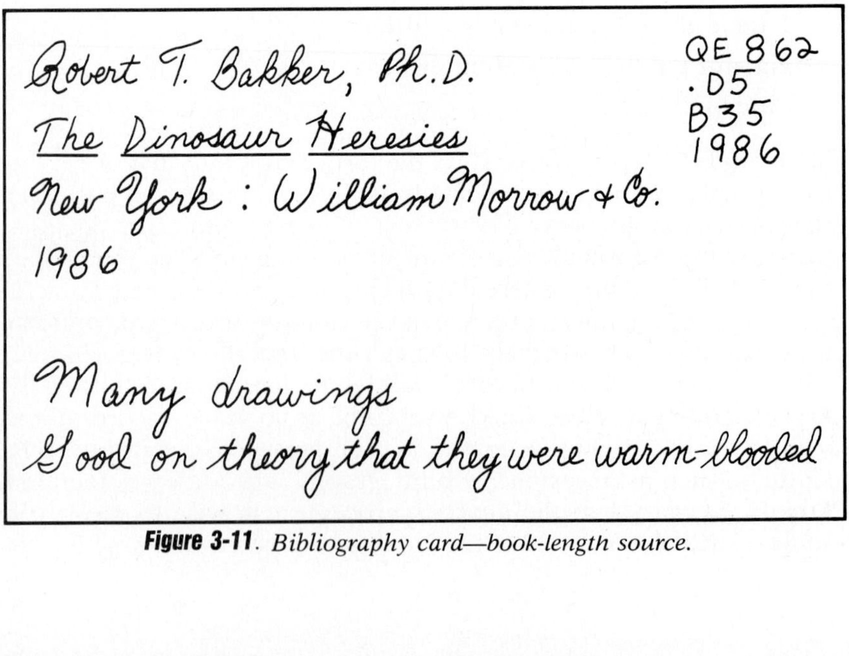
Robert T. Bakker, Ph.D.
The Dinosaur Heresies
New York : William Morrow & Co.
1986
QE 862
.D5
B35
1986
Many drawings
Good on theory that they were warm-blooded

**Figure 3-11**. *Bibliography card—book-length source.*

required items of information; an optional item which you record frequently probably deserves a prompt of its own; others can be entered, when appropriate, into a general COMMENT area.

**Recording Bibliography in a Database** As we shall see in Chapter 4, on analyzing information, the electronic database has even greater advantages as an information-gathering tool than the word processor. Using the database, you can effortlessly select and sort your notes and bibliography in ways almost impossible to the unaided user of note cards.

A bibliography database file should contain records which have, at a minimum, the following fields:

Author's last name

Author's first name and initials (first and last names are kept in separate fields to facilitate the sorting process)

Title (this will serve for either article or book title; be certain to allow enough space, say, fifty characters)

Journal name (left blank for books, but it must be there because of the necessary uniformity of record structure)

Volume and issue number

Date (the last two will be filled in for periodicals only)

Year (for both book and periodical items; separated from date for sorting purposes)

Pages (again, for periodicals only)

Place of publication

Publisher (these two fields will be completed for books)

Comments (for the optional items mentioned earlier)

Once you have created this structure for a bibliographic database, you can add any number of records to it over a period of days or weeks. You can even clone the structure and use it for a different research project. Entering data is as simple as filling in the blanks, and when a record is completed, a new one immediately pops into place, ready to be filled with information on the next source.

## Recording Information Found in the Sources: The Note-Taking Process

**Paraphrase and Summary** A major element of the research paper is the recording of the results of a range of readings from a variety of sources. When reporting the results of readings, writers have three options available: direct quotations, *paraphrases*, or *summaries*. Inexperienced writers tend to give readers lengthy quotations that are often difficult to understand in the context of the paper. It is usually more effective to paraphrase or summarize the material.

Although there is a distinction between a paraphrase and a summary, the difference between them is actually quite slight. A paraphrase is often the same length as the original and is usually expressed in the writer's own words. A summary is briefer than the original and can reflect the language and tone of the original. Both attempt to restate the ideas of others in a more easily understood form, and both sometimes include short quotations. Although there are occasions for paraphrase (when you want to include many of the details in the original, for example), we recommend that you summarize whenever possible.

Summarizing is a skill successful college writers have mastered. Any pattern of thought can be summarized—a speech, a film, or a mathematical proof. While these thoughts *can* be expressed in writing (a film, after all, has a script), we need not have encountered them in written form to summarize them. Summarizing is a means of communicating clearly and concisely important aspects of your intellectual experiences to both yourself and your readers.

The most frequent reason for summary is not, as you might expect, to save space. If full and direct quotation is the most effective way to present your material, space considerations should not prevent you from quoting. Rather, successful writers summarize because by doing so they make material more accessible to their readers by expressing ideas in more familiar language, or combining materials from several sources in the same summary section, or increasing emphasis by rearranging material and omitting those portions which are not important to the purpose of *their* writing.

Writing clear, effective summaries requires careful, attentive reading and attention to detail in your presentation. You should keep the following points in mind when preparing a summary.

1. Determine *your* purpose in writing the summary. Often, your goal may be an objective summary of the original, but there are occasions when your intentions may be quite different from those of the original author. For example, if you are summarizing as part of a justification for your own research, your goal may well be to point out the deficiencies of the original. As a result of this determination, you may focus on certain points in the original, and you may organize the details in your summary in a pattern different from that in the original.

**2.** Identify the essential ideas in the original and incorporate them into your summary. While your purpose in summarizing may lead you to an emphasis or organization different from that in the original, there is *no* justification for a distortion of the essential ideas found in your source.

**3.** Minimize your use of direct quotation. Quote only if you are certain that the original author's exact language is significant. For example, specialized technical vocabulary, a coined word or phrase, and the source author's expression of opinion couched in terms which would be distorted if you provide a summary are all justification for direct quotation. If a source says: "The New Deal was the most blatant political charade ever foisted on a trusting American public" and your note says "Professor X disapproves of the New Deal," you have certainly lost something by summarizing.

Here is a paragraph from a biology paper. It includes both a lengthy quotation *and* a summary of the quotation.

> Inheritance theories (Mayr's theories 1, 2, and 3) explain evolution in terms of changes effected in a parent which are passed genetically to succeeding generations. This theory is most closely identified with the eighteenth-century natural historian Jean-Baptiste Lamarck, who, in the *Philosophie zoologique* (1809), stated as a law:
>
> > All that nature has caused individuals to gain or lose by the influence of the circumstances to which their race has been exposed for a long time, and, consequently, by the influence of a predominant use or constant disuse of an organ or part, is conserved through generation in the new individuals descending from them, provided that these acquired changes are common to the two sexes or to those which have produced these new individuals. (Burkhardt 166)
>
> In other words, as an organism uses a part of its body to meet the needs of its surroundings, it causes changes in that part which are passed along, genetically, to its children (Eisley 49). In Lamarck's famous example, the giraffe which stretched its neck to reach leaves on branches above its head caused a gradual increase in its neck length and, finally, a generally longer neck in the species.

When it came time to revise the paper, the writer decided that the quotation was not essential to her point. In fact, she thought the quotation might even detract from the paragraph. Here is the same paragraph after the writer revised it to omit the quotation:

> Inheritance theories (Mayr's theories 1, 2, and 3) explain evolution in terms of changes effected in a parent which are passed genetically to succeeding generations. This theory is most closely identified with the eighteenth-century natural historian Jean-Baptiste Lamarck who, in the

*Philosophie zoologique* (1809), stated that, as an organism uses a part of its body to meet the needs of its surroundings, it causes changes in that part which are passed along, genetically, to its children (Eisley 49). In Lamarck's famous example, the giraffe which stretched its neck to reach leaves on branches above its head caused a gradual increase in its neck length and, finally, a generally longer neck in the species.

Note that the writer includes the source of the reference ("Jean-Baptiste Lamarck, who, in the *Philosophie zoologique...*") with the summary. The writer did that because most major style manuals now recommend that the author's name and the title of the source be included as part of the text.

**Using Note Cards** Whether you are using electronic tools or pencil and 3 by 5 cards for taking notes on your research reading, you must understand the logic that lies behind the process. Remember, during this stage in your research your goal is to *quickly* and *accurately* collect information which you will later analyze and possibly incorporate in the draft of your paper. For a note to be usable, it must contain three essential items: (1) the source from which the note was obtained, (2) the research information, and (3) the *exact* location of the recorded information within the source.

Many students unnecessarily record extensive bibliographic information on each card; if they take fifteen notes from the same source, they write the author's full name, article title, journal name, volume number, and so forth fifteen times. What a waste of time, effort, and pencil lead! Remember, for each note there already exists a bibliography card with complete information on the source. Your note card need record only enough information so that you can associate the note with its source. In most cases the author's last name and initial will suffice. If you are examining two or more publications by the same author or collective authors, a short title *only long enough to distinguish the work's identity* must be added.

Some students attempt to streamline this process even further by assigning a code number to each record in the working bibliography and then writing this number on each note. We don't recommend this method of source identification. It may actually cost time, since it often requires you to check the "code" for a given work as you prepare your notes, especially for longer works to which you must return for more than one session of note taking. Additionally, when the time comes to analyze and organize your notes or draft the paper, it is often necessary to know who was the author of a given idea and the code does not provide this essential information, forcing you to interrupt your analysis or writing and turn to the bibliography for the necessary information.

No matter what else you may miss in these suggestions, never, under any circumstances, forget to record the page(s) on which you found the material. To do so is to ensure a return to the library, and with Murphy's law as the prime operative force in the universe, it is guaranteed that someone will have the source you need checked out. So *don't forget the page references.*

Don't fall into the trap of pushing too much into a single note. The way some students work to make use of every square centimeter of space on the cards leads some instructors to believe that the cost of a pack of 3 by 5s places a severe financial strain on student researchers. Some conserve cards by taking multiple notes on full sheets of paper—all this despite the fact that it will lead to difficulty when the time comes to arrange ideas.

No matter what the medium, keep your notes short and focused: fifty to sixty words might seem a reasonable maximum to shoot for. When in doubt, spread it out. It's far easier to place two cards together than it is to try to separate a single card into distant parts of the paper.

Keep the "one idea per card" concept fully in mind at all times. The goal of each note should be to record a single item of information; at most, a note should contain a short series of very closely related facts. If you adhere to this principle, you will be able to effectively organize your notes by idea rather than falling into the "here's all the information I found in source A; now here's all the information for source B" trap. A paper organized by ideas leads the reader to believe that you not only collected information but also understood it well enough to see the connections between disparate sources and to condense, combine, and compare material from many sources to form a presentation uniquely your own.

As you are reading and taking notes, put a keyword (or keywords) in a prominent position in your notes to facilitate the selection and analysis process. You won't have to read the entire text of the note to discover it's about "Lamarck" and "inherited characteristics," if those keywords were prominently displayed in your note.

Make certain that you distinguish between direct quotation and passages of paraphrase or summary by the use of quotation marks. The fact that you will indicate the source of your material does not relieve you of the responsibility of clearly distinguishing between your words and those of your sources. It is also useful when quoting a long passage that crosses a page boundary to indicate the point of the page break with a special symbol (for example, two slashes: // ). When you come to incorporate the note in your writing, you may decide that only a portion of the quotation that lies on one page is useful, and then the moment it took to indicate the page break will allow you to accurately reference the quotation.

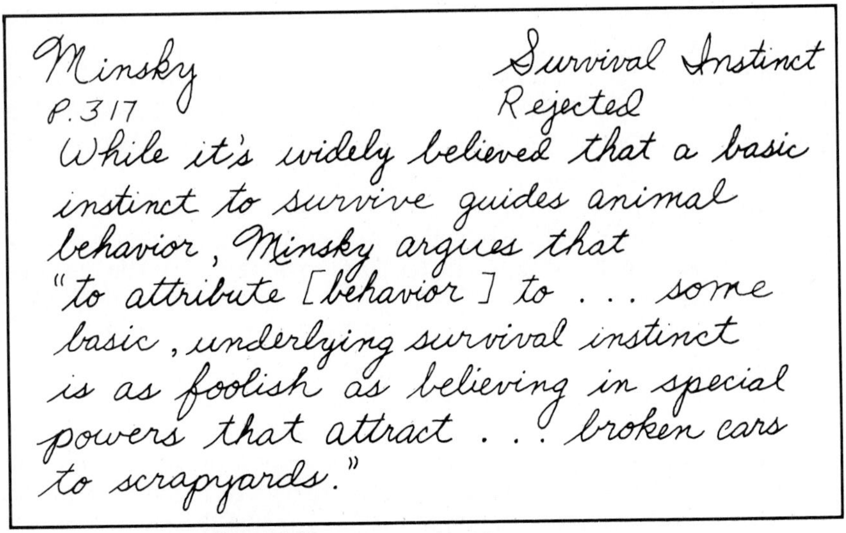

**Figure 3-12**. *Note card with a summary.*

The sample note card in Figure 3-12 effectively and concisely integrates quotation and summary.

**Taking Notes with Your Word Processor**   When using the word processor to collect notes, set up a template file (perhaps called NOTE-TEMP for "note template") as described earlier when we introduced the concept of templates. This file might hold the following prompts:

```
NAME:
TITLE:    (Remember, a short title to be
          completed only if necessary.)
TEXT:     (Six or seven lines should be about
          right; any more and your note is proba-
          bly too long, containing too many
          ideas.)
PAGE:
KEYWORD
KEYWORD
KEYWORD
```

A keyword is a word or phrase which captures an important concept in the note. Used as targets for the word processor's FIND function, they allow an elementary selection of material during the analysis process. Since the selected notes are already in word processor form, they can be easily merged into your draft, avoiding the dreaded, and error-prone, task of retyping.

After merging a copy of NOTETEMP into the note card file, enter your information with insert off and press RETURN to end each line; this will eliminate word wrap and the resultant addition of new lines. As a result, you will be forced to stay within the maximum length you have set for yourself.

**Taking Notes in a Database** Like the word processor, the database implementation of note taking differs only minimally from its use in recording the working bibliography. The only significant difference is in the fields that make up a note record. We suggest you create database fields and lengths such as the following:

```
NAME      (A field length of thirty should con-
          tain even multiple authors; remember
          initial and last name only.)
TITLE     (Again, only filled in when two or more
          works by the same author are
          encountered.)
TEXT      (The actual note: put a limit of 400
          characters on the text field, and you
          have ensured yourself that you won't be
          recording excessively long or complex
          notes.)
PAGE      (A length of nine characters will allow a
          page spread up to 9998-9999, a limit your
          sources are most unlikely to exceed.)
KEYWORD1
KEYWORD2
KEYWORD3
```

The keyword implementation deserves a brief discussion. First, decide how many different keywords to allow for on the basis of the maximum number of important concepts you might wish to assign to any single note. Remember, the more keyword fields you allow, the more specifically you can focus your selections by searching on multiple fields. However, excessive keyword fields slow down the process and require careful phrasing of your selection questions. Observe that even though the information assigned to the keyword fields can go in any of the three fields, the fields must have slightly different names; no database manager allows duplicate field names.

# ▰▰▰▰▰*EXERCISES*

*1.* Using resources in your library, provide complete bibliographical information for the following:

**a.** Two articles written by Crick and Watson on DNA which were published in *Nature* in the same year.
**b.** An article on international monetary policy published within the last year and another published before 1952.
**c.** A *book* which suggests that the dinosaurs were warm-blooded rather than cold-blooded.
**d.** A critical view of Charles Dickens's *Dombey and Son* published within the last five years and another published during Dickens's lifetime.

**2.** Select one of the following areas for investigation. Create a working bibliography of as many entries as you can. Do not consider whether your library contains the publication; the bibliography should contain all *possible* sources.

**a.** The Tellico Dam controversy
**b.** The morality of the use of violence in film
**c.** The role of vitamin C in preventing the common cold
**d.** The effect of the loss of rain forest on world climates
**e.** The role of politics in the awarding of the Nobel Prize in literature

**3.** For each of the following questions, prepare a note card (electronic or otherwise) which answers the question as well as a bibliography card for the source where you obtained the information.

**a.** What was the population of your home state in 1910?
**b.** What is the annual production of steel in the United States for the most recent year for which information is available?
**c.** What films did William Faulker work on as a screen writer?
**d.** What evidence suggests that Vikings landed in North America before Columbus's voyage of 1492?
**e.** When did the last passenger pigeon die? What was her name?
**f.** What was the value of one share of General Motor's common stock on September 19, 1983?

**4.** Prepare a card or cards effectively annotating the information in the following passage. *Do not* use direct quotation.

We're normally quite unaware of how our brain-machines enable us to see, or walk, or remember what we want. And we're equally unaware of how we speak or of how we comprehend the words we hear. As far as consciousness can tell, no sooner do we hear a phrase than all its meanings spring to mind—yet we have no conscious sense of how those words produce their effects. Consider that all children learn to speak and understand—yet few adults will ever recognize the regularities of their grammars. For example, all English speakers learn that saying "big brown dog" is right, while "brown big dog" is somehow wrong. How do we learn which phrases are admissible? No language scientist even knows whether brains must learn this once or twice—first, for knowing what to say, and second, for knowing what to hear. Do we reuse the same machinery for both? Our conscious minds just cannot tell, since consciousness does not reveal how language works. (Marvin Minsky, *The Society of Mind*)

# PAPERS IN PROGRESS: GATHERING INFORMATION

## Jonathan's Paper on an Emily Dickinson Poem

Since Jonathan's topic had been so tightly focused by his instructor's assignment, he did not need to carry out a preliminary analysis in order to focus his research efforts. He was ready at once to begin his information search.

A traditionalist at heart, he turned first to the card catalog. As we might expect, he found nothing directly relating to the poem that was his subject; however, he did find a few books that looked promising.

The books were generally not very helpful; those few which did discuss the poem, "I Heard a Fly Buzz When I Died," did not examine the imagery of the fly in any detail. Jonathan moved on to periodicals.

As he began his search through the indexes in the reference room, Jonathan wondered how long it would take him to review eighty-five years' worth of the *Readers' Guide;* it seemed his library had the full set. That said nothing of the time for a manual search of the *Humanities Index* and the *MLA International Bibliography.*

The library's computerized magazine index, *InfoTrak,* failed to produce any useful leads. Since it indexes general-readership periodicals and those with a technical or business orientation, there were no references to Jonathan's target poem.

Then he learned that his library allowed students evening access to the Dialog information retrieval service. Using Dialog, he searched the *MLA International Bibliography* online. He first searched using the key "Dickinson, Emily." This netted 559 matches. Against these 559, he asked for a match on the word "fly"; four fit the combined pattern. He downloaded the full bibliographic information on each and went to the stacks.

Of the four periodicals, all proved useful but the earliest was written in 1979. He had no earlier entries because the computer version of the *MLA Bibliography* has been extended only to 1970. Realizing that he needed more information and that there was no help for it, Jonathan carried out a manual search of the earlier years of the *MLA Bibliography.*

Beginning with 1969, he extended his search backward, locating eleven additional sources with the earliest dating from 1955. Continuing back to 1940 yielded no additional sources, so he ended his search. Later, after reading his fifteen sources, he confirmed the wisdom of terminating his search when he did, as no critic mentioned any views of the poem published before 1950.

Since he did not have access to a database, Jonathan kept his working bibliography and notes on 3 by 5 cards. In taking notes he limited himself to a single card for each note; in fact, in most cases he restricted the note to one side of the card. Each note contained up to three keywords in the upper right corner, a feature which became very useful when he turned to the next stage in the process: analysis.

## Jennifer's Paper on the Confederate Navy

Jennifer's assignment was to research some area of Civil War military history. The paper was to be relatively short—six to ten pages, but no other conditions were given.

Jennifer began by looking through indexes for articles. Since she found very little in the *Readers' Guide to Periodical Literature* and nothing at all in the *Humanities Index,* she decided to look through the university library card catalog. She found that the university had dozens of books on military aspects of the Civil War; several of them were multivolume sets.

She found the area of the stacks where the books on this subject were stored and began browsing. She found several books reviewing the various battles of the war. Another set, *The History of the Confederate States Navy,* was dedicated to naval battles. She pulled out the first volume of the naval battle series and began skimming. One of the first topics in the book was the preparation for war. The book emphasized that the South had no naval resources at all, while the North, to avoid provoking the South, had purposely distributed its ships throughout the world. Jennifer considered developing some kind of paper on that.

Then she saw some information on U.S. Navy officers who resigned their commissions and joined the Confederate Navy. She was impressed by the fact that only a minority of officers from Southern states chose to resign from the U.S. Navy. Here are the figures she saw:

|  | Total | Total South | Resigned | Stayed | Resigned, % |
|---|---|---|---|---|---|
| Captains | 93 | 38 | 16 | 22 | 42.11 |
| Commanders | 127 | 64 | 34 | 30 | 53.13 |
| Lieutenants | 351 | 151 | 76 | 75 | 50.33 |
| Surgeons | 43 | 31 | 11 | 20 | 35.48 |
| Math Profs | 12 | 7 | 1 | 6 | 14.29 |
| Assistant Surgeons | 36 | 18 | 7 | 11 | 38.89 |
| Paymasters | 64 | 27 | 10 | 17 | 37.04 |
| Chaplains | 24 | 6 | 1 | 5 | 16.67 |
| Masters | 45 | 16 | 6 | 10 | 37.50 |
| Midshipmen | 55 | 20 | 5 | 15 | 25.00 |

She began looking through other books for accounts of officers resigning from the U.S. Navy. She was able to find several other accounts of them and began recording such resignations on note cards. In the course of four hours of skimming books in the library, she found four sources that specifically described efforts by the Confederacy to get soldiers and sailors from Southern states to resign from the U.S. military and join the Confederate forces. The four books gave her twelve different descriptions of resignations or efforts to cause resignations. She recorded a summary of each description on a card.

With so many good sources to choose from, Jennifer was especially selective about which sources to use. She discovered that many of the books in the library were fictional accounts of the war or were based on earlier works. She decided to bypass such books and use as many original sources as she could. These sources included autobiographies and reports written only fifteen or twenty years after the war.

One impressive source she found was *The War of the Rebellion: a collection of the official records of the Union and Confederate Armies.* She found that the set was created by the U.S. Government in 1880 and contained nearly 100 volumes of letters, proclamations, and other documents from the war. Because these were actual documents of the war, she felt they would have more authority than other, interpreted, sources she might be able to find. So she spent two hours looking through the index of the first volume for any references to Confederate efforts to induce resignations of U.S. military personnel. She found nearly a dozen references, including direct correspondence from Jefferson Davis, regarding specific instances in which his aides attempted to induce resignations.

Even though she had used only five different sources, she felt comfortable about the direction her research was taking and was pleased with the quality of her sources.

## Kris's Paper on the Mechanism of Evolution

Given the relatively vague nature of her biology professor's assignment ("Write a paper on some aspect of evolution"), Kris's first problem was clearly to select a more specific area for investigation. Had she not done this, the initial job of locating information would have been insurmountable. Her library's card catalog subject section contained over 200 evolution-related entries; the *Readers' Guide* for the previous year had 176 entries, and the *Biological and Agricultural Index* contained 624 (not counting the entries she might have found had she examined the many secondary cross-references).

To focus her investigation, Kris reviewed her lecture notes and read the article on evolution in an encyclopedia. Her notes reminded her that her professor expected a thesis paper, one that would consider some controversial issue in order to form and support her own conclusion on the matter. Since she really was not aware of controversies on the issue of evolution, other than the creationism-versus-evolution debate which she quite wisely decided was beyond her ability to cover adequately in the time available, she began reviewing the *Readers' Guide* to collect background information. She hoped that the subheadings and titles she found there would reveal some pattern of discussion that she could pursue.

As she reviewed this basic index, she noticed that she was collecting many working bibliography cards for reviews of Ernst Mayr's *The Growth of Biological Thought: Diversity, Evolution and Inheritance.* Since this work was reviewed so frequently, she decided to begin her more directed reading there. There she discovered her topic: Mayr points out that while evolutionary biologists are agreed that evolution is a fact of the natural world, there is profound disagreement as to the mechanism by which the process occurs. Although Kris had heard of "the survival of the fittest" as the force that drove evolutionary change, she wasn't sure exactly what this meant and really had no idea if that was, in fact, an accurate assessment. Thus she began her more focused research not with a thesis to be proved but with a question the answer to which she would ultimately determine to her own satisfaction and support in her paper.

Armed with a more directed area of investigation, she returned to the library to compile a more limited working bibliography and to begin the reading and note-taking process. As she read she took note of researchers whose views were mentioned frequently in the works she encountered and returned to the indexes to see if they had authored works that her subject search had missed.

Fortunately, the library at Kris's university had computers available for student use, so she could gather her bibliography and notes directly into her database. Since past experience had taught her the danger of including too much information in a single note, her record structure allowed a maximum of 300 characters (about fifty words) for the text of each note; she also included fields for three keywords.

By the time she was ready to begin analyzing her information, her note database contained over 100 entries from twenty different sources. Of these twenty sources, only three were book-length studies (the most recent was published four years earlier), the remaining seventeen were from journals, and only one of these predated the most recent book.

# Chapter 4

# ANALYZING AND INTERPRETING RESEARCH INFORMATION

*I*n Chapter 3 we discussed several ways of gathering and storing research data. A logical next step is to try to form some conclusions about the information gathered. Once done with that, it would seem we would begin writing. This seems like a very reasonable sequence.

However, for better or worse, research work is seldom that simple. To begin with, the idea that researchers gather information first and form conclusions second just doesn't match up against what really happens. Our vision of the biologist looking at slide after slide until suddenly noticing a particular characteristic of cancer cells is very romantic. It assumes that researchers have no prejudices, no previous ideas, no "hunches." That would make researchers not only very unusual but probably also very poor researchers.

As we mentioned in Chapter 3, a much more usual process is for researchers to begin an inquiry with a question and a possible answer and then do enough research to confirm or deny their first hunch. Usually the research will help them understand their question better, enabling them to form another possible answer and do some more research, which helps them restate their question, and so on. The result is a cycle: (1) make a tentative hypothesis about a problem, (2) do research to prove or disprove the hypothesis, (3) analyze the research, and (4) make another hypothesis about the problem.

The research you originally do on a subject helps you to understand the general area and may raise questions for you. You then analyze the research you have done to form conclusions about the subject. Your analysis will then have to be supported, so you find yourself doing more research. This research leads to more analysis. To do a full analysis may require more research. To put it simply, one trip to the library isn't enough.

This chapter describes the primary analysis techniques used in writing. Some of these techniques you can use before you ever go to the library—as a warm-up or preparation for research. Some of the same techniques can be used after you have collected much of your data as a way of helping you make sense of what you have collected and to help you decide what additional data you will need. You may also find yourself using a few of these analysis techniques when you are almost done with your paper as a last-minute check to see if you have been complete.

So consider the techniques described here less as a stage you go through and more as a process you return to as needed. Analysis simply means trying to understand, and that's something we all do constantly.

The procedures described in this chapter fall into three main groups: general questioners, analysis of authority, and computer tools. Each group has its own advantages. You may prefer to use procedures from each group or to limit yourself to just one group. Your subject will also help to determine which group is best for you. If your subject involves numbers, the computer tools may be your primary choice. For other subjects, the general question techniques from two thousand years ago may be just as effective.

## GENERAL QUESTIONERS

Long before computers and other advanced forms of technology had even been thought of, speakers and writers were faced with the same problem we have today: "How can I discover what is really central in this subject? How can I determine what matters most? What other ways are there of looking at the information I already have?"

Previously writers used lists of specific questions to thoroughly and effectively describe a subject. Aristotle was one of the first to create such a list for orators. His *Topics* helped speakers prepare for Athenian debates. Some of the questions were tied to specific topics, while others were for general analysis of topics. These general questions asked for such things as definition, partition, comparison, analogy, antecedent, consequence, cause and effect, genus, and species (D'Angelo).

Since then a number of question sets have been created, all with the purpose of helping a writer be insightful, complete, and original. Most of these lists don't require a computer at all. They are just lists of questions writers ask themselves as they prepare to write. By the time they have reached the end of the list, they should have a better understanding of the subject and be better prepared to write. Some of these lists have been computerized in the last few years, and a few additional computer prompting techniques have been invented. We'll look at the traditional questioners first.

## Tagmemic Matrix

Beginning during World War II, three professors at the University of Michigan developed a theory of observation and description called the *tagmemic matrix*. Central to the matrix is the belief that to understand something we have to know three things: what makes the thing unique, what possible forms it can take, and where it fits in a larger world.

To reach this understanding we might ask questions such as these:

What makes $X$ special?

How is $X$ important?

What are the major features of $X$?

What are some of the forms $X$ can take?

What is the most unique form of $X$?

Is $X$ different from what it used to be?

Will $X$ change in the future? How?

What makes $X$ different from $Y$?

What else relies on $X$?

What causes changes in $X$?

This became known as the *particle-wave-field approach* to observation. While this set of questions can help people think more clearly about their own experiences, it can also help researchers become better observers. For example, suppose that you have been reading about social castes. You know that social groups often break into levels, and you believe that there are levels in your own world. Your readings describe income levels and education levels. Are those the levels that determine caste, or are there others? How would you know?

You start with the American middle class and begin asking "particle" or contrastive questions about it. What features make it different from the upper or lower class? What is unique about the dress of middle-class people? What are their primary occupations? Where do they live? What is different about their leisure activities? If you saw two people walking down the street, how would you know whether they were middle-class?

"Wave" or variation questions check for the range of traits your subject can have and still be the subject. For instance, what range of dress is still "middle-class?" What range of incomes? What range of leisure activities? "Wave" questions also consider a subject over time and might include questions such as, "How has the income of the middle class changed in the last hundred years? In the last ten years? Are their political views changing?"

"Field" questions that try to view the middle class in a larger context might include issues such as what distinguishes the American middle class from the middle class of countries such as Japan, Mexico, and England; what economic and political role does the middle class play in the United States; what major institutions grew as the power of the middle class grew; what social events would disappear if the middle class were to disappear; and what would supermarkets look like if there were no middle class?

Asking and answering all the questions of the tagmemic matrix can be time-consuming, but they should leave you with a much clearer understanding of your subject. You can be reasonably sure you haven't missed any important aspects of the subject, and you may discover a question or two leading you in new directions for research.

How can you use the tagmemic matrix when writing a paper? You would probably want to use it several times. The first might be before you have done much research at all. You have an idea for a subject and just want to "play" with it before you start. You might begin by asking yourself the ten questions above plus any other questions that help you look closely at your subject. Can you determine what is unique about your subject? Can you define it in some detail? Can you see that something is changing? Something tied to a larger world? This first use of the matrix should help you think more clearly about your subject and think of new approaches to it.

A second time to use the matrix is after you have begun your research. You have been reading for several days and are beginning to collect a fair amount of information. How does that information fit together? If you ask yourself the matrix questions again, try to note which ones are easiest to answer. If most of your reading has led you to think that your subject is totally unique, you may not be able to say much about how your subject has changed over time or how it connects with other subjects. Now that you look back on it, is your subject that unique? Are your sources being fair in not mentioning how your subject ties to others? Or have you been looking in the wrong places for information? Do you feel comfortable taking this approach to your subject?

What if you are less able to determine how your subject is unique but readily able to say how your subject interconnects with others? It seems that the more you study your subject, the more it seems to be tied to several others. You find yourself being unable to explain your subject without describing these others, too. This should give you an important insight into what direction you will take with your research paper and a major point you will have to make to your readers.

As you use the matrix, you should find that it helps you determine how much you really know about your subject and which aspect of your subject is primary: its uniqueness, its range of forms, or its connections to other subjects.

## Burke's Pentad

Another set of questions that can help you analyze your subject is Kenneth Burke's pentad. To a certain extent you have done much of Burke's pentad if you have ever tried to answer the "five W's and an H" questions journalists use: who, what, when, where, why, and how. In the case of an automobile accident, a journalist might ask: "Who was involved?" "What happened?" "When did the accident occur?" "Where was the accident?" "Why did it occur?" "How did it occur?"

Kenneth Burke reframes these questions slightly, using "agent" instead of "who," "action" instead of "what," "agency" instead of "how," "scene" instead of "when" and "where," and "purpose" instead of "why." This gives him five primary questions, or a pentad of questions.

What is unique about Burke's use of these questions is that he adds two more aspects to his pentad: ratio and circumference. *Circumference* refers to the general background of the event—in the case of the auto accident, it might be the American love of cars, current problems with overconsumption of alcohol, and questionable safety standards for American products. *Ratio* is the truly unique area of Burke. It simply asks, of all the areas of the pentad, which is most important? Which is central? If you were to draw an event as five petals on a flower, which of the five would be largest and which smallest? Would "agent" or "who" be crucial in our accident—a person with a history of drunken-driving arrests? Or might it be the scene—a hilly road covered with fog? As we try to draw the relative sizes of the pentad petals, we are forced to make judgments about what was crucial and what was incidental.

Here is how Burke's pentad might work if we were studying the problem of teenage pregnancy:

*Agent:* Who is getting pregnant? What are the rates for various ages 13 to 19? Are the rates the same for city and rural, urban and suburban? Are the rates the same for all income levels? All races or nationalities? What do we know about these girls and about the responsible boys?

*Action:* What are teenagers doing about their pregnancies? Are they aborting or keeping their babies or giving them up for adoption? How well are they handling the fact of their pregnancies? How are their parents responding? Their friends?

*Agency:* How are they getting pregnant? Did they attempt contraception? Did they want to get pregnant? Was this the first time they were sexually active, or was it part of a history of such activity?

*Scene:* When and where are teenagers becoming pregnant—in their parents' homes? In cars? During school? Late at night?

*Purpose:* If the pregnancy was an accident, was the girl involved in order to please a boyfriend? To act older? Because "everyone" does it? To anger her parents? If the pregnancy was planned, was the purpose to establish independence? Gain social status? Find love?

*Circumference:* What is the general social climate in which teenage pregnancy is occurring? Does it have anything to do with the increase in divorce? Is it tied to economic trends? How does it connect to sexually explicit movies and television shows? Are there other countries with similar problems, or is this uniquely American? Has this always been a problem in the United States, or are we seeing something new?

*Ratio:* What is key to understanding teenage pregnancy—the people involved, or the general social atmosphere of the United States? Should we focus most on the reasons girls are getting pregnant, or look first at how girls end up pregnant? Which area tells us the most about the problem? Where should we begin to look for solutions?

The idea of a "ratio," the attempt to rank reasons for a problem in some order, is especially helpful with complex problems. Without a ratio, we gather increasing amounts of information about a subject and may create a long list of research questions, but we may still be confused about what is central to a problem. If we are going to research a problem, it only makes sense to try to research the main cause. Identifying the ratio is one way of forcing ourselves to look for the main point. We may not find it right away—the key point is seldom obvious—but trying to find the key point can guide our research in a specific direction and help us avoid wandering aimlessly through endless facts.

How do we determine the ratio, or central point of a subject we are researching? This may be a very difficult task. Fortunately, there are methods readily available to us. One approach to take is to look at the volume of information available. You are seldom the first person to research a certain subject. What area of that problem have most others looked at? If you look in your database and discover that most of the notes you found were descriptions of the teenagers currently getting pregnant, that may be the ratio or central issue. But if most information is about the "why" rather than the "who" of pregnancy, the reasons why teenagers are suddenly becoming pregnant in growing numbers, then that may be the ratio.

Maybe all the other researchers on teenage pregnancy are wrong. You feel they have emphasized the wrong issue. Okay, there is no reason why you have to go with the crowd. Maybe what strikes you is not the volume of information, but one very dramatic description you find in an article. That becomes your ratio. You are free to decide for yourself what the central issue is; all that is important is that you do decide, and you do prepare to defend your choice.

One place to start is with the table in Figure 4-1. Choose a subject and try to fill in as many of the boxes as you can. Then try to rate the boxes on importance from top (1) to bottom (6).

Here again you may want to fill out such a table twice: once before you do much of your research so that you can use this as a guide, and then again after your research is well under way. When you use the pentad the second time, it will help you see how well you know your subject (how easy it is to fill in each of the six areas). You can also compare your ratio to the ratio you created before you started. Did you start out thinking that the agent was most important, only to

SUBJECT: _____

| Rating | Type | Answer |
|---|---|---|
| | Agent | |
| | Action | |
| | Agency | |
| | Scene | |
| | Purpose | |
| | Circumference | |

**Figure 4-1.** *Burke's pentad.*

change to circumference as your reading progressed? What made you change your mind?

Repeatedly using the pentad can help serve as a map of your progress with your subject. As your ideas change, the pentad will change. Later when you start writing your first draft, the pentad will serve as a checklist of information to include and should help you determine the focus for your paper—the ratio will tell you which aspect of your subject is most important, most necessary to communicate to your readers.

## Metaphors

While the tagmemic matrix and Burke's pentad create a very orderly method of analyzing a subject you have been researching, there are more playful ways to explore ideas. Ray and Dawn Rodrigues have invented a procedure they call "visual synectics." It is a way to think about your subject by drawing comparisons to items in a picture you randomly select.

For instance, let's say that you happen to select a picture of a family picnic. You would begin by making a list of things you see in the picture. You might list a picnic table, a volleyball net, potato salad, ants, and a barbeque grill.

Now that you have a list of visual images, you would try to make a connection between your subject and those images. For example, if your subject were television violence, you might use your images to create this list of questions:

How is television violence like a picnic table?
   *(Hundreds of directors and producers are eating from it.)*
Compare television violence and a volleyball net.
   *(So many cars are flying through the air all the time they begin to look like volleyballs.)*
What do television violence and potato salad have in common?
   *(By the end of most chase scenes, the cars look a lot like potato salad.*
Why is television violence like ants?
   *(They both are constant irritants.)*
How is a barbeque grill like television violence?
   *(They are both used to heat something up. In one case it is dead meat; in the other case it is dead ideas.)*

As you can see, this approach doesn't work as scientifically as the others, but it does start you thinking in ways that might be productive. You make connections you might otherwise miss, and you may get a creative slant on a subject others might miss. Visual synectics isn't as comprehensive as the other approaches we have seen, but it is easy to try and may help you get started in analyzing a new subject.

Another approach using metaphors was developed by Peter Elbow. He created a series of ten question sets such as questions to help you write about a place, questions to help you write about a group, and questions to help you write about a problem. Here are a few of the questions he lists to help develop metaphors about a subject you are studying:

Imagine _____ were the opposite sex. Describe the life_____ would have lived.

Make up or guess the most important childhood event in _____'s life.

Describe _____'s life if that event hadn't occurred or something entirely different had occurred.

Tell a recurring dream that _____ has.

Imagine _____ is a machine. Describe how it works.

What is the most important part of the machine? Which part breaks down most?

Describe _____ as a poison; its effects; its antidotes.

Describe _____ as a weapon. How do you make it go off? What does it do? Who invented it? (Elbow 1981, 90)

The point of these and the other questions is to get you thinking about your subject in a wholly new way. By stretching your ideas about a subject enough to compare it to something totally different, you test your understanding of the subject and discover new approaches to what may have seemed an "obvious" report.

When should you use metaphors? An obvious time is when your subject has gone "dead" on you. You've been reading for so long that the magic is gone. It's all just words, words, words. To breathe some life back into your subject and to see how much you really know about your subject, just stop and ask five metaphorical questions about your subject. If you can't think of better ones, try these:

Guess the most important childhood event in the life of X.

Compare X to a chalkboard.

Image X is a machine. Describe it.

How is X like an eraser?

If X were a weapon, how would you set it off?

Ultimately, whether you use the methods devised by Dawn and Raymond Rodrigues or those of Peter Elbow, your analysis of your subject will be much richer if you take a little time to be a little "crazy." Make an effort to look at your subject in a whole new way. It may be the only way to arrive at a useful analysis. It will certainly lead to a fresher view of the subject.

# ANALYSIS OF AUTHORITY

The purpose of the question sets we have just discussed is to check our knowledge about a subject. Have we looked at it fully? Is there a pattern to what we know? Will a "crazy" question or two lead us to fresh insight? This is a very common approach to analyzing research information. But there is also a very different approach people can take. It is based on this question: do you trust what you know?

Rather than just gather facts, you analyze the facts themselves. You decide that not all facts are created equal. Supposedly they are. All science is based on the principle of replication—the idea that anyone should be able to perform any known experiment and achieve exactly the same results as the first experimenters. The fact that these results can be repeated proves their accuracy.

But are all experiments repeated? No, because this would be very expensive and time-consuming. Some social experiments seem almost impossible to repeat because conditions have changed. So we often end up having to trust the experimenter. Occasionally, this is a mistake. Several times a year one scientist or another is discovered to have "fudged" data in order to force a preferred result. Other times additional examination shows that the experimenter simply misunderstood the results. Just because work is done at a prestigious university doesn't always mean that it is accurate.

So how can you respond to the research materials you are gathering? You certainly can't duplicate all the experiments you read about. So how do you decide which reports to trust? And even if you decide to trust all of them, how do you decide which materials are more substantial, more important? If you read four studies about a problem, which results should you give most credence to? In general, you will have to trust the accuracy of what you read. You can use any of several means to help to determine which evidence is most substantial, which studies carry most authority.

1. Consider the source. Suppose that you are reading a report published in a professional journal. The report will have been judged by a panel of experts in that field. Those experts may be wrong, but at least they have checked the report for accuracy and have judged that the ideas presented in the article are significant.

In comparison, suppose that you are reading a report in *Newsweek*. The report was written by a reporter with a deadline who may have checked the facts, but how can we be sure the reporter has the *right* facts? For example, a reporter wants to interview an expert on economics. How will a reporter know which expert is the most expert? A panel of leaders in the field would have a much better sense of whose ideas are most accurate and significant.

2. Look for detail. If a report you are reading cites specific sources for information and uses detail, you at least know that the author has done some work on the subject. If the report is long on generalizations, it's difficult to know whether the author's observations are based on anything other than active imagination and good intentions.

3. Follow the leader. After you have been reading for a while, you will almost always find one study or article cited by other researchers. The more frequently that article is cited, the greater sense you get that others in the field judge the work to be important. Some articles even come to be labeled as "seminal," meaning that they formed the basis for a whole field of inquiry. If others are quoting such an article, you should, too. Find the article and read it. Use it as the basis for your analysis.

The overreliance on authority can be dangerous in that even leaders in a field can make mistakes. However, as you analyze your research, you should at least begin to sense who the leaders are. Not all the information you have gathered has equal value. In determining your own analysis of your research, you, too, will have to weigh the evidence and decide which reports to base your conclusions on. You must consider the authority of your evidence now while you are forming your conclusions, and you will have to think again about the authority of your evidence when you are presenting your ideas to a potentially hostile audience.

If you choose this form of analysis—checking the authority of your "facts"—you may find yourself taking a very different road than you would if you spent most of your time answering the questions of the matrix or pentad. Your approach now is to read for authority. With a stack of note cards on your desk or a list of entries in your database, how do you rank the articles you have read and summarized? Which were most important? Which did you believe?

One procedure to try at this point is to review your bibliography. Can you order your entries by importance? Which article or book do you find yourself coming back to again and again? Which article or book do you think you will quote most often? Which article or book did you use as a basis for further reading?

If you can identify your primary sources, you may already have found a focus for your research. If your best source sees the major problem as being *X*, you may, also. If you trust their facts, you may also trust their priorities.

You are still expected to have your own ideas about a subject and to use information from more than one source, but your ideas (and everyone else's) are based on ideas that came before. Choosing which existing information is most valid and useful is a skill. If you can effectively evaluate the information you are reading, you have made major advances in your research and are much closer to being able to write research of your own.

# COMPUTER ANALYSIS TOOLS

The general questions we discussed earlier in this chapter and the analysis of authority we just discussed are two of the analytic techniques that have been with us for millennia. The students of Aristotle were just as eager as you are to learn how to fully analyze a subject, and their approaches were very similar to yours. However, in the last decade we have gained access to some techniques that are truly new. These techniques use the computer to store and manipulate data in ways that help people more clearly understand the information they have gathered. All of these new techniques make analysis easier, faster, or more accurate.

## Computer Questioners

Since it can be time-consuming to think up questions for such approaches as the matrix or the pentad, several computer programs have been created to do this. Typically, such programs ask one question at the top of the computer screen and then have you type in an answer as you would on a word processor. Here are a few questions you might get from one such program: INVENT by Major Hugh Burns of the U.S. Air Force Academy.

> COMPUTER: Now I need to find out what you are writing about. So would you please type in your subject. I am looking for one to three words.
> STUDENT: Protest against materialism.
> COMPUTER: Hey, that's neat, Wally! We'll have a good time thinking about protest against materialism.
> A comment about purpose:
> During this exploration process, you will be asked to clarify the purpose of your paper on protest against materialism.
> So now would you briefly describe what the purpose of your paper is by completing this statement: the purpose of this paper is to . . . (limit: one line)
> STUDENT: Explain how the myths about materialism come about and how it has improved the world.
> COMPUTER: Anymore? (If so, type whatever it is, if not, type 'no.')
> STUDENT: No.

COMPUTER: Fine, Wally, you and I will talk again about your purpose. Relax now, Wally, and enjoy this brainstorming session.

What special experiences made you select protest against materialism as your topic?

STUDENT: The study of medieval man. The way in which he was led to believe at the time. The influence of the church.

COMPUTER: That's the idea, Wally. Give me some more info now. (Burns, 1984, 18–19)

This kind of dialogue could last from ten minutes to as long as an hour, depending on the number of questions built into the program. The purpose of the questions is to help you think about your subject in a productive manner. When you are done, generally the programs will print out a transcript of your "conversation," so you have a record of both the questions and your answers.

There are other programs which use the capabilities of the computer to ask you questions in ways that are impossible with pencil and paper. The most extensive information analysis program available is WRITER'S HELPER. This program includes twenty analysis activities to help you think about ideas before you begin writing. Several of them are much like the question programs already shown. They try to help you understand a subject by asking you a series of questions about it. Several others take advantage of the computer's ability to randomize and create unique displays on the screen.

One such activity is called "Random Revelations." It tries to help you gain new insight into your research subject by making random connections between your subject and a set of traits. Some of the connections will be silly and may not lead to any greater understanding. But others may start you thinking about your subject in new ways.

For example, if your subject were "product liability laws," the program would create this screen:

```
                          would          bore children
                          could          raise certain fears
                          should         improve some situa-
                          won't          tions
          Product         might                               
          liability laws  can't  <==>  confuse, confuse,      <=
                          will           confuse
                          could          bring out greed
                          would          quickly fade
                                         disappear entirely
                                         appeal to only some
                                         enlighten totally

                          [1]            [2]

Enter any response to a connection or press 1 or 2.
RESPONSE: [  ]
```

The two lists of words and phrases act like "wheels" and turn on the screen until they are stopped by pressing a 1 or a 2. Each time they stop, a new alignment is created. One time the alignment reads "Product liability laws will appeal to only some," and another time it may stop at "Product liability laws should confuse, confuse, confuse." The writer has the choice of writing a small response to the random sentence or to start the wheels spinning again. The hope is that by randomly connecting a subject with a verb and a consequence, writers will find one or two new ways of looking at their subject. Will product liability laws confuse? Why might they only appeal to some? Trying to respond may give you good ideas for further research, test how well you already know your subject, or help you think of responses your readers might make.

Another one of these randomizing activities is "Connections." This activity tries to help you see connections between areas of your research. It begins by asking you to list as much as you can about your subject. Let's say that your subject was the English Romantic poet William Blake. You might create a list like this:

Angels
Experience
Chimney sweeps
Imagination
Engravings
Songs of Innocence
Eternity
Salvation
Little lamb
Tyger! tyger!
Newton
Realms of day
Mind-forg'd manacles
Senses

Connections would take this list and put it in two wheels on the screen:

| | |
|---|---|
| angels | engravings |
| experience | Songs of Innocence |
| imagination | salvation |
| engravings | little lamb |
| senses ⟨==⟩ | tyger! tyger! ⟨= |
| realms of day | Newton |
| mind-forg'd manacles | senses |
| salvation | chimney sweeps |
| chimney sweeps | Eternity |

[1]                    [2]

Each wheel spins independently and stops whenever you enter a 1 or a 2. As items line up across from each other, you can try to determine what connection there is between them. For example, knowing Blake's attitudes toward the senses, you might compare the typical sensory description of a tiger and Blake's description in his famous poem. What about "salvation" and "chimney sweeps"? What connections would Blake make? What connections would anyone else make?

The point of the activity is to explore connections that wouldn't normally be made. Using more typical techniques, we might group Blake's ideas or compare them to another person's, but here we are making random connections between items that would not normally be associated at all. Maybe an interesting connection will be found. Maybe a connection will start you thinking of other connections. In any case, the activity gives you one more way to look at the information you have collected about your subject.

Other computer programs are available to help you analyze a subject you are researching. All the ones currently available operate by asking a series of questions to get you thinking in a productive direction or spur your own creativity by making new visual connections between ideas you already have about your subject.

If you have access to such programs, expect to spend between thirty and forty-five minutes each time you use them. You should also be prepared to answer lots of questions. Such programs don't know any answers—just questions. Be prepared to be prodded like you might be by a tutor. With luck you'll finish your computer session with new ideas about your subject and fresh questions to research.

## Invisible Writing

One approach to analysis that has been used effectively in many research situations is *brainstorming*. The central feature of brainstorming is speed. You write or speak as quickly as you can, jotting down notes as you go. The hope is that if you go fast enough, you can overcome the "censor" that lives in most of us. This censor can be helpful later in determining which conclusions are more valuable, but if we begin censoring too early, we end up with almost no ideas—all our effort goes into thinking why our ideas are wrong instead of finding new ideas.

So we brainstorm. You may have worked in groups that brainstorm. The group uses a large sheet of paper, and everyone tries to put as many ideas as possible on the sheet. No one is allowed to say anything negative about any of the ideas until later. By the time you were done you may have had many more ideas than anyone would have imagined possible.

You may have done brainstorming in the form of "free writing." This method works by having an individual write out ideas as fast as possible for a period of five or ten minutes. During that five or ten minutes you are not allowed to stop writing or to go back and correct anything you have written. Normally by the end of five minutes you have written well over a page, and while some of the writing may be silly, there are often surprising and useful ideas buried in your writing.

Lately a number of people have begun using a new form of brainstorming: invisible writing. Invisible writing uses a word processor as a means of entering ideas quickly but adds a new twist—the writer turns off the computer screen (while leaving the rest of the computer on). Now the word processor will still work and will still record what you write, but nothing will be displayed on the screen. With nothing to see on the screen, your internal censor can't take over. There are no distractions—nothing to see, no errors to correct—so you write undisturbed for five or ten minutes. At the end of this time, you turn the screen back on and see what you have written.

In between the typos and dangling sentences, you will almost always find ideas you wouldn't expect—you were brighter than you thought you were. Since your censor wasn't able to keep a lid on your ideas, a few new ones got out.

To improve the value of invisible writing, you might start with some initial idea. You are concerned about why immigration patterns are so volatile. You might want to start by writing a beginning sentence first, with the screen on. Just a few words will do; all you want is a starting place. Now shut the screen off and start writing. Remember to write as fast as you can and not to stop for anything. With luck, by the time you finish, you will have pages of ideas about immigration trends. If one of the ideas seems especially useful, rewrite that one at the top of the screen and try invisible writing again, this time trying to elaborate on that idea. You don't want to put too much focus on your writing—that will limit you, too—but having a starting point may help you get below the surface of your topic.

Invisible writing has limitations. It is no substitute for reading and research. It will only help you discover conclusions about information already in your memory. If your research has been limited, your conclusions will be limited. If, however, you have been reading for days and are beginning to feel overwhelmed, invisible writing may help you form initial conclusions about your subject. It may be that a useful analysis of your reading is buried in your memory just waiting for a chance to come out. Brainstorming can be that chance.

## Spreadsheets

Often your research will turn up masses of numbers. Research in sociology gives you hundreds of income levels. A psychology report gives you a whole table of reaction times. A discussion of poetic style finishes with a list of word frequencies for a certain poet.

These numbers are a powerful ally in achieving precision. Without them you are left with vague claims such as "real income has declined for the last ten years." That seems like a simple statement, but it will lead many to ask questions like, "How much has the decline been? Has it declined every year in the last ten, or just as a total? Has it declined in all occupations or just for a few?" The original statement answers none of these questions. A detailed look at income figures should let you make much more precise analyses of what happened to income over the last ten years.

However, there is a problem. While numbers can give precision and a much clearer understanding of what is really happening, numbers themselves can be confusing. For example, here is a set of figures on gross hourly incomes for various industries. Just by looking at the set of numbers, what conclusions can you draw?

Hourly Wages (in 1977 U.S. Dollars)

| Industry | 1970 | 1980 | 1984 |
|---|---|---|---|
| Manufacturing | 5.23 | 5.34 | 5.42 |
| Mining | 6.01 | 6.74 | 6.86 |
| Construction | 8.17 | 7.30 | 7.15 |
| Transportation | 6.01 | 6.52 | 6.55 |
| Wholesale trade | 5.37 | 5.11 | 5.29 |
| Retail trade | 3.81 | 3.59 | 3.47 |
| Finance, insurance | 4.79 | 4.25 | 4.50 |
| Services | 4.38 | 4.30 | 4.51 |
| Average | 5.04 | 4.89 | 4.91 |

These figures are from the U.S. Census Bureau and have been adjusted to remove the effects of inflation. Even with all the work the Census Bureau has done, it is no easy task to determine a pattern in these numbers. Some industries seem to have done better over the last fifteen years, while others have done worse. Analyzing these numbers will not be easy.

There are tools especially designed to help with numbers. One of the most powerful is the spreadsheet. The spreadsheet is a computer program that lists numbers in rows and columns in a similar manner to an accountant's ledger sheets. The first spreadsheet was designed by a college student in 1979 and went on to sell over half a million copies. All spreadsheet programs currently available are modeled on that first program.

Since 1979 spreadsheet programs have grown to be very common. They almost always have the same appearance and capabilities. The program presents a large grid of rows and columns, and users are able to type in names and numbers anywhere they would like on the grid. Initially at least, the program operates much like a word processor: you enter the text you would like.

One difference between word processors and spreadsheets, however, is that spreadsheets have built-in mathematical capabilities. If you wanted, they could add up a column of numbers you had typed in. They could also tell you the average of a column. You simply tell the program which column of numbers you want added and where to put the sum and it will do the mathematics for you. Here is how one spreadsheet might add up a column of numbers:

```
A          B              C
1          MONTHLY EXPENSES
2
3          PIZZA          57.54
4          MOVIES         15.00
5          POP CORN        3.50
6          BOOKS          12.30
7
8          TOTAL   @SUM(C3...C6)
```

The program now knows to add all the numbers in column C from row 3 to row 6 and put the total where the formula is. Spreadsheets can do much more advanced mathematics than this, but most of it is accomplished in the same manner—you say what you want done to which numbers.

Besides performing simple mathematics, spreadsheets will let you manipulate blocks of numbers in ways that help you make sense of them. For instance, one way to help understand the wage figures above might be to sort them. We could list the industries from best- to worst-paying. In fact, we could do this twice: once based on 1970 earnings and once based on 1984 earnings to see if there is much change. Doing all this sorting by hand would be so time-consuming that no one would attempt it. But all spreadsheets have built-in sorting capability, so we could sort these numbers in just two or three minutes. By the way, here are the figures after they have been sorted by a spreadsheet:

Hourly Wages (in 1977 U.S. Dollars; Sorted by 1970 Hourly Wages)

| Industry | 1970 | 1980 | 1984 |
|---|---|---|---|
| Construction | 8.17 | 7.30 | 7.15 |
| Mining | 6.01 | 6.74 | 6.86 |
| Transportation | 6.01 | 6.52 | 6.55 |
| Wholesale trade | 5.37 | 5.11 | 5.29 |
| Manufacturing | 5.23 | 5.34 | 5.42 |
| Finance, insurance | 4.79 | 4.25 | 4.50 |
| Services | 4.38 | 4.30 | 4.51 |
| Retail trade | 3.81 | 3.59 | 3.47 |
| Average | 5.04 | 4.89 | 4.91 |

Hourly Wages (in 1977 U.S. Dollars; Sorted by 1984 Hourly Wages)

| Industry | 1970 | 1980 | 1984 |
|---|---|---|---|
| Construction | 8.17 | 7.30 | 7.15 |
| Mining | 6.01 | 6.74 | 6.86 |
| Transportation | 6.01 | 6.52 | 6.55 |
| Manufacturing | 5.23 | 5.34 | 5.42 |
| Wholesale trade | 5.37 | 5.11 | 5.29 |
| Services | 4.38 | 4.30 | 4.51 |
| Finance, insurance | 4.79 | 4.25 | 4.50 |
| Retail trade | 3.81 | 3.59 | 3.47 |
| Average | 5.04 | 4.89 | 4.91 |

With the help of this sort we can now answer questions about individual industries much more easily. We can see at a glance not only which industries paid best and worst but also how they fared during the last fifteen years. For instance, while construction paid the best and retail trade the worst both in 1970 and 1984, most of the other industries changed relative positions. Mining and transportation started out tied for second, but mining improved much more than transportation. Manufacturing wages improved in relative position, as did services, while wholesale trade and finance wages faded. So just our simple sort helped us to quickly make some comparisons between industries.

Besides repositioning information to facilitate our analysis, spreadsheets also do many calculations automatically. We have already seen how they can add up a column of numbers. We could just as easily have them calculate the exact amount of change in wage rates between 1970 and 1984. This involves giving the computer a simple formula (column C minus column B) which it applies to our figures. Here is what those calculations look like on our spreadsheet:

Hourly Wages (in 1977 U.S. Dollars)

| Industry | 1970 | 1984 | Change |
|---|---|---|---|
| Construction | 8.17 | 7.15 | −1.02 |
| Mining | 6.01 | 6.86 | 0.85 |
| Transportation | 6.01 | 6.55 | 0.54 |
| Manufacturing | 5.23 | 5.42 | 0.19 |
| Wholesale trade | 5.37 | 5.29 | −0.08 |
| Services | 4.38 | 4.51 | 0.13 |
| Finance, insurance | 4.79 | 4.50 | −0.29 |
| Retail trade | 3.81 | 3.47 | −0.34 |
| Average | 5.04 | 4.91 | −0.13 |

Spreadsheets were designed specifically to perform that kind of calculation, so they do it quickly and easily. And now that the mathematics have been done for us, we can see for ourselves exactly how much change in wages occurred during the last fourteen years. Of course, to help make these changes even more meaningful to us, we can sort the chart one more time, this time sorting by amount of change. Here is the result:

Hourly Wages (in 1977 U.S. Dollars)

| Industry | 1970 | 1984 | Change |
|---|---|---|---|
| Mining | 6.01 | 6.86 | 0.85 |
| Transportation | 6.01 | 6.55 | 0.54 |
| Manufacturing | 5.23 | 5.42 | 0.19 |
| Services | 4.38 | 4.51 | 0.13 |
| Wholesale trade | 5.37 | 5.29 | −0.08 |
| Finance, insurance | 4.79 | 4.50 | −0.29 |
| Retail trade | 3.81 | 3.47 | −0.34 |
| Construction | 8.17 | 7.15 | −1.02 |
| Average | 5.04 | 4.91 | −0.13 |

Now suddenly we can see that while construction paid the best in 1984, it had actually fallen the most in wages paid. Mining and transportation, both tied for number 2 in 1970, were the big winners over the period. Sadly, retail trade, which paid the worst in both 1970 and 1984, was also the second-worst loser in terms of average wages. This chart gives us a whole new way of looking at the information we had buried in the original chart.

Now that we have seen how various industries fared during the last fourteen years and quantified their gains and losses, one tempting thought is to project how these industries will do over the next fourteen years. True projections are very complicated and usually involve formulas for inflation and industry maturity and such, but we could try a simple projection quite easily. For instance, how would wages look if they changed just as much in the next fourteen years as they did in the last? Of course, the odds of the next fourteen years being exactly the same as the last fourteen years are very slim, but what if they were? We could have our spreadsheet do a simple calculation and then sort the results. Here's what we would get:

Hourly Wages (in 1977 U.S. Dollars)

| Industry | 1970 | 1984 | 1998 |
|---|---|---|---|
| Mining | 6.01 | 6.86 | 7.71 |
| Transportation | 6.01 | 6.55 | 7.09 |
| Construction | 8.17 | 7.15 | 6.13 |
| Manufacturing | 5.23 | 5.42 | 5.61 |
| Wholesale trade | 5.37 | 5.29 | 5.21 |
| Services | 4.38 | 4.51 | 4.64 |
| Finance, insurance | 4.79 | 4.50 | 4.21 |
| Retail trade | 3.81 | 3.47 | 3.13 |
| Average | 5.04 | 4.91 | 4.78 |

Our simple projection shows that if current trends continue for another fourteen years, mining would become the best-paying job, while construction would fall to third place, and that workers in retail trades will actually be earning less than the minimum wage by 1998.

Will these projections be correct? Probably not. Many circumstances can change in fourteen years, but the projections do help to point out general trends which might warrant further exploration. Why is mining doing so well and construction so poorly? Why is retail trade consistently at the bottom of the list and falling?

Spreadsheets can't answer these questions, but they can help us understand blocks of data sufficiently to at least note that these trends are occurring. We aren't faced with a matrix of lifeless numbers any more. We can manipulate numbers quickly and easily until they have been repositioned and recalculated enough to be meaningful to us. Clearly, the spreadsheet is a powerful tool for analysis and interpretation.

When should you use a spreadsheet? First, of course, spreadsheets are useful only for numbers. Second, they are more useful for many numbers than they are for just two or three. If you encounter only a few numbers in your research, there will be little need to "analyze" those numbers with a spreadsheet—you can do it mentally just as well.

A spreadsheet becomes valuable when you face an array of numbers and have one of two problems: no clear pattern is visible in the numbers, or you want to manipulate the numbers to evaluate them for trends. Now is the time to find a spreadsheet program on your campus and learn to use it. It will be well worth your effort.

## Spreadsheet-Based Graphics

Spreadsheets, which have the capacity to sort, reposition, recalculate, and manipulate numbers, are also used for graphics. When the spreadsheet work is done, the numbers should be easier to understand. They are still numbers, however, and for people and some applications, this is a problem.

In 1981 Jonathan Sachs and Mitch Kapor took the next step and wrote a spreadsheet, Lotus 1-2-3, that not only manipulates numbers but also converts them to graphics. Now you can see not only the numbers themselves, but also these numbers reconstructed as bar graphs, pie charts, line graphs, and more. Besides having the computer calculate the difference between two numbers, you can have it draw the difference.

The ability to graph numbers has become so important to people who analyze data that most spreadsheets now have the ability to draw graphs on command. To understand the usefulness of graphics in interpreting data, study the following data on alcohol consumption and the four graphs that follow.

Frequency of Alcohol Consumption

|  | Age | | | Income | | |
|---|---|---|---|---|---|---|
|  | 20–34 | 35–54 | <55 | <$6,000 | $6,000-$15,000 | $15,000-$30,000 |
| Less than once per year | 22 | 28 | 45 | 46 | 38 | 27 |
| Less than once per week | 36 | 35 | 28 | 29 | 32 | 38 |
| Once or twice per week | 18 | 14 | 9 | 13 | 14 | 13 |
| Three or more per week | 24 | 23 | 18 | 13 | 16 | 21 |

This spreadsheet combines two sets of information: the effects of age and income on drinking. We might be able to see several trends just by looking at the chart. Younger people seem to drink more than older, and poor people drink less than do middle-income people. However, the differences we see could be much more clearly defined for us if they could be translated into pictures. Most graphics programs will do just that with spreadsheet information. For example, let's take one age group, 20- to 34-year-olds, and make a *bar graph* of their drinking habits. (See Figure 4-2.)

Now we see clearly that there is not an orderly transition from those who never drink to those who frequently drink. The bars make it obvious that there is a major group of people who apparently drink only on special occasions. We also can see that only one-fourth of the people in this group could be called "regular" drinkers. Of course, we could also learn this from the spreadsheet, but the bar graph makes the information even easier to interpret.

Another graph that clarifies information is a *pie chart*. In this case we are looking not at raw numbers but at percentages of a whole, or pieces of a total pie. For example, if you spent $20 one day, you could either look at your expenditures as specific numbers ($4.95 for pizza, $6.50 for a book, 44 cents for stamps, etc.), or you could view your $20 as a pie, with the largest slice going for books, a smaller slice going for pizza, and just a sliver going for stamps.

We can do the same thing with heavy drinkers. We can list the numbers of people for each age group, or say, of the total pie of heavy drinkers, how big a slice comes from young people, middle-age people, and old people. (See Figure 4-3.)

From this pie chart, it seems each age group has a roughly equal slice. The percentages may vary slightly, but in general it appears there are as many in each age group. Again we could have seen roughly the same information by just looking at the spreadsheet, but here the graph reinforced and clarified what the spreadsheet showed us.

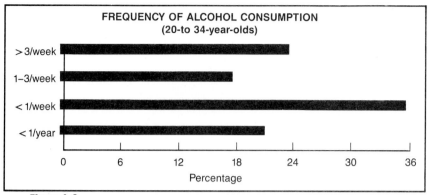

**Figure 4-2.** *A bar graph of alcohol consumption by 20- to 34-year-olds.*

Sometimes graphs can be used to plot two different trends to see how they offset each other; these are called *line graphs*. For example, in our case we might be interested in knowing how the trends look for heavy drinkers, as measured by both age and income. One quick way to discover this would be to create a line graph with one line for income and the other for age. Where the lines meet should tell us what ages and income are equally likely for heavy drinkers. This is something our spreadsheet cannot show us, but the graph can quite easily. Figure 4-4 is a line graph for heavy drinkers.

In this case the line graph was able to show the relative effect of two trends quite easily. The lines also let us project out for ages not on the spreadsheet. As people get older, what happens to their alcohol consumption? What happens as they get wealthier? The lines created by the graph make general trends pretty clear. So line graphs can be used not only to make information easier to see than it might be on a spreadsheet but also to allow easy viewing of multiple trends and long-term trends.

Graphs can help to clarify information also by showing the combined effects of two different trends. In our example we know the effect now of age and of income, but what is the effect of them both? Is a young poor person more likely to drink than an old wealthy person? The answer to such questions can usually be found through the use of a *layer graph*. It adds the effect of one trend on top of the other and colors them so we can see the combined influence of two or more trends. Figure 4-5, for example, shows the combined effect of age and income on heavy drinking.

In this case the combined effects produces an almost even result. There is slightly more heavy drinking when we add high income to old age than there is when we add low income to youth, but the difference is not very great. It appears that the trends almost totally

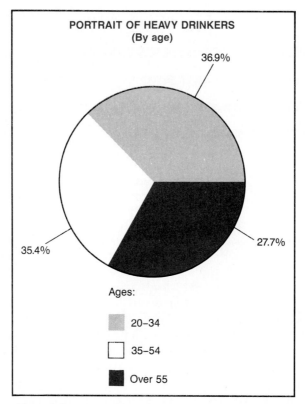

**Figure 4-3**. *A pie chart showing percentage of heavy drinkers by age.*

offset each other. Layer graphs let us see this where spreadsheets would only do it with difficulty.

Are graphs essential to an understanding of numeric information? No; by studying spreadsheets carefully enough, we could obtain most of the information that we would otherwise get from graphs. However, graphing multiple trends does show us certain combined effects that we could detect only with difficulty by spreadsheet analysis, and even simple bar graphs reinforce any conclusions we might make about the data. Graphs make complex blocks of numbers much easier to understand.

Fortunately, most current spreadsheets include graphics right in the program so there is little additional expense or effort required to create graphs. If you think a graph would help you understand a set of numbers, go ahead and make it. Here, for instance, is the information that was required to generate our bar chart on alcohol consumption:

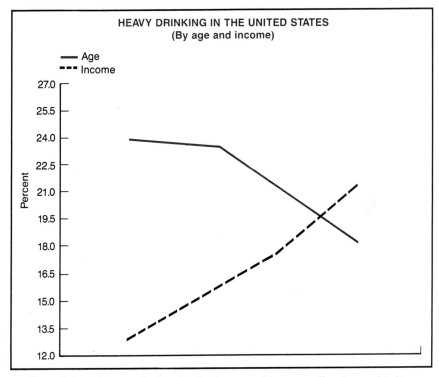

**Figure 4-4.** *A line graph showing how age and income affect heavy drinking.*

*Title:* "Frequency of Alcohol Consumption"
Data block: B1...B4
*Title block:* A1...A4

The "Data block" refers to the column in our spreadsheet where we stored the numbers about alcohol consumption. "Title block" refers to the column where we stored the labels. Here is part of the spreadsheet that was used:

| A | B | C |
|---|---|---|
| 1 | 1/YEAR | 22 |
| 2 | 1/WEEK | 36 |
| 3 | 1-3/WEEK | 18 |
| 4 | 3/WEEK | 24 |

Once the graphing program knew where in the spreadsheet to get the numbers for the graph, it did the rest automatically.

In Chapter 8 we'll discuss how graphs can be useful in explaining data to your readers as well.

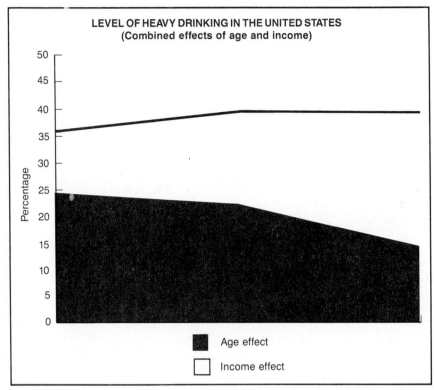

**Figure 4-5**. *A layer graph showing the combined effect of age and income heavy drinking.*

## Personal Databases

As we described in Chapter 3, there are three main functions for microcomputer databases: collecting information in a convenient format for later transfer to a word processor, ordering information so that it's easier to understand, and selecting information according to some criterion.

Remember, the primary advantage of using databases is convenience—rather than having to recopy your note cards, you simply transfer the information directly to a word processor and no retyping is needed. Ordering information is a convenience, too, but it can also help you see the extent of the information you currently have. For instance, if you had set up your data format as SUBJECT, SUBHEAD1, SUBHEAD2, INFORMATION, SOURCE, you could ask the database to list all the SUBHEAD1 labels in alphabetical order. This would very quickly let you see what information you had collected, where there seems to be some duplication, and where there might be a few holes.

However, the real role of databases in analysis is in their ability to select information—to query the database. Once your database reaches a significant size, you should be able to ask it questions. Questions are in the form of selection criteria and usually take the form "Are there any countries in our database with gross national products above $50 billion?" The database now does a search looking for GNPs above the number we gave and prints out information about every country that meets the criteria.

We have a great deal of control over this search. For instance, we can tell the program where we want it to look for our information— which field is the important one and what information we want if it finds a match, the whole note card we made or just part of it.

Let's use an example to illustrate the searches available. If you were doing a study of immigration patterns into the United States, you might have database entries that looked like this:

```
COUNTRY: China
1961-1970:  96,700
1971-1980: 202,000
1981-1983: 105,000
NOTES: Numbers include both People's Republic of
China and Taiwan
SOURCE: U.S. Census Bureau
```

Now a database query might take the form:

```
LIST COUNTRY for 1961-1970    100,000
```

This question would be asking for the names of all the countries that sent more than 100,000 people to the United States during the 1960s. It is the second half of the line above, "1961–1970 > 100,000," that determines the selection. The first half, "LIST COUNTRY," tells us what to do with those countries selected: list them to the screen for viewing. We could also have asked that those countries be printed out on paper or saved on a computer disk. Once we had that list of countries, we could ask the database to put the names in alphabetical order to facilitate reading.

Our queries could be even more rigorous if we wanted to use combinations of criteria. For example, if we wanted to know the names of the countries that had sent us over 50,000 people in both the 1960s and the 1970s, we could state our question as

```
LIST COUNTRY for 1961-1970   50000 .AND.
1971-1980   50000
```

Here "AND" tells the database that we want only countries for which both selection criteria are true: list the country if it sent us over 50,000 people in 1961–1970 *and* in 1971–1980. This will be a fairly restrictive list; both selection criteria must be met before a country will be listed. Here is the list we would get, based on U.S. Census figures:

Germany
Greece
Italy
Portugal
United Kingdom
China
Philippines
Canada
Mexico
Cuba
Dominican Republic
Jamaica
Columbia

If we wanted a more general list, we might use "OR." In this case we want to know which countries sent us over 50,000 people in either 1961–1970 *or* 1971–1980. This will be a much more substantial list. Here is what we would see:

Germany
Greece
Italy
Poland
Portugal
United Kingdom
China
India
Korea
Philippines
Vietnam
Canada
Mexico
Cuba
Dominican Republic
Haiti
Trinidad and Tobago
Jamaica
Columbia
Ecuador

Seven additional countries fit into this list because they sent us 50,000 people in 1961–1970 *or* in 1971–1980. Now if we have the database subtract one list from the other, we obtain a list of those countries not on both lists, or the countries that sent us 50,000 people in only one of the two decades we are looking at:

Poland
India
Korea
Vietnam
Haiti
Trinidad and Tobago
Ecuador

Just by creating three lists, we know all the countries that have sent us significant numbers of immigrants (one decade *or* the other), the countries that consistently send us large numbers of people (one decade *and* the other), and those countries that are more inconsistent in terms of immigration (our last list). Selection procedures helped us analyze the information in our database.

Such questioning can serve two functions for us. If we are just getting started and aren't too sure what our evidence shows, we can ask a series of questions to help us spot trends (e.g., whether certain countries have consistently sent us large numbers of immigrants).

Later, if we have preliminary conclusions about our data, we can question our database to see if we have facts to back up our initial ideas. For instance, we might conclude that most immigration from Asia comes from China. Will our database give us information to support this conclusion? If we look at our list of countries that gave us over 50,000 people in 1961–1970 *and* in 1971–1980, we will find both China and the Philippines. Then if we have the database order the countries that sent us immigrants in the most recent decade, we will find that China is really a distant third behind the Philippines and Korea. By either measure we see that there is no support for our initial conclusion.

How would you decide which query to use? You might begin with a list of statements that seem to apply to your subject. For example, you might make statements such as "Nitrate pollution is very common," "Most hijackers are from the Middle East," and "Hemingway drank himself into insanity." Now the problem is to determine whether these statements are true.

One way to find out is to check your own database of information. You enter queries such as: LIST ALL for SUBJECT = "nitrate pollution." COUNT for HOME = MIDDLE EAST. LIST ALL for SUBJECT1 = "Hemingway" AND SUBJECT2 = "insanity." The effect is exactly the same as if you were looking through a deck of 3 by 5 cards and pulling those out that were related. The difference is the database will do the selecting for you and do it much faster. Of course, this assumes that you have a fair number of entries already made in your database. The whole project is hardly worth the trouble if you have only ten or twelve entries. In that case you could probably look for the information you wanted faster than you could write a query to do it for you. But if you do begin to collect mountains of notes, the database query will be a real aid in pulling the right information out of your mountain.

As we will see in the next chapter, databases are also useful in creating the first drafts of research papers.

## Outliners

You probably began writing outlines in fourth or fifth grade and remember numerous rules about roman numerals and capital letters and indentations, all seeming sufficiently complex and arbitrary to be worthy of an Emily Post. Outlines were required and rules about their form enforced.

The basic premise for that kind of outline is that you know in advance what you intend to say. You know your major ideas and their order, and your supporting ideas and their order, and you won't be making any last-minute additions or deletions. If all that is true, then writing a paper is easy. You merely follow your outline and write, knowing what each paragraph will be about and what support it will contain.

As it turns out, there are actually some people who can write that way. They so thoroughly understand a topic they are describing that they know exactly what they will say before they say it. But how often will that be the case? How often will we ever be writing about a subject that is that familiar to us?

Fortunately, an outline system has been developed recently whose entire function is to help people who don't yet know what they want to say.

Computer outliners are simple programs that are similar in some ways to word processors. The first apparent difference is that they generally expect ideas to be just one line long—a few words or a phrase. You enter the idea on a single line and then put subsequent ideas on the following lines. It's all very simple.

Where it becomes more interesting is that since the outliner works much like a word processor, when you want to add ideas in the middle of your list of ideas, for instance, the program will automatically insert a new line for you. The program will also let you change the order of ideas in your list by using a block move function similar to the one in your word processor. So at this level we have a program that uses the functions of a word processor to make list creation easy.

What about all those roman numerals and capital letters for subitems in an outline? Some outliner programs will insert them automatically for you. You press one key to have a new line indented, or you type in a few initial spaces and the program puts in roman numerals or such for you. Other outliner programs don't use such formalisms. In either case, since the program handles such matters automatically, you can worry about what ideas go with other ideas and let the computer take care of the rest. When you are done, your outline might now look like this:

Computer history
   Biographies of early developers
Computer sizes
   Mainframe
   Mini
   Micro
Current architecture
   Random-access memory (RAM)
   Secondary memory
     Tape
     Disks
   Input-output (I/O) devices
     Monitors
     Keyboards
     Printers
     Digitizers
     Card readers
   Central processing unit (CPU)
Current applications
   Educational uses
     Drills
     Word processors
     Spreadsheets
     Vocational education aids
       Robotics
       Computer-aided design (CAD)

Note that no formalisms such as roman numerals are required. Subordinate ideas are indicated by the degree of indentation. Major ideas are those that are farther out toward the left margin. So we have the original concept of outlines but in a much cleaner form.

We have some additional power. Thus far we have been able to use standard word processor features in building our outline. We could add lines in the middle if we wanted or move lines around. Outliners, however, usually have one capability that word processors don't—the ability to "collapse" down to a certain level. For example, the preceding outline is just the beginning of what we might create if we wanted to list and organize our ideas about computers, but already the top portion is getting so large that it is difficult to view all of it at once. If it increased and spread over several pages (and several screens), it would be difficult for us to remember the main ideas of the outline. We would be working on one idea, such as current applications, and might forget about the first ideas we had listed. It's the old problem of not being able to see the forest for the trees—we get so caught up in the details of the moment that we often forget where we started from and what we were trying to do in the beginning. Enter "collapse."

The collapse feature of outliners collapses an outline like an accordion so that only the major headings are visible. The minor points still exist, but they are hidden for the moment, so we can look once again at our main ideas. In the case of our outline above, collapse would yield this listing:

Computer history
Computer sizes
Current architecture
Current applications

Now that we can see our main ideas again, we can decide whether our groupings are correct (whether sizes and architecture should be combined), whether the order should be changed (whether we should describe applications first and then architecture), or even whether our ideas are still on target (whether we are wandering too far from our initial efforts to describe computer history).

Collapsing is our way to put distractors aside temporarily and decide where our ideas are going. We can instantly get an overview—a look at the forest—and make decisions about where to go next and what to do with what we have done so far. If we are satisfied, a simple command to expand will build the outline back out to its original form and we can go back to adding items to our list. If we see problems, we can correct them now and then go back to building our lists. Clearly this kind of outliner is simpler and more powerful than the outlines we remember from grade school.

Outliners of this kind are so simple that we can use them to analyze information about a topic we are currently exploring. Let's say that we started with a handful of notes or a printed listing from an online database search. To organize the information in those notes, we might begin by creating an outline. We start by making the first idea on the first note the first line in the outline. We take the second note. Should it be grouped with the first? Is it subordinate or equal to the first? Are both of them examples of some larger concept? Just deciding where to put the second, third, or twentieth idea in our outline will force us to study how this idea relates to all the other ideas that have come before. Our outline comes to represent our current analysis of the ideas we have encountered. Luckily, if our analysis changes as we do more thinking or reading, our outline is easy to change.

As our collection of ideas builds into a longer and longer outline, with increasingly intricate groupings and subgroupings, we can collapse our outline and see if we are still on track or are creating unneeded groups. When we look at our main headings, are they really equal? Or should one or two be grouped under the others? Are they in an order that still makes sense, or should we use the block move capability of the outliner to change the order?

An outliner used this way not only provides a guide for writing our first draft but also helps us analyze the information we have collected. We start with a series of notes and end up with an ordered set of grouped ideas. The outliner will make it easy for us to create that set of grouped ideas and to change it if needed. In either case, just making the outline will help us see the connections between our information and also where we need to do more research—a heading with only one subheading is a good indicator that we still have more digging to do on that idea.

Because outliners are such useful ways of organizing research information, they have become increasingly available. Initially they were designed as a specialized program; now there are word processors and questioner programs which include them as just one more feature for writers.

One additional feature of an outliner program—whether designed as a separate program or as part of a word processor or planning program—is that its output can be transferred to any word processor. This means that you can use the outline you create as a guide when you are writing, or even as a skeleton to be fleshed out during the first draft. We'll discuss this function of outlines again when we examine new tools for writing a first draft.

What if you don't have access to an outline program? You can use a word processor to make an outline. You won't have the ability to collapse or expand your outline automatically, but you will be able to mimic most of the functions of an outliner.

For example, you could use a word processor to write the example outline shown above. A word processor won't indent automatically for you or insert roman numerals automatically, but it will still let you enter words or phrases easily. You will be able to insert new lines if you need to, and deletion is quick and easy. All word processors allow quick block moves for moving blocks of an outline into a new order. So if you find writing outlines useful in grouping information and ordering ideas, use a word processor.

## CONCLUSION

Whether you use one of the computer questioners, sift through your data with database queries, generate an outline, manipulate a spreadsheet, or brainstorm with invisible writing, your purpose is the same—to form conclusions about the information you have gathered. Your conclusions may be tentative and lead you into further information gathering. Your conclusions may take final form and lead into the writing of a preliminary draft of your paper. In either case, a wide variety of tools are available to help you form your conclusions. This chapter has outlined the most common tools.

## EXERCISES

1. Do a tagmemic matrix analysis (particle, wave, and field) for the following subjects
   a. Your part-time job
   b. College composition classes
   c. Microcomputers
   d. A major city near you

2. For the subjects in question 1, decide whether particle, wave, or field questions are easiest to answer. Suppose that you were writing a paper about each. What would that suggest?

3. Use Burke's pentad to investigate these subjects:
   a. Your part-time job
   b. Factory automation
   c. Groundwater pollution
   d. The last party you went to

4. Working with a partner, write a random list of items you see around you. Then compare your partner's subject against each item in your list.

5. Which sample paper in Appendix A shows the most authority?

6. Which source did the author of that paper rely on most?

7. Are the tagmemic matrix and Burke's pentad equally useful for all subjects? Try to name one subject that seems best analyzed by each method. What are the differences between the two subjects?

**8**. Use one of the subjects below, and try to make a list of information about it. Then copy the list. Put the two lists next to each other and cross-compare them item by item.

 **a.** The Super Bowl
 **b.** Japanese work habits
 **c.** Air pollution
 **d.** Newspaper reporters

**9**. Use a word processor to create a small outline of your choice. Don't bother with roman numerals and such. After you have created a short twelve- to twenty-line outline, try inserting new ideas and moving groups of lines around.

**10**. Try brainstorming any of the topics below. Brainstorm first in a group. With the help of three or four people, list every idea you can on a sheet of paper. Then try invisible writing to see what you can say about the subject without the distractions of words on the screen.

 **a.** Future immigration
 **b.** The best movie ever produced
 **c.** A law of physics that needs changing
 **d.** A new legal voting age

**11**. List the computer analysis tools available on your campus.

**12**. What conclusions can you form from the data on rates of cigarette smoking? If possible, graph the data and see if your conclusions change.

Cigarette Smoking, % Total Population

| Number of cigarettes/day | 1970 | | 1980 | | 1983 | |
|---|---|---|---|---|---|---|
| | Males | Females | Males | Females | Males | Females |
| 1–15 | 11.5 | 11.8 | 8.7 | 10.2 | 8.3 | 10.1 |
| 15–24 | 18.4 | 12.9 | 15.2 | 12.1 | 15.0 | 13.2 |
| 25–34 | 5.1 | 3.0 | 5.3 | 3.2 | 5.2 | 3.1 |
| >35 | 6.4 | 2.5 | 6.7 | 3.4 | 5.9 | 2.5 |

**13**. What levels of cigarette smoking would you expect to find in the 1990 census according to data from the graph you constructed?

# PAPERS IN PROGRESS: ANALYSIS

## Jonathan's Paper on an Emily Dickinson Poem

After Jonathan finishedgathering his information about Emily Dickinson's poem, "I Heard a Fly Buzz When I Died," he began to think about interpreting what he had. Jonathan had little problem with sources since all the references to the poem were from works Jonathan considered reputable: articles in recognized journals and books published by recognized publishers.

The task of analyzing was relatively simple. Because Jonathan's topic was a chronological survey of critical interpretations of the poem, the form dictated itself. Jonathan used his word processor as an outliner. Since his topic was chronological, he first listed all the dates for the references in chronological order.

1955 Friedrich

1955 Johnson

1956 Ciardi

1956 Ransom

1961 Hogue

Then he looked at the entries to determine what the critic's attitude was toward the poem. At this point, Jonathan looked for one word. Here is what his computer screen looked like at this stage:

| | |
|---|---|
| 1955 Friedrich | nasty |
| 1955 Johnson | cadaverous |
| 1956 Ciardi | disagrees with Friedrich |
| 1956 Ransom | between Friedrich and Ciardi |
| 1961 Hogue | agrees with Friedrich |

After listing all the entries, Jonathan looked for a pattern. There was one. It seemed to Jonathan that most critics perceived the fly as something terrible. He felt that he now had a synthesis of the opinions he had read and a position from which to develop his paper.

## Jennifer's Paper on the Confederate Navy

Jennifer had collected a good deal of information on efforts of the Confederacy to attract U.S. Navy personnel from Southern states. One of her sources even gave a specific description of resignation rates by rank. She wanted to form some conclusion about how many officers actually resigned and served in the Confederate Navy, but she found that the resignation rates varied considerably by rank. Here are her figures:

| | Total | Total South | Resigned | Stayed | Resigned, % |
|---|---|---|---|---|---|
| Captains | 93 | 38 | 16 | 22 | 42.11 |
| Commanders | 127 | 64 | 34 | 30 | 53.13 |
| Lieutenants | 351 | 151 | 76 | 75 | 50.33 |
| Surgeons | 43 | 31 | 11 | 20 | 35.48 |
| Assistant surgeons | 36 | 18 | 7 | 11 | 38.89 |
| Paymasters | 64 | 27 | 10 | 17 | 37.04 |
| Chaplains | 24 | 6 | 1 | 5 | 16.67 |
| Mathematics professors | 12 | 7 | 1 | 6 | 14.29 |
| Masters | 45 | 16 | 6 | 10 | 37.50 |
| Midshipmen | 55 | 20 | 5 | 15 | 25.00 |
| Gunners | 47 | 11 | 2 | 9 | 18.18 |
| Carpenters | 45 | 20 | 1 | 19 | 5.00 |
| Sailmakers | 40 | 14 | 3 | 11 | 21.43 |

Two facts seem to stand out in this cart: there is a great range in the percentage of officers who resigned to serve with the Confederacy (5 to 53 percent), and the majority of officers with Southern origins did *not* resign.

Since there is a great deal of information in this chart, one way to aid analysis would be to give it some order. This is a common spreadsheet operation and one of several that Jennifer could perform to help her understand numerical data of this sort. She chose to begin by sorting the chart by resignation rates. Here is the chart that resulted:

| | Total | Total South | Resigned | Stayed | Resigned, % |
|---|---|---|---|---|---|
| Commanders | 127 | 64 | 34 | 30 | 53.1 |
| Lieutenants | 351 | 151 | 76 | 75 | 50.3 |
| Captains | 93 | 38 | 16 | 22 | 42.1 |
| Masters | 45 | 16 | 6 | 10 | 37.5 |
| Paymasters | 64 | 27 | 10 | 17 | 37.0 |
| Assistant surgeons | 64 | 27 | 10 | 17 | 37.0 |
| Surgeons | 43 | 31 | 11 | 20 | 35.5 |
| Midshipmen | 55 | 20 | 5 | 15 | 25.0 |
| Sailmakers | 40 | 14 | 3 | 11 | 21.4 |
| Gunners | 47 | 11 | 2 | 9 | 18.2 |
| Chaplains | 24 | 6 | 1 | 5 | 16.7 |
| Mathematics professors | 12 | 7 | 1 | 6 | 14.3 |
| Carpenters | 45 | 20 | 1 | 19 | 5.0 |

The sorted data makes the differences in ranks even more obvious. A majority of commanders resigned, while almost all carpenters, professors of mathematics, chaplains, gunners, and sailmakers stayed in the U.S. Navy, even if they were from Southern states. A graph of the data makes the differences even more clear. Figure 4-6 is a graph generated from the spreadsheet. The dramatic differences in resignation rates are obvious from the graph.

At this point Jennifer could begin to make some conclusions about resignations: the rates were generally under 50 percent but they differed greatly according to rank. If she wanted to, she could take this data and use it as the basis for a paper. Or she could process the data a little more first. For example, she might choose to focus more closely on command ranks. It is one thing for carpenters to resign; it is another for captains to resign. Jennifer decided to examine command ranks more closely. Here is the part of the spreadsheet relevant

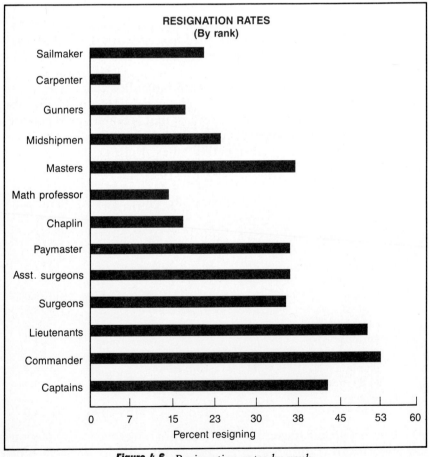

**Figure 4-6.** *Resignation rates by rank.*

to the three command ranks, followed by a line graph showing their rates of resignation:

|            | Total | Total South | Resigned | Stayed | Resigned, % |
|------------|-------|-------------|----------|--------|-------------|
| Commanders | 127   | 64          | 34       | 30     | 53.1        |
| Lieutenants | 351  | 151         | 76       | 75     | 50.3        |
| Captains   | 93    | 38          | 16       | 22     | 42.1        |

Figure 4-7 has been scaled to help emphasize the differences in rates of resignation. It makes a very clear point: officers in the command ranks did not all resign at the same rate—53 percent of commanders left and 50 percent of lieutenants left, but only 42 percent of captains left. Why? Looking through her note cards, Jennifer finds this description of promotion problems in the U.S. Navy:

> The excessive accumulation of older officers at the head of the list was felt as a heavy drag all the way down to the foot. Promotion was blocked, as there was no provision for retirement; and the commanders and lieutenants, many of whom were conspicuous for ability and energy, were stagnating in subordinate positions. The commanders at the list were between fifty-eight and sixty years of age—a time of life at which few men are useful for active service. The upper lieutenants were forty-eight or fifty—some indeed were past fifty—and very few were in command of vessels, as there were two hundred officers above them. (Soley 5)
>
> This enforced continuance in subordinate positions could not fail to tell upon even the best men. The tendency in such a system is to make mere routine men, and to substitute apathy and indolence for zeal and energy. (Soley 5)

Commanders are in their late fifties with no hope of promotion. Lieutenants are in their late forties with little hope of promotion. Is

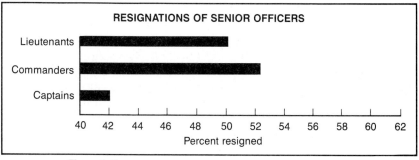

**Figure 4-7.** *Resignation rates for senior naval officers.*

lack of promotion sufficient motivation for an officer to resign his commission and join the Confederate Navy? Maybe not, but it is one possible explanation for differences in resignation rates. Jennifer will want to scan her notes for other explanations, but at least she has found a focus for her paper and has analyzed her data sufficiently to have a feasible conclusion.

Her cycles of analysis are not complete—she will want to use Burke's pentad or some other questioner program to help her think through possible explanations; she may want to try invisible writing to brainstorm for other ideas. Even if she begins writing her first draft now, she will probably need to gather additional information as she writes and perform additional analyses as she struggles to get all her ideas on paper. Nevertheless, her paper has evolved considerably since she began her research.

## Kris's Paper on the Mechanism of Evolution

As we have seen, Kris began the analysis of information as a first step because her initial assignment was in need of significant focus before she could even begin to collect her information. Even though she had focused her topic on the specific question "What is the mechanism of the evolutionary process," she still had work to do to analyze the information she had acquired.

Even while continuing to collect information, Kris found herself analyzing the information in her notes to resolve two central issues: which theories was she going to discuss in her paper and which would she finally offer as the most reasonable. Since she was faced with a wide range of expert opinion on these theories, Kris decided to employ a structured approach to reaching her conclusion.

After reviewing the analysis tools we have just discussed, she elected to try applying the journalist's "who," "what," "when," "where," "why," and "how" to both concerns. Note how the questions she asked reflect the six questions of that approach.

First, she had decided which theories of evolutionary mechanism she was going to include. In her reading she had encountered far more explanations than she could possibly examine in the five- to six-page paper her instructor had requested. As a result, realizing the importance of current information in the sciences, she eliminated those older theories which were no longer being supported in the current literature ("when"); here the dates recorded in her working bibliography cards were a determining factor. She searched her bibliography database and selected all entries older than ten years (later she would reconsider the Eldridge and Gould article of 1972 since it was acknowledged to be a major document in the evolutionary debate.) Additionally, she focused on those theories which were supported by several different authors and were debated in professional rather than popular journals ("who" and "where"). Finally, she considered that any theory which was widely debated, even if authors argued against its validity, was important enough to warrant a place in her paper; she did this by selectively retrieving all notes which contained selected words in the keyword fields ("how" others view this theory). Once she had done this, she was able to compare the number of references to each concept; this analysis narrowed her focus to three major explanations of the process.

Once she decided on the players in the evolutionary debate, Kris had to analyze the claims of each and decide which of the three her paper would offer as the most reasonable explanation. Again she used breadth of published support and the source of such support as guides in reaching her conclusion. As before, she considered both the reputation of the author and the place of publication as important indicators. But a new factor, logical support, entered her deliberations. In asking the final two questions, "Why do my experts support this view?" and "What evidence do they offer in support of their views?" Kris had arrived at a stage where she could decide on her own conclusion.

# Chapter 5

# WRITING THE FIRST DRAFT

**Y**ou've been collecting information about your subject, learning as much as you can about it. You've analyzed the data using the most appropriate tools available. You've formed some preliminary conclusions about your subject. The time has come to begin writing your report.

Or is it time? Sometimes actually choosing when to begin writing can be difficult. Some people may feel that they know enough about a subject to begin writing part of their report before they have even completed all their research—they are confident about what they will find and where it will fit in the report. Others put off writing until they have read all possible sources, done one analysis after another, and formed a whole series of conclusions about the subject. Others find other reasons to postpone writing the report.

Writing is not like working on an assembly line. There may be no clear distinction between researching and analyzing and drafting. You may be doing some of each at the same time. If you get a good idea for an introduction, you may want to write it, even though you are still collecting some of your information. If one part of your paper seems clear, you may want to write a first draft on that area even though you are still unclear about another area of the paper. There may be no clear signal that research and analysis is done—the time for writing has come.

No matter how or when you start, however, there is one major difference between writing the first draft and what you have done before. When you start writing, you begin to express *your* ideas, *your* conclusions about the subject. Before, you were evaluating what others said. Now you will have to explain your own stand on the subject. Your ability to understand your subject and explain your ideas will be evident to all your readers. There will be no hiding how much you really know. Writing can be very public and at the same time very personal.

Fortunately, you will have several opportunities to improve your report. With each draft you will have an opportunity to revise and edit the report to make sure that it clearly explains and expresses your ideas on the subject. The first draft doesn't have to do that. It isn't public; no one will see it except you unless you ask people to read it and give you ideas for revision. It is your chance to experiment with different methods of description, different organizational forms, and different content.

What should you hope to accomplish in your first draft? It can't do everything, but there are three goals you should set for the first draft. It should (1) solidify your ideas about the subject, (2) determine an order of presentation, and (3) get your ideas down on paper. There will be time to revise and rework, to clarify and correct. For the moment, just satisfying these three goals is sufficient.

## ▓▓▓▓▓DEVELOPING YOUR IDEAS ABOUT A SUBJECT

Even though you may do extensive and systematic analysis of your data, you may find that your ideas change as you begin writing. Just putting your ideas on paper may cause them to shift. This seems to be true for most people—they find new ways of looking at a subject as they write.

Many professional writers have commented on this aspect of writing. Here is what a few of them have to say about writing and discovery:

> *Edward Albee:* Writing has got to be an act of discovery. I write to find out what I'm thinking about.

> *Frank Conroy:* Most often I come to an understanding of what I'm thinking about as I write it.

> *Robert Duncan:* If I write what you know, I bore you; if I write what I know, I bore myself, therefore I write what I don't know.

> *E. M. Forster:* How do I know what I think until I see what I say?

> *Christopher Fry:* My trouble is I'm the sort of writer who only finds out what he's getting at by the time he's got to the end of it.

> *Shirley Hazzard:* I think that one is constantly startled by the things that appear before you on the page when you're writing.

> *Bernard Malamud:* A writer has to surprise himself to be worth reading.

> *Henry Miller:* Writing, like life itself, is a voyage of discovery.

> *Kurt Vonnegut:* It's like watching a teletype machine in a newspaper office to see what comes out. (Murray 1978, 101–103)

These authors are primarily describing fiction writing, but much of what they say applies to report writing as well. I'm not sure report writers would want to go as far as Christopher Fry and know "what he's getting at [only] by the time he's got to the end of it," but there is a fair amount of discovery that goes on for report writers, too. Describing research in detail, organizing disparate ideas into a sequence, grouping and selecting information, all the actions of writing a first draft will help in leading you to new ideas about your subject.

These new ideas may seem like an annoyance. You had the paper all worked out, and now it seems to be changing as you write it. Maybe the new ideas seem like good luck. You were unsure about what to say, and now the ideas seem to be springing up from nowhere. In either case, you should expect that writing will generate ideas. No matter how sure you were of your conclusions before, some of them will change as you write. This is one reason why many people find writing exciting—it is one kind of exploration.

While most discoveries will come automatically as you write, you can increase the exploratory aspects of writing. One way is to turn off the internal "censor" you developed over the years. Don't worry if ideas are too silly, or if they are grammatically correct; you can always make corrections later. Your goal is to try out new ways of stating an idea just to see how they look. Of course, the word processor aids in this effort. If an idea doesn't work out, you can totally erase it in seconds. If only part of a paragraph seems worth keeping, you can erase the weak parts. The word processor makes text manipulation quick and easy.

You can also use specific techniques to increase the amount of discovering you do while you write. You can use these techniques with any part of the paper whenever you seem to be bogged down or unhappy about the way a section is going. Maybe the best time to use these techniques is when you are just getting started with your paper and face a blank sheet of paper or a blank computer monitor.

## Invisible Writing

We discussed the invisible writing technique in Chapter 4. The idea is to turn off the word processor screen and write as much as you can for a set period of time—perhaps ten or twenty minutes. The point is to reduce distractions. With the screen on, it is tempting to look back and reread sections or correct typos or other errors. With the screen off, you see nothing to reread or correct—you stay with your current thought and push that as far as you can.

With that approach in mind, to leave corrections and rewriting for later and just focus on getting initial ideas entered into the computer, you should find that two things happen to your writing: you write more, and you write things that surprise you. You write more because you are spending more time writing and less time correcting, and you have fewer distractions to break your concentration. You write things that surprise you because when the screen goes off, so does much of your internal censor.

This is one way to begin writing your paper. Too often writers have all kinds of ideas but can't seem to get started because they are so worried about having the "right" first sentence that they never get past it. They work through one idea after another in their minds, and nothing ever gets on paper. Invisible writing drops that barrier. You begin writing, continue writing, and worry later about what parts of your writing are worth keeping. After twenty minutes of writing with the screen off, you have three or four screens full of text. In those screens you may have several different passages that you like. Now your choice is not what to say, but which idea to place first. This is a much easier choice to make and a more productive one, because now instead of having a jumble of conflicting and often paralyzing thoughts, you have pages of text—components of your first draft.

In short, the best way to start writing is not to think about writing, but to write. Invisible writing makes that easier for some people.

## Loop Writing

In his classic book, *Writing with Power,* Peter Elbow describes a set of activities for getting the first draft down on paper. He calls these activities "loop writing" because they start with a set subject in mind, drift temporarily away from the subject while the writer explores aspects of the subject, and then loop back to the subject as the writer gains new insight. These twelve activities are worth examining in detail because they were created especially for people writing research reports. You should be able to find one or two that you will want to try for yourself.

**First Thoughts**   You may prepare a short two- or three-page draft before you have done any research at all, or before you have formed any final conclusions about the research you have done. This is called the *first thoughts.* The point is not to be accurate or particularly glib, but to clear the air. What ideas do you already have, what conclusions have you already reached, even before you have begun your research or formally analyzed all your data? As you collect your information or analyze your data, you will probably change your ideas (if new facts won't change your ideas, how will they ever change the ideas of your readers?), but for now you are putting all your cards on the table—"Here's what I already know and what I have already decided about the subject."

For instance, if you were researching the use of pesticides in a particular ecosystem, even if you had never formally researched this area before, you might write a short draft describing what you know about pesticides in general (even if it turns out what you "know" isn't true) and how you feel about their use. As your research develops, this first draft can serve as a starting point for your paper. It can remind you of your initial reactions to the subject (and the likely initial reactions of your readers) and give you initial conclusions that you can either respond to now that you know better or support more fully now that you understand your subject more.

**Prejudices** What do you *want* your data to prove? If your research is on remedial teaching methods, do you want the research you are doing to prove that specially trained teachers are the only solution? Or that schools are powerless and that only effective parenting will prevent learning problems? What are the biases you have? Don't pretend that you are a neutral observer—you're not, and neither are your readers.

Taking time to write a two- or three-page draft of your *prejudices* about your subject will have several advantages for you as you begin writing the report itself. First, it will help you be honest with yourself. You'll recognize where you are trying to twist evidence and why you may be reacting in a certain way to certain studies. Second, it will help you separate evidence from bias. As you write your report, it should be easier for you to see where your conclusions are supported by solid evidence and where they are supported only by your desires. You'll never be convincing to others until you can evaluate the quality of your own evidence. Third, your report will be read by others. How they receive the ideas you present will depend in part on the biases they have when they start reading. A good way to prepare a response to those biases is to recognize your own.

**Instant Version** There are a few people who can sit down and write a report straight out. This is called the *instant version*. They begin at page one, and after two or three hours have the whole thing. Few people can do this, but sometimes it's useful to pretend that you can do it even if you can't. You start writing and put in research if you have it or make up the research if you don't. If you have a conclusion you state it; if you don't, you invent one as best you can. In either case you pretend as if this were your research paper and you were going to turn it in tomorrow.

Why write a "pretend" research paper? First, it may surprise you to see that you are a lot closer to being done than you realized. By not worrying about all the details, you get your draft on paper much faster and probably much closer to an acceptable "real" paper than you might expect. Some of the paper might be pretty rough, but other sections might be nearly completed. This lets you focus your attention on just those sections that need it and gives you some idea of which methods will work and which descriptive approaches are less useful. For instance, if you look back at your "pretend" paper and find that the best sections are those that use a rhetorical question followed by data summary as response, you have discovered an organizational technique that you may want to use more often in the paper.

Probably the best reason for writing a pretend research paper is reassurance. You see that you can do it and that some parts of it are almost complete. Now you don't have to worry about writing the whole paper, just those parts where you didn't have facts or completed conclusions. The job ahead of you has just been reduced.

**Dialogues**   One barrier that may prevent you from writing your first draft is a conflict over which of several conclusions is best. You have analyzed your evidence over and over, and you still find that there are two different conclusions you can form. You can resolve this conflict by constructing a *dialogue*. Let's say that you are researching factory automation and one body of information leads you to support it since it will produce better products at lower cost and at less danger to factory workers. Another body of evidence leads you to worry about unemployment and the erosion of the middle class. How can you write a paper if you can't even decide what position to take?

One way to help you form a conclusion is to personify the two sides. Create a dialogue in which a factory worker who favors automation discusses it with a factory worker who doesn't. As you supply facts for each one to speak, you will be reexamining those facts, deciding which ones are most powerful and true. You will consider your facts in a new way. You should find that it will only take five or ten exchanges between your "characters" before one side has won and your conclusion has been formed.

One additional advantage to this approach is that you will have looked very closely at the arguments against your conclusion. This should make it much easier for you to respond to those arguments and convince your readers.

**Narrative Thinking**   If you remain confused about what conclusion to reach from your research, you may try to straighten it out by writing a history of your ideas on the subject. This is referred to as *narrative* *thinking.* For example, you might write something like: "I began as opposed to capital punishment, mostly because it just seemed too ugly to me. Why would you ever want to kill someone? Then I started reading about some of the horrible crimes some people have committed and I just got mad about those people either getting out on parole or escaping and being out in public again after doing what they had done. But then I found some statistics on how many convicted murderers are actually found to be totally innocent years later...."

By tracking the development of your ideas, you should see why you are confused, which events or readings changed your stand from one side to another, and which facts changed them back. Now you can decide which of those facts was the strongest. Should you have changed your mind? Looking back, did you let one article influence you more than it should have? Once you know where your confusion originated, it is much easier to eliminate. You should also find that tracking your reaction to various articles and arguments makes you much more sensitive to the kind of reactions your readers will have when they read about them in your report.

**Stories** The information you have collected for your report may seem like an endless series of dates and places and numbers. But buried in those facts are real people doing real things. If you wanted to, you could probably write pages of *stories* about the people in your report, or stories about your own life that occurred to you as you read.

Take the example of a research topic that seems totally cold and scientific: artificial cellulose production. What could be drier than that subject? But you start writing stories about people and events. You begin by describing the chief investigators and tell a little about how they started their research. You add a story of your own about a research project you once did and what it meant to you. You add a story a professor once told you about a crash research project that took her eighteen hours a day for months. Next you think of a statement made by a logger about how synthetic cellulose will affect business. This gets you thinking about a ghost town you visited in the mountains, or the time someone in your family was laid off from a job.

Each story leads to another until you have thirty or forty vignettes. What do you do with the stories? First, rereading the stories will help you see your attitudes toward the subject. Do your stories seem more sympathetic toward the researcher? Or the logger? You may want to use those attitudes to form the conclusions you will present during your paper, or you may form a totally different conclusion, but those stories should remind you of the biases you have as you present your facts, biases your readers are likely to share.

Those stories will also serve as a source of illustrations as you write. Carefully selected anecdotes are acceptable in almost all research reports and help to both enhance your writing and clarify points you are trying to make. Now you have a set of illustrations from which to choose.

**Scenes** If you were going to present your paper as a series of photographs, what would the photographs contain? Try writing a few pages in which each paragraph is a picture to be included with your report. How many pictures would be needed? Which picture would come first? You are writing a report on the economic effects of shopping malls. Is the first picture that comes to mind a huge new mall in the suburbs or empty streets downtown? Do you see independent merchants working for their piece of the economic pie or endless shop girls being paid minimum wage by remote corporate offices? The picture you describe will help you clarify your own ideas about the subject and later explain your ideas to your readers.

**New Audiences** If you are having trouble getting started on a paper, one way to get rolling and learn more about your subject at the same time is to write the paper to a totally *new audience*. For instance, how would you explain the Russian Revolution to the friends you had back in third grade? You are all sitting around your tree house talking baseball and Saturday cartoon shows, when someone mentions the Russian Revolution. Not very likely, of course, but what could you say to kids that age? What would be most important to them? What would they be capable of understanding? Where would you begin? Has there been anything in their lives that would help them understand the event?

Even if you write only a page or two, you will have viewed your subject in a totally new way. You will see sides of the subject that might otherwise have escaped you. Now return to your original audience—college-educated adults—and see what effect they have on what you say and how you say it.

**New Writers** Having trouble writing as yourself? Try writing the first two pages of the report from the perspective of Ronald Reagan. What would Ronald Reagan have to say about the cultural effects of in vitro fertilization? If Ronald Reagan is too tough, how about Madonna or Bruce Springsteen? The point is not to slave over a perfect characterization, but to see what effect the writer has on the report—what gets said, as well as when and how. Once you've admitted that the writer makes a difference, you are more prepared to honestly deal with how *you* affect the report. You should also see your facts in a whole new light, assuming that you can keep a straight face long enough to continue writing.

**New Times** Let's suppose that you are writing about groundwater pollution. What would the report have been like if it were written in 1776? Would people during that time be upset about the pollution or astounded that chemistry had gone so far? Would they be more concerned about health and water than we are, or less? What would their priorities be? Would they want more government involvement, or not? Just two pages of writing for history should give you some new perspective about your subject. Are the things that matter now even remotely similar to the things that mattered most 200 years ago or that will matter most in another 200 years? If they are different, how can we justify our concern? If they are the same, what makes these problems so universal?

**Dangerous Errors** Now that you know something about your subject, what are the biggest mistakes people can make about it? If people continue to be wrong about the causes of teenage pregnancies, what is the worst error they can make? Write a page or two about their error and what effect it would have on the problem. Understanding their errors first forces you to think about your readers—what ideas they may have when they start reading your paper, and also makes you order the responses you make. What should be the first point you make in your report? What can safely be left for later? You should find it much easier to determine the beginning of your paper now.

**Lies** Can any good come from *lies?* You might find out by writing two or three pages of lies about your subject. Just make up as many as you can. Some may be elaborate lies going on for a paragraph or two. Others might just take a sentence. Air pollution is caused by hamburgers being grilled by the millions in fast-food restaurants. Pollution would go away if we all inhaled at the same time. Cigarettes are a solution to pollution because their concentration in the lungs prevents lung damage from other kinds of pollution. Try a page or two of lies—enjoy yourself.

What's the good of lies? Besides giving you a nice break from a long assignment and a chance to clear your head, the lies themselves may help you make some connections you hadn't made before, or clarify some connections you had made but not admitted. For instance, what is the connection between cigarette smoking and air pollution? Does it make any sense to force businesses to pay billions for air treatment if people willingly pay money to destroy their health with cigarettes, anyway? Why should the business down the street have to clean the air when the person next to me can legally blow smoke in my face?

After you write your lies and make your connections, you may find that your conclusions about your subject change. Your perspective is different now. Your lies led you to a new truth.

The purpose of these loop writing techniques is to use writing as a mode of exploration. Using one of these techniques for ten or fifteen minutes should help you discover new ideas about your subject. You may be able to use what you write later as part of your actual paper, or the writing may just give you new ideas and a new perspective. In either case, two or three pages created through loop writing or invisible writing will help prepare you for your first draft. Most importantly, it will get you past the dreaded blank screen. You will already be past the stage of researching and immersed in the stage of writing. You will have switched from discovering what others have to say to discovering what you have to say.

# ORGANIZING YOUR IDEAS

While you know the first draft will change many times before you complete the final report, one goal you want to satisfy with this draft is to at least begin forming some organization for your ideas. As you begin developing this organization, you will find that your organization will be one of two types: *content-driven* or *format-driven.*

A *content-driven* organization is one that is determined mainly by the information you have gathered. For example, in the course of gathering data about the problem of teenage pregnancies, you find an endless series of stories about individuals who have faced severe difficulties because of early pregnancies. As you sit down to write your report, it seems the best way to present the information you have is to retell those stories—to make the paper a collection of individual examples. You may have some initial material and some concluding remarks, but most of the paper will be the examples you found.

*Format-driven* organizations are those determined by various professional journals or by individual professors. For instance, reports of educational research almost always have five parts: (1) introduction to the problem being studied, (2) descriptions of former studies, (3) procedures used in this study, (4) results of the study, and (5) conclusions.

You still have some flexibility in this kind of paper. For instance, you can decide which of the former studies to present and what order to use for them, but in all cases it will be assumed that you will describe former studies before, not after, you describe your current study.

Formats such as these are very common. They have the advantage of presenting information in a form that has been found useful over a period of time. They also ease the burden of the reader. Since readers know in advance what form your report will take, they can more easily scan your work and find the data that is most important to them. They might begin by reading your conclusions first and then leaf back to the results part of your report if they want to see the data on which you based your ideas. Since your paper follows a standard format, searching for particular parts is very simple.

To give you an idea of the range of formats research papers can take, here are some sample formats popular in several different fields:

### Scientific Paper (General Format)

1. Title
2. Abstract
3. Introduction
4. Materials and methods
5. Results
6. Discussion
7. Acknowledgments
8. Literature cited

### Chemistry Laboratory Report

1. Title of the experiment
2. Introduction
3. Procedure
4. Data and observations
5. Calculations
6. Summary
7. Discussion of errors

### Biology Laboratory Report

1. Abstract
2. Introduction
3. Methods and materials
4. Results
5. Discussion and conclusion

### Physics Laboratory Report

1. Title of the experiment
2. Purpose
3. References
4. Procedure
5. Data
6. Graphs
7. Calculations
8. Conclusions

### Sociology Report

1. Formulate a hypothesis
2. Gather data and statistical information
3. Analyze results
4. Present implications

### Clinical Psychology Report

1. State the problem
2. Collect relevant data
3. Generate alternative solutions or answers
4. Determine consequences of various solutions
5. Identify the "best" solution and support the choice

### History Report

1. Begin with a question
2. Find historical evidence
3. Determine credibility or reliability of the evidence
4. Analyze the usable evidence
5. Arrive at a conclusion

### Analysis of a Problem for Economics

1. Introduction
2. Statement of the specific question
3. Literature review
4. Data sources
5. Analysis

**6.** Results

**7.** Conclusions

Most of these formats have common elements, but it is clear that each discipline has developed its own way of ordering some of the information usual to reports in that field. As you prepare to write your first draft, you will want to look carefully at the formats standard to your kind of report. It makes sense to write a report that generally adheres to the format common for psychology reports if the area you are researching is psychological. These formats have been developed over decades and are commonly accepted practice.

If you are unsure what kind of format is most appropriate for the kind of report you are doing, consider in retrospect the articles you read as you did your research. The format they used is probably close to the format you will want to use. If you can find the main outline for that and similar articles, enter the outline in your word processor and use it as a template for your report. The specific use of such templates is described below.

Whether you are free to develop an organization of your own based on the content of your paper or need to follow the standard organization always used for reports of the type you have chosen, there are several tools available to help you both find and adhere to a selected organization.

## Use of Templates

Templates are outlines based on standard formats for reports. In situations where you know what the standard formats are, you can create a template by means of a word processor. Here is one you might create if you are reporting research using the recommended format of the American Psychological Association:

Abstract
Introduction
  Overview of the problem
  Previous studies
  Controversial issues
  Your position
Method
  Subjects
  Apparatus
  Procedures
Results
Discussion
References

Since this is the format recommended for reports of this type, one way to guarantee that you follow this organization when you write your report is to type the format into your word processor and save it on your disk. Now it becomes the outline or template for this or any other research report you have to do.

When you actually begin writing, you first load the template in from your disk, position the cursor after one of the topics, and begin entering the information appropriate for that section of the report. The template will be your organizational guide. It reminds you of all the parts your paper will have, shows you the order these components must be in, and helps you see where each piece of information you have collected should be placed.

If the report you are writing is heavily formated like this, the template almost lets you "write by the numbers." Each heading becomes a space that has to be filled in, and the heading tells you what kind of information has to be placed there. We gradually build the report by filling in the headings like this:

Abstract
Introduction
   Overview of the problem
   Previous studies
   Controversial issues
   Your position
Method
   Subjects
     Subjects were 120 first-year college students enrolled in an introductory psychology class. Sixty-three were female; fifty-seven were male. All were between the ages of eighteen and twenty-three. These students were participating in the study as part of a course requirement. None reported any prior experience with studies of this type.
   Apparatus
   Procedures
Results
Discussion
References

When the template is very specific, as in this example, writing becomes very easy. You know what has to be said and where it has to go. Other areas of the template may be more vague and leave more room for experimentation. For example, the introduction says that you should describe the problem but doesn't say much more than that. It is up to you to decide how to introduce the problem. Should you use a specific example? Give a few statistics about how prevalent the problem is? Use an anecdote you found in your reading? Those decisions are still left to you. All the template shows you is where the material you use for an introduction should go.

## Use of Outliner Programs

In the last chapter we described outliner programs and how they can be used to help you organize information. These programs operate much like word processors in that you can insert and delete and move information at will. Their advantage is that you can collapse or expand the outline when necessary. If you want to see only major headings for the most important ideas, you collapse the outline. If you want to examine the details of your outline, you expand it.

Such outlines make an excellent tool for finding an initial organization for your report. In some cases you will find that the outline is nearly identical to the outline you will use for your paper. You can simply transfer the outline to your word processor and begin writing.

In some cases you may find that the outline served a useful purpose in helping you collect information and group it, but some changes have to be made before the outline can be used for the report itself. For example, consider this outline:

Computer history
   Biographies of early developers
Computer sizes
   Mainframe
   Mini
   Micro
Current architecture
   RAM
   Secondary memory
     Tape
     Disks
   I/O devices
     Monitors
     Keyboards
     Printers
     Digitizers
     Card readers
   CPU
Current applications
   Educational uses
     Drills
     Word processors
     Spreadsheets

Vocational education aids
Robotics
  CAD

This outline holds all the information from our readings about computers. Depending on the purpose of our report, it may serve as a very good writing outline as well. But if we "collapse" the outline, we see that the main ideas are a bit disjointed:

Computer history

Computer sizes

Current architecture

Current applications

Each of these topics is rather broad and could be covered separately in a report. Several books have been written on computer history. There must be hundreds of books on current applications of computers. Surely we wouldn't want to try to cover that much information in one research report.

So the first thing that we might do with our outline when we prepare to write our first draft is to reduce it. We look back at the outline and decide to concentrate on one area only and eliminate the rest. We still have one section of the outline to use as the basis for our report, but now we have pared it down to a size that is more reasonable.

Even if we pare the outline down, we may have to modify it in other ways as well. Let's take this section of the outline:

Current applications
  Educational uses
    Drills
    Word processors
    Spreadsheets
    Vocational education aids
      Robotics
      CAD

Current educational uses of computers might be a good topic for a paper. There has been quite a bit of growth in that area and some recent changes that might surprise most readers. However, while the outline segment shown above gives possible headings for the report, we might want to reconsider it before actually using it for writing. For instance, do we want to adhere to that order? In our reading we may find descriptions of drill programs first and place them at the beginning of our outline, but do we want to describe them first in our paper? It may be that the increased use of word processors in schools is more important than some of the other developments. You may have read about word processors being used by kindergarten children and think that this would be an interesting way to begin your report. In either case, you will want to look at your outline to see what order would be best to meet your purposes and achieve the desired response from your audience.

Now that we are using the outline as a presenter rather than a collector of information, we might want to make some additions. The two obvious additions are an introduction and a conclusion. We may also see the need for some transitional material between major headings. As a result, our outline may end up looking something like this:

> Educational uses of computers
>> Introduction with current examples
>>> Word processors
>>>> Grade-school uses
>>>> Typical middle-school uses
>>>> The new high-school English class
>> Other uses gaining in popularity
>>> Spreadsheets
>>> CAD
>> Uses in decline
>>> Drills
>> Conclusion reviewing interesting applications and major trends

Besides paring down an outline and rearranging it prior to the first draft, another approach to take is synthesis. In studying the major headings of the outline, do we find any central theme that links them together? Our outline starts out looking pretty disjointed, but there may be a central theme running through the outline that isn't apparent yet. If we can find it, we might be able to arrive at our synthesis. Let's take another look at that outline:

> Computer history
>
> Computer sizes
>
> Current architecture
>
> Current applications

Currently all four headings have equivalent status. If you think back to your reading, however, you might question whether they really are equivalent. Does computer architecture determine the application potential of computers? (It does.) Or does the historical development of computers affect current applications? If you think about it, you may decide that a proper synthesis of your outline would be this:

Computer history: its effect on
    Computer sizes
    Computer architecture
    Computer applications

Now your outline shows a common theme, a theme that you can develop throughout your report.

Outliner programs make this kind of movement and insertion easy to do, thus facilitating the transition from collecting ideas to presenting them. Whether you adjust your former outline through narrowing your focus, changing your order, or finding a unifying synthesis for your ideas, some adjustment in your outline will probably be necessary as you prepare to write. The purpose of your outline has changed, so its form will also change.

Incidentally, if you don't have access to an outliner program, you can use a word processor to do most of what outliner programs do. You won't be able to expand or collapse your outline, but you will still have the power of the word processor to insert, delete, and move ideas around. And since you are creating your outline right in a word processor, it will be even easier to flesh out your ideas when the time comes.

## GETTING THE FIRST DRAFT ON PAPER

Prior to writing the first draft, you may have tried one of the looping techniques described earlier in the chapter to test out an approach to the subject. You may also have started developing an organization by creating a template if your paper will be highly formatted or using an outliner program or making a rough list in a word processor if your report will be less formally organized. In either case, you probably acknowledge that your paper will change considerably as you write it, but the only way to achieve that final form is to start writing. You need to get a draft done. It is that first tentative draft that will tell you whether you need to do more research or whether your conclusions make any sense at all. There is no substitute for writing.

How you generate that first draft will depend partly on your personality and partly on the tools you have available when you write. Here are four different methods for writing the first draft:

The instant draft
Drafts with windows
Drafts from outlines
Database transfers

There is no known research proving that any one of these methods is superior to the others. Choose whichever approach seems most reasonable to you and is most easily achieved with the writing tools you have available.

## The Instant Version

The instant version is one of the loop procedures described earlier in the chapter. The technique here is to ignore any place where you aren't too sure of your facts and just write. When in doubt, leave a blank or make up a "fact." Write as long as you can, and try to complete one whole draft of the paper even if a few places are a little weak or fuzzy. With luck, this approach could help you discover your position on a subject and test one possible form of organization. It could be used before you have done much of your research or after your research is completed.

If you are writing with a word processor, this approach is even more attractive because little extra work is involved in rewriting sections of the report that turn out to be unacceptable. You simply erase the sections that are weak, save the sections that are stronger, and rewrite where needed. There is never a need to redo the entire project, as there might be if you were typing the report. With a word processor the good lines can be easily separated and saved for another day.

One advantage of this approach to the first draft is reassurance. If you tend to get so concerned about what you will write that you end up writing nothing at all, this approach helps you get over that hurdle. You know that this isn't a "serious" draft, so you write instead of worrying about writing. When you have a draft done, you may have to change much of it but you are no longer staring at a blank sheet of paper or a blank computer screen—you have a draft in front of you to improve, a draft to encourage you to continue writing.

Several techniques can help you continue writing while you are working on this draft. You want to avoid situations where you spend so much time selecting just the "right" word or repeatedly rewriting the same sentence that your whole draft bogs down. The point is not to be perfect the first time, but to finish the first draft so that you can go on to the second draft.

To keep yourself moving, Peter Elbow suggests making up facts if you don't know them. For people who have been doing lengthy research on a subject, this advice might be hard to follow. Several techniques can be used to achieve the same effect—keeping you writing instead of endlessly searching through piles of note cards or database indexes.

The first is to insert notes to yourself as you write. If there is a special character at the beginning of the note, you can use the search and replace capability of your word processor to find the note quickly later. For example, if you were writing about groundwater pollution and couldn't quite remember the statistic you needed, you might try something like this:

> One of the most dangerous aspects of polychlorobenzene pollution is that whenever concentrations rise above [[get the amount from the Clark article]] parts per million, water fowl suffer major reproduction problems.

You can continue writing and wait until later to get the exact figure you need. When you have finished the first draft and want to put in the details you need, you have the word processor search for "[[." It will find those two brackets in an instant and put the cursor right at that spot, so you can erase the note and insert the figure you have found. As a result, you can concentrate on expressing the major ideas of your paper and wait until later to insert the supporting details.

A similar approach works with long names or titles. Instead of concentrating on typing the entire name out, you give it some easy abbreviation while you are writing, and then use the search and replace mechanism of the word processor to put in the complete name later. In the following example, this method is used to avoid the time necessary to repeatedly type out the formal name of an herbicide:

> The weed killer *ATZ* has caused thyroid cancer in laboratory animals. This chemical was misused by a number of cranberry growers in 1959, producing residues on some of the marketed berries. In the controversy that followed the seizure of contaminated cranberries by the *FDA*, the fact that the chemical actually was cancer-producing was widely challenged, even by many medical experts. The scientific facts released by the *FDA* clearly indicate the carcinogenic nature of *ATZ* in laboratory rats. (Carson 1962, 200)

Here ATZ is an abbreviation for aminotriazole, and, of course, FDA is short for Food and Drug Administration. In either case, using the abbreviation during the first draft not only saves time but also lessens the likelihood of spelling errors. (What are the chances of typing out "aminotriazole" ten or fifteen times and getting it right every time?) After the rough draft has been completed, you can use your word processor's search and replace function to replace every abbreviation with the full word or phrase desired. On most word processors the whole process would only take a minute or two.

Another shortcut to use if you write with a word processor is a *macro*. A macro can be used as a substitute for a block of text or for a series of commands. Not all word processors have this capability, but it is becoming increasingly common. It is essentially the capability of having the word processor run special instruction sequences for you.

A fairly standard place to use a macro as a substitute for a block of text is in return addresses. Since they are always the same three lines, rather than enter them over and over again, you set up a macro definition telling the word processor that when you press some special keystroke (e.g., Alt-R), you want the word processor to enter the return address for you. You could do the same thing for any other substantial group of words you found yourself using repeatedly. For instance, if your research made repeated mention of the work of "Professor Joyce Hartford, University of Miami," you could set up a macro that would enter that whole phrase every time you pressed a key combination (e.g., Alt-H). Now, as you type along, rather than have to pause every time you get to some reference to Professor Hartford and type in that whole long phrase, you simply press Alt-H and the entire phrase is put in by the computer.

Not all word processors have macro capabilities, but when it is available, this feature can let you write much faster than you ever thought possible.

## Windows and Drafts

While developing one section of a paper, writers often lose track of the rest of the paper. This situation is even worse for people writing on a word processor. As has been pointed out by more than one researcher, "the size of the display screen makes it difficult to see many things simultaneously or in juxtaposition." (Bridwell 1984, 111) With only ten to twenty lines of text visible at any one time, it is easy to lose track of what came earlier in the report, and where these lines fit. This is one place where people who use pen and paper or typewriters may have an advantage over those with word processors—they can see thirty or so lines on a page and can spread several pages out to examine at the same time.

One solution to this problem is to print out the text of a report often so that you have the paper version of the report to examine, but this is time-consuming and distracting. Another approach is to use windows.

*Windows* are subsections of the computer screen. Not all word processing programs support windows, but they are so useful they are becoming increasingly common. They can be horizontal or vertical and can usually be whatever size you would prefer. Essentially you are splitting the screen up so that part of your text appears in one section of the screen and part in another.

What do you put in your windows? One common practice is to put a note to yourself in the top window while you write as usual in the bottom window. This note could be a statement you are trying to prove throughout your report, a section of your introduction, or a brief outline. Here are three examples showing what the windows might contain:

```
Teenage pregnancies have increased dramatically
in the last ten years. They are a major cause of
increased poverty rates for children.

Another study conducted at the University of
Ohio showed that rates of teenage pregnancies
were growing fastest among working-class white
girls.
```

Top window used for main point

```
The United States has done a great deal to im-
prove the quality of its groundwater. Both fed-
eral and state legislation has been passed forc-
ing polluters to clean up known danger areas,
and much more stringent tests must be passed be-
fore new chemicals can be used.

In addition to the federal legislation, many
states have passed codes even more stringent in
their limits of potential pollution. For exam-
ple, Louisiana fishermen were concerned about
the potential damage new cotton pesticides could
have on shrimp beds, so they
```

Top window used for introduction

```
Twain's disgust with people
     Cowardice
     Stupidity
     Greed

Another example of cowardice comes in the Colo-
nel Sherburn episode in which one man forces a
mob to back down and insults them while he does
it. The episode begins with
```

Top window used for outline.

In these examples the top window is used to hold the main point, a section of the introduction, or a section of an outline, while the rest of the screen functions as a normal word processor. Whatever you put in the window, it should help you remember your central point and how what you are writing fits into the report. You can ask yourself whether this sentence supports your main point or whether you are drifting away from your subject or whether a particular paragraph belongs in a particular location in the report. The contents of the top window are always there to remind you of what you are doing.

While windows can be used to help you with your organization and keep you on track, they can also be used whenever you need to look back at earlier sections of your report. For instance, as you described conclusions about some research, you might want to put the specific results of that research in a window to use details from the results in your discussion. If you had already included these results in an earlier portion of your paper, you could make that section of your paper visible in one window while you continued writing your paper in the other window.

Whether you use windows to guide your writing or to make connections within your report, they should aid you in making your report more coherent.

## Drafts from Outlines

We have already described outliner programs and generating outlines in a normal word processor. Some will find these new tools helpful; others will continue to avoid outlining before they write. For those who do create outlines, there is no need to begin at the beginning.

Even if your "outline" is just a list of ideas you want to include in your report, there is no need to start writing with the first idea. For example, if we were writing a paper on *Huckleberry Finn*, we might say that Twain saw three major vices in humans: cowardice, stupidity, and greed. Our outline might look like this:

Human weaknesses described in *Huckleberry Finn*
    Cowardice
    Stupidity
    Greed

If you decided that cowardice was described more often than any other failing, you might want to have it first in your report. Does that mean that you have to write about it first? If you are using a word processor, you are free to move the cursor down one line and start with "stupidity." Later you can move the cursor up and enter your ideas about cowardice in the appropriate spot. The order in which you enter ideas does not have to be the order in which they appear.

With a word processor you are relieved of the tedious task of having to begin at the beginning. You can start wherever you want and always make room back at the beginning for ideas you bypassed temporarily. This should give you some additional freedom during the creation of your first draft. If you are more interested in an idea that comes later in your paper, write about it first. If you have completed most of your research in one area, write about it, even if you still have some work to do on a topic that comes earlier in the paper. You are no longer required to write in any specific sequence— let your interests be your guide.

## Database Transfers

In Chapter 3 we examined how personal databases could be used to collect information. In Chapter 4 we discussed how these databases could be used to sort through and analyze that information. It should be no surprise that a tool that powerful can also be used to generate first drafts.

You'll remember that the general sequence for use of personal databases is putting data into records, determining possible questions or queries, and sorting or retrieving information based on those queries. As you did your original research, you put your data into the database records. During analysis, you did some queries to see what conclusions could be supported by your data. Now that you have completed your initial analysis, you'll want to retrieve that data and transfer it to a word processing document where it will become a part of your report.

As you pull your data and other notes from the database and put them into your report, you perform two steps. First, you identify which information you want and what order you want it in, and then you do the actual transfer. Let's take one example and watch the process.

Suppose you were writing a paper on Mark Twain's *The Adventures of Huckleberry Finn.* You notice that Twain seldom has anything negative to say about nature but almost never says anything positive about people. You begin taking notes and putting them in a personal database. Your database records look something like this:

Subject: People

Topic: Cowardice

Topic: Mobs

Topic: Lynching

Character: Colonel Sherburn

Quote: I was born and raised in the South and I've lived in the North; so I know the average all around. The average man's a coward. In the North

he lets anybody walk over him that wants to, and goes home and prays for a humble spirit to bear it. In the South one man, all by himself, has stopped a stage full of men, in the daytime, and robbed the lot. Your newspapers call you a brave people so much that you think you *are* braver than any other people—whereas you're just *as* brave, and no braver. Why don't your juries hang murderers? Because they're afraid the man's friends will shoot them in the back, in the dark—and it's just what they *would* do.
Page: 118

*Huckleberry Finn* is full of such passages. It would be a very simple matter to collect forty or fifty such quotations, some bemoaning the nature of the human animal, some praising the beauty of nature. As you collect such quotations from the book, you know that some will later be included in your paper to support your interpretation of the book, while most will be abridged or ignored if they turn out later to be less relevant to your central point.

How do you determine your central point? Some of the methods of analysis described in Chapter 4 could be used here. You might begin by having the database count how many passages concern "cowardice," how many focus on "greed," and how many portray "ignorance." Your query might resemble this:

```
COUNT ALL for TOPIC = ``cowardice''

COUNT ALL for TOPIC = ``greed''

COUNT ALL for TOPIC = ``ignorance''
```

If the respective counts came back 13, 4, and 8, you might begin by concluding that Twain thought that the major weakness of humans was cowardice. Or you might decide that both ignorance and cowardice bothered Twain, while greed seemed less important to him. In either case, you have used the summarization abilities of a database to help you form at least a tentative conclusion about your data.

The next step is to transfer those supporting quotations over to the word processor so that you can use them to help convince others of your conclusions about Twain. This transfer process will occur in one of two ways, depending on the kind of database you are using.

If you are using a word processor that is "integrated" with a spreadsheet and database (such programs are becoming increasingly popular), you would have the database select all the records that match your needs. In our example, you might have the database select all the records in which "cowardice" is the topic. Most databases can also arrange these records according to page number.

Once these records had been selected and placed in an order, you could move them to the word processor just as you might move paragraphs around within the word processor. The process is nearly identical and very simple.

If your database is separate from the word processor, generally you have to transfer the selected records to a data disk first and then have the word processor pull them in from the disk. Such transfer can be a little more complicated since the records you entered on the disk must be in the same format that your word processor can read. Since not all word processors can read all formats, this can be a little tricky. In general it is best to check in advance whether the database and word processor you choose are as compatible as possible.

Whichever method you use for transfer, the data from the database will be added directly to the word processing document you are creating. In the case of our Twain example, we might have written an introduction like the following:

> A major feature of *The Adventures of Huckleberry Finn* is the constant criticism of human nature. Twain spends whole pages accusing humans of one weakness after another. The weakness he dwells on most often is cowardice. In thirteen different passages Twain specifically accuses humans of being cowards. Here are three which are typical:

Three of the passages from the database are included here, followed by abridged versions of several of the other passages. By directly transfering the passages from the database to this point, there is no need to retype those sections, and they can be ordered automatically as they are selected.

When the transfer is made from the database to the place marked above, all the records that contain comments on cowardice will be selected and inserted into your report. You will certainly not want to use each passage in its entirety. The result would be a paper containing endless series of poorly connected quotations. To use your passages to best effect, you would probably select the best two or three to demonstrate your point and summarize the rest. After using the passages you need the most, just erase the rest and move on to the next major section of your paper.

## ▆▆▆▆▆ CONCLUSION

One of the primary goals of the first draft should be to explore. As you write, you test the "feel" of ideas, knowing that these ideas might change when you put them into words. Various techniques, such as loop writing, will aid in that process of exploration.

A second goal of this draft is finding a tentative organization.

Some organizations are common to specific kinds of writings. Such formats are expected for some kinds of writing and will directly guide the order of presentation you choose.

The final goal of the first draft is to get your ideas down on paper so that they can be further developed and refined. There are many ways of doing this; the techniques described in this chapter are designed to make the draft easier to create and more coherent to work with.

## ▬▬▬▬EXERCISES

*1*. Name the three primary objectives of the first draft.

*2*. Select one of the quotations on discovery and discuss why it seems more accurate than the others.

*3*. Select three of the loop writing techniques that you think most useful and discuss why they seem more helpful than the others.

*4*. Use the three loop writing techniques on the report you are creating.

*5*. Select one of the reports you have been reading. What would be different about the report if it were written by one of these authors?

    *a*. Abraham Lincoln

    *b*. A sportscaster

    *c*. A romance writer

    *d*. A TV newscaster

*6*. Now adjust the report to one of these media:

    *a*. The Sunday paper

    *b*. "Saturday Night Live"

    *c*. A television commercial

    *d*. A television documentary

*7*. Identify the standard format being used by three of the reports you have read.

*8*. What other kinds of writing seem to follow a fairly standard format?

*9*. Look quickly at the sample reports in Appendix A. Can you tell what abbreviations the authors of those reports might have used when they were writing their first drafts? How does the search and replace function work on your word processor?

*10*. Find out whether the word processing programs available for your use are capable of making windows. If they are, write the command sequence to create a window.

11. If your word processing program can use "macros," write the command sequence to define and use a macro.

12. What disk format does information have to be in before your word processor can read it in? Can your word processor read in information created by any other programs such as databases and outliners?

# PAPERS IN PROGRESS: DRAFTING

## Jonathan's Paper on an Emily Dickinson Poem

Jonathan analyzed the poem "I Heard a Fly Buzz When I Died" by listing the year each interpretation was published, the author, and a brief characterization of the interpretation. His list looked like this:

| | |
|---|---|
| 1955 Friedrich | nasty |
| 1955 Johnson | cadaverous |
| 1956 Ciardi | disagrees with Friedrich |
| 1956 Ransom | between Friedrich and Ciardi |
| 1961 Hogue | agrees with Friedrich |

He decided this list could serve as an outline for his paper since the orientation he had chosen for the paper was a chronological view of the various interpretations taken over the years.

However, there was a problem with the list. How should he order the interpretations that appeared in the same year? For example, should he leave Friedrich and Johnson the way they were? Or was there a more effective order? It appeared to Jonathan that a good transition, ultimately, would be from Friedrich to Ciardi, since Ciardi mentioned Friedrich in his article. Jonathan decided to move Johnson to the first entry and Friedrich to the second entry to make the transition easier. Because he wanted to capitalize on the Ciardi-versus-Friedrich controversy, Jonathan left Ciardi and Ransom where they were. His new order looked like this:

| | |
|---|---|
| 1955 Johnson | cadaverous |
| 1955 Friedrich | nasty |
| 1956 Ciardi | disagrees with Friedrich |
| 1956 Ransom | between Friedrich and Ciardi |
| 1961 Hogue | agrees with Friedrich |

Jonathan then went through the rest of the entries looking for similar relationships, focusing on the writer's attitude toward the fly. When he found no obvious order, he listed the entries as he found them.

With his initial outline complete, Jonathan already had a good start on a first draft. While he did not yet have clear topic sentences, he did have some sense of the paragraphs of the paper and a fairly good idea of just what was going into each paragraph. For Jonathan, whose ideas about the subject were clear and who had already determined the order of presentation, drafting meant getting these ideas onto the screen.

Because Jonathan used the word processor outline, he chose to write his draft by adding to the outline already in the word processor. This meant transferring his research from his "note cards" in another word processor file to the right place in this word processor file. As a result, he very quickly fleshed out the original outline.

## Jennifer's Paper on the Confederate Navy

Jennifer had created two spreadsheets and several graphs to help her examine the different rates at which officers joined the Confederate Navy. She decided that the best way to write her first draft was to create a simple outline with her word processor and then pull in the spreadsheets and graphs where most appropriate. Her word processor was fully compatible with the spreadsheet and graphics she was using, so this merging was fairly direct.

She began by creating this rough outline with her word processor:

Southern officers who joined the Confederate Navy
    Preparations for war
    Experience with U.S. Navy
    Changing sides
    Enrollment by rank
    Reasons for differences by rank
        Conditions in the U.S. Navy
        Salaries in the Confederate Navy
    Strategies for keeping more Southern officers

She decided to begin writing near the end of her outline giving the reasons why officers from the South chose to join the Confederate Navy. She started with a description of conditions in the U.S. Navy at the time the Civil War began. She had saved several direct quotations in a word processing file and "read" them into her report at the appropriate place in her outline. She then began adding material to explain the quotations.

When she had done this for two pages, she moved on to the question of salaries in the Confederate Navy. This information was stored in a spreadsheet. She transferred this information to her word processor and began writing an explanation of the figures in the chart. This section of her draft look like this:

Enrollment by rank

|              | Total | Total South | Resigned | Stayed | Resigned, % |
|--------------|-------|-------------|----------|--------|-------------|
| Commanders   | 127   | 64          | 34       | 30     | 53.1        |
| Lieutenants  | 351   | 151         | 76       | 75     | 50.3        |
| Captains     | 93    | 38          | 16       | 22     | 42.1        |

Reasons for differences by rank

CONDITIONS IN THE U.S. NAVY

The excessive accumulation of older officers at the head of the list was felt as a heavy drag all the way down to the foot. Promotion was blocked, as there was no provision for retirement; and the commanders and lieutenants, many of whom were conspicuous for ability and energy, were stagnating in subordinate positions. The commanders on the list were between fifty-eight and sixty years of age—a time of life at which few men are useful for active service. The upper lieutenants were forty-eight or fifty—some indeed were past fifty—and very few were in command of vessels, as there were two hundred officers above them. (Soley 5)

This enforced continuance in subordinate positions could not fail to tell upon even the best men. The tendency in such a system is to make mere routine men, and to substitute apathy and indolence for zeal and energy. (Soley 5)

Once finished with this section of her draft, she moved up to the beginning of her report and wrote the introduction, including an explanation of the general circumstances of the Confederate Navy when the Civil War began. By writing the introduction after she had worked on the later sections of her paper, she felt more comfortable about where she was going and how well her research would hold up.

She knew that her first draft was very rough and would change as she revised her paper, but at least she had an initial order for her ideas and had integrated her notes and charts.

## Kris's Paper on the Mechanism of Evolution

Like most successful writers faced with a large body of material, Kris decided to prepare an outline first. She felt that this would be especially useful in helping her to organize her presentation. Some papers have an inherent organization. For example, a study of the reactions of various presidents to economic crisis seems to fall automatically into a chronological order. Kris, however, had three major theories to examine and no clear reason for treating one before another. She decided to outline to decide whether moving sections of the outline around would help to determine an organization. Of course, the use of an outline program allowed Kris to painlessly reorder her discussion of the three theories she had selected as the focus of her paper. The outline allowed her to "hide" subordinate sections so that she could focus on overall organization yet move them automatically as the main heads were manipulated.

She finally selected a chronological organization. She opened up an outline section at a time and began elaborating and adding detailed support for each theory; she felt comfortable doing this because later she would move the entire outline to her word processor and thus avoid retyping. When she was satisfied with the form of a section, she would hide all except the section heading to eliminate distraction and move on to developing another portion of the paper.

When she was satisfied with her outline, she printed a copy for reference and moved the outline to her word processor. She added detail and fuller sentence structure for support on the way to her first draft. Thus, the outline gradually grew into a first draft.

# Chapter 6

Revising is the process of checking to see that what you have written is, in fact, what you want to say. Revising is not what writers do *after* a paper is written; it is what writers do *while* a paper is being composed.

There are two primary approaches to revising. The first is to use revising as a time to "resee" (see again) something you have written. During the course of writing an early draft your ideas about the topic might have changed, or you might have been concerned about how your information looks on a page and question whether your earlier analysis might be wrong. This kind of revising can occur at any time: while you are gathering information, while you write initial drafts, or after you have allowed a project to sit for a day or two to cool. These discoveries can be exciting if they lead you in valuable new directions, but troublesome if you begin to feel that much of your previous work was in error.

A second kind of revising is much less accidental. When we speak we don't have to be exact because if people have questions, they can interrupt and ask. When we listen we don't listen only to what is being said but also to how it is being said and by whom. We listen for tone of voice and traits such as sincerity and authority. But writing has to stand alone. A reader can't ask for additional information; the writer isn't there to supply it. Readers can decide only on how well information has been presented.

This second kind of revision is based on three features: coherence, clarity, and sufficiency. If your writing is coherent, readers will be able to follow the logic of your ideas. If your writing is clear, readers will be able to completely understand your message. If your writing is sufficient, you will have provided enough facts, details, examples, references to authorities, or reasons to support the point you are making. The purpose of revising is to make sure that readers accept, rather than reject, what you have written.

One way to determine how coherent, clear, and sufficient a piece of writing is would be to have someone else read it. Unfortunately, finding good readers is not always easy. Most people are already busy, and friends may not be willing to be as honest about a paper as needed. They may say that it looks fine to them when they can't really comprehend it. Friends may also be the wrong audience. If you are trying to make a point about literature, a friend who never opens a book might be too easily confused, while the English major down the hall may understand everything you are saying about *The Sound and the Fury*, but only because that person has already read three books on Faulkner.

Fortunately, there are a number of computer aids available to help you revise.

# REVISING FOR COHERENCE

One of the first steps successful writers take in revising is to make sure that the overall organization of their writing is coherent. "Coherence" refers to the clear and logical connection between ideas. The connections can link words, sentences, or paragraphs. It is not enough to have all the words carefully chosen and all the sentences carefully crafted if they do not clearly relate to each other and develop logically.

## Questioner Programs

One excellent way to check the overall organization of your writing is to use a questioner program. While questioner programs are generally used prior to writing, they make effective revising tools as well. Answering these questions after writing a first draft can help you see whether you have been complete and coherent. When you are done you will be able to determine whether you covered the questions, where you covered the questions, and where your writing needs to be strengthened.

Here is one group of questions generated by a popular questioner program. The first group of questions asks about your goals in writing.

GOALS

Before you decide how to organize your ideas, it helps to outline your goals. Which of these statements is most true for you?

1. My readers should be impressed by my style.
2. I want my readers to easily understand this paper.
3. I want to persuade a hostile audience.

4. I want to demonstrate all I know about this.
5. I only want to satisfy a boss or a professor.
6. I don't care if readers have to work; this subject is important.
7. I want to share some experiences that are important to me.
8. I want any reader to easily understand this paper.
9. I know my readers will have fun reading about this.
10. I want to generate some real interest in this subject.

After listing the goals, the program allows you to add any goals not mentioned. For example, your goal might be simply to inform readers. What is important is that you have a clear sense of why you are writing and what you hope to accomplish.

The questioner will then ask you to list your two most important goals for that particular piece of writing. The purpose of this exercise is to encourage you to distinguish between the many goals that exist. If, for example, one of your goals is to impress your readers by your style, you will be even more concerned than usual with typical questions of style such as word choice and sentence structure. Similarly, if one of your goals is to persuade a hostile audience, you will have to be very careful with the language you use, the evidence you offer, and the tone you adopt.

The program that asks these questions also has an audience analysis component that will help you determine how well your writing matches your audience.

Here is another group of questions from the same questioner program. These questions focus more specifically on an analysis of your intended audience and on your thesis.

1. What is your subject?
2. Who are your readers?
3. Try to give a concise description of your readers. (How many are there? What are their ages? Their education? Their interests?)
4. What's the best thing to be said about your readers?
5. What's the worst?
6. Do they already know something about the subject?
7. What is it that your reader doesn't know?
8. How does your audience feel about your subject? (Are they friendly? Hostile? Disinterested?)
9. How do you want them to feel when they have finished with what you have written?
10. How can you make them feel that way?
11. What is the main point you want to make to your readers?

## Concern for Audience

At this phase in your writing, a concern for audience is essential. The purpose of the questions listed above is to encourage you to think about your audience in as many ways as possible. If your readers are not experts, how much background information will you have to give them? Will you, for example, have to tell them what the objections are to the old plan? What will you need to define? (Will they know what a "bifurcated strut" is?) What will you need to illustrate? (Do you really want to take the time to explain "cross-nut hatching" when a simple diagram will suffice?) If your readers are experts, they know their field intimately and will want lots of facts, and they will want complete facts. They will also appreciate the use of specialized vocabulary and abbreviations.

Often, in presenting the results of research, it is not sufficient to communicate facts and figures. While your audience might not be hostile, it might certainly be disinterested. It is your job to make what you write interesting enough to hold the reader's attention. The wider the audience, the harder you'll have to work to make your writing interesting. Here are the introductions to three research papers. From the introductions alone, how many of the ten goal questions or the eleven audience questions can you answer?

> Ever since the first city was built, humans have been searching for a way to dispose of their waste materials. At first it was easy; just let the nearest river carry the waste to someone else's property. Today the solution is not that simple. Each year our society produces three to four billion tons of waste materials. (Grosswirth 16) As land disposal sites reach capacity and become dangerous, the waste disposers turn to the oceans for an answer. Can the oceans safely accept waste? Many believe that the answer to this question is no. Dumping of wastes into the ocean will only lead to an unhealthy environment. Still, the most intense research supports the idea of ocean waste disposal. It shows that the oceans have the capacity to accept sewage sludge and other toxic wastes. The research concludes that with a carefully studied and well regulated plan, ocean dumping will be a viable solution to some of the world's waste disposal problems.

This paper was written for a freshman English class. The subject of the paper is probably clear to you. Is the main point equally clear? Can you tell from the introduction which of the ten goals is most important to the writer? How many of the eleven audience questions can you answer?

Here is another introduction to a research paper, this time from an economics course.

> "I'll trade you a Ted Williams for a Pete Rose," said an eager-eyed ten-year-old as he shuffled through his collection of baseball cards. Twenty-five years later, the same scenario is repeated with significantly higher stakes: "My 2,500 pounds of roots should bring enough to buy a Mercedes." World trade is an extension of this scenario.

Do you like this introduction? Does it catch your attention, or does it make you wonder about the academic credentials of the writer? Can you tell what the writer's goals are? Can you tell what the writer's attitude is toward her reader?

Here is an introduction to a research paper written for a sophomore literature class. Is the intended audience clear? Do you think that this paper was written for the class or for the teacher? What makes you think so? From the introduction, would you be interested in reading the rest of the paper? Why? Why not?

> It has been suggested that the history of Shakespeare criticism forms a self-contained world of thought and feeling. As one studies *The Tragedy of Hamlet, Prince of Denmark*, one is left with the impression that this play, perhaps the most analyzed work in English literature, lures both students and critics into a self-contained world indeed—the world of the conundrum. A conundrum is, by definition, a question or problem having only a conjectural answer. As the play contains evidence insufficient for definite knowledge, critics over the years have formed opinions and made judgments rather than conjectures.
>
> Just as the two gravediggers in *Hamlet* (V, i) discuss the circumstances under which a man drowns himself in or is drowned by the water, *Hamlet* scholars rely on a similar type of reasoning as they "cudgel their brains" over the "most problematic of problem plays." (1) Although the play commands critical statements, the statements, once compared, are but groping thoughts and feelings.

Do the lengthy sentences bother you? Are any of the words unfamiliar? What do you think of the use of words such as "one," "indeed," and "rather"? Do they add to or detract from the writing?

Your purpose in clarifying, expanding, and connecting your thoughts is to make sure that you have a reasonable, logical, and defensible attitude toward your subject. The writer's attitude toward the subject is sometimes called the "thesis."

## The Thesis

The thesis is the chameleon of composition. When the thesis is clear and obvious, your reader will have little or no trouble picking it out from its surroundings. It can sometimes even be in the first paragraph, as it is in the paper on ocean waste disposal ("The research concludes that with a carefully studied and well regulated plan, ocean dumping will be a viable solution to some of the world's waste disposal problems.").

If the thesis is not clear and obvious, however, your reader will find it difficult (if not impossible) to grasp the point of your paper.

Whether it appears in the first paragraph, the last paragraph, somewhere in between, or even not at all, or whether you call it the main idea, the core idea, or the major conclusion, the thesis is your statement about the subject, and almost all writing should have one.

*Almost* all writing should have a thesis. However, certain types of writing, although having a controlling idea, in fact seldom have a thesis. If you are preparing a chemistry laboratory report, an encyclopedia entry, or a shopping list, for example, you will probably not be making a statement about the subject.

In most writing, the thesis answers the question a reader asks when faced with a mass of information—"So what?" The thesis clarifies the connection among all the bits and pieces of information you have offered. If you are arguing a point, the thesis is a statement of the main idea of the argument. If you are presenting the results of research, the thesis is a general statement of the major conclusions uncovered through your research.

At this stage of your writing, in order to maintain a clear focus and a consistent point of view, we suggest that your thesis be as full as possible. Some students include the full statement of the thesis as part of the paper; others simply keep it handy at the beginning of the document. Here is an example of a fully developed thesis for a research paper on the subject of competence testing for high-school seniors:

> Competence testing for high-school seniors should be mandatory because such comprehensive final examinations (1) help to unify the curriculum, (2) provide a strong motivation for students to learn, and (3) help to strengthen academic standards.

Note that the fully developed thesis includes a general outline for the paper. That general outline can help you maintain a clear focus and a consistent point of view. If you include a fully developed thesis in your paper, your readers will have a clear picture of the stages of thinking going on in the paper.

*A note of caution:* At this point in your writing, and at every point in your writing, your thesis is tentative. It may stay the same, but it may change. Don't become committed to it. As you write, and as you add and delete information, you will be reshaping and refining your ideas. If your working thesis is "Acupuncture is a cure-all that should be endorsed by the American Medical Association and immediately introduced into all medical schools," and you read several seemingly plausible articles that question the effectiveness of acupuncture, you should seriously consider modifying or qualifying your thesis accordingly.

## Outline Generators

Once you are satisfied that you have a thesis and that you are, in fact, making a point, a valuable next step is to outline your paper. Outline generators redisplay your text so that only the first sentence of each paragraph, or the first and last sentences of each paragraph, are visible. Using an outline generator will allow you to check for transitions, unity of thought, and logical development.

Here is an outline generated by David, a student writing a narrative for his freshman English class. The paper describes an experience David and his brother had "playing" the stock market.

> We had scanned the *Wall Street Journal* commodities page for a year.
>
> After securing the services of a Chicago-based trading firm called Murlas and filling out the proper trade forms, we forwarded them a check for $6,700.
>
> Because the company we traded with was located in Chicago, we had to call them via a WATS line to keep track of the market trends.
>
> Few people knew we had invested into the commodities; fewer knew the amount of money.
>
> The first trade we made was a small one, buying September 1981 oats in June of that year.
>
> From then on it was mostly bad trades and an unbelievably stable world.
>
> Slowly the money in our account became less and less.
>
> A year and five months later the trades were finally over.

Such an outline lets you see whether you have been consistent. Is there a general development of ideas, or do you seem to jump around wildly? Such outlines are not perfect; for instance, if your writing is highly stylized, there may be no obvious connection between paragraph leads. These outlines do, however, indicate whether your writing will be easy or difficult to follow. It is necessary to remember that how you structure a piece of writing will often determine the effect on the reader.

When David analyzed the preceding outline, he focused only on the development of the ideas. At that stage of his writing, David's teacher told him not to worry about the comma splice, the wordiness, or the mechanical errors that appeared here and there in the sentences. David thought that all the sentences seemed fine except the third one, which seemed out of place. When he went back and looked at the draft, he decided that the third sentence was, in fact, irrelevant.

## Paragraphs

After you are sure that the overall organization of your writing is coherent, that you have a main idea, that the parts of the paper clearly relate to your main idea, that the parts of the paper develop according to some clear plan, and that you have a clear sense of your intended audience and goals, you should check for coherence between paragraphs.

Although a paragraph can be as short as a sentence or even one word, we are referring to a group of sentences focusing on one idea or topic. Sometimes a paragraph is the entire piece of writing; more often it is part of a longer piece of writing.

Why do we need paragraphs? They provide a break for the reader. More importantly, however, they signal the reader that the writer is moving from one idea or topic to the next.

A successful paragraph reflects the writer's obligation to the reader and to the demands and conventions of the discipline. All public writing involves a "contract" between the reader's expectations and the writer's promises. If, for example, you begin to read an article in *People* magazine on Ike and Tina Turner, you could reasonably expect a slick, superficial exposé about the once-married rock stars. You would not expect a scholarly treatise on monogamy in the twentieth century. If, however, you are reading an article in the *Journal of Personality and Social Psychology* on monogamy in the twentieth century, you would be surprised to find a slick, superficial exposé about Ike and Tina Turner.

Whether the paragraph is in *People* magazine or the *Journal of Personality and Social Psychology*, one of the major clauses in the reader-writer contract states that after reading a paragraph, readers expect to know what the writer's controlling idea is and expect to be able to recognize the relationship that each of the other sentences has to the topic sentence. In a coherent paragraph, a point is made and there is a clear and logical connection between the sentences.

## Topic Sentences

As a rule, a successful paragraph has a topic sentence. One well-researched article searched for topic sentences in twenty-five essays published in the country's leading journals and magazines. While not all the paragraphs in the articles contained a topic sentence, the author of the article, Richard Braddock, concludes that, "In my opinion, often the writing in the 25 essays would have been clearer and more comfortable to read if the paragraphs had presented more explicit topic sentences." (301)

The topic sentence (or controlling idea) is a general statement that

ties together the information contained in the paragraph. We are not suggesting that all paragraphs have topic sentences, or that all good writers always use topic sentences. A paragraph that continues an idea started in the previous paragraph or that is part of an ongoing narrative does not always need a topic sentence. Moreover, certain kinds of academic and professional writing (such as case histories and laboratory reports) often do not need consistent topic sentences. We agree with Braddock, however: much of the professional and academic writing we have seen that does not use topic sentences would have been clearer and easier to read if the paragraphs had used topic sentences.

There are two kinds of topic sentence: stated and implied. A stated topic sentence expresses the central (or controlling) idea of the paragraph and tells the reader what the paragraph is about. It can be a simple statement of the subject of the paragraph ("Many European countries developed sheepdog breeds"; "Some vegetarians select their diet for ecological reasons") or a more complex statement that conveys an attitude toward the topic-subject of the paragraph ("One argument in support of a redirection of funds currently spent on the artificial heart program is that the technology is too expensive to be considered a valid treatment option for cardiac disease"; "There is some evidence to suggest that preschool education has little effect at all on the social development of young children").

An implied topic sentence, in contrast, must be inferred by the reader and is thus more demanding of the reader. Because the lack of a clearly stated topic sentence can render a paragraph unclear or misleading, writers should use implied topic sentences sparingly, if at all.

Here are two paragraphs from an article on the mutually beneficial relationship between plants and animals. The first sentence of the first paragraph is a stated topic sentence. It summarizes the results of an experiment and relates that experiment to the overall purpose of the article, which is to argue that the thick wall surrounding the pit of the fruit of the *Calvaria* plant evolved through coevolution with the now extinct dodo (*Raphus cucullatus*). The second paragraph has no one sentence that helps to tie together all the information in the paragraph; rather, it has an implied topic sentence.

Perhaps the most convincing evidence that seed-coat dormancy in *Calvaria* can only be overcome naturally by passage through a bird's digestive tract comes from experiments in which I force-fed single, fresh *Calvaria* pits to turkeys. Some of these pits were retained in the turkey's digestive tract for as long as 6 days, and 7 of seventeen ingested pits were eventually crushed by the bird's gizzard. The remaining ten pits were either regurgitated or passed in the feces after being reduced in size through abrasion in the gizzard. I planted the ten recovered seeds under nursery conditions, and 3 subsequently germinated. These may well have been the first *Calvaria* seeds to germinate in more than 300 years.

The fruits of *Calvaria* are large, single-seeded drupes about 50 mm in diameter. Anatomically, the fruit is composed of a thin exocarp; a pulpy, succulent mesocarp; and a hard, woody, thick-walled endocarp. The seed is depresso-globulose in shape and is completely enclosed in a stone or pit formed by the walls of the endocarp, which can be as thick as 15 mm. Some other sapotaceous plants also have relatively thick endocarps covering their seeds, but the endocarp surrounding a *Calvaria* seed is extraordinarily thick even for this family. Apparently, *Calvaria* seeds fail to germinate because the thick endocarp mechanically resists the expansion of the embryo within. (Temple 885)

Stated topic sentences often appear somewhere near the beginning of a paragraph, as in the first paragraph in the preceeding excerpt; they can also appear at the end or even in the middle of a paragraph. Here, for example, is a paragraph from Kris's paper on evolution. The paragraph ends with the topic sentence (paragraphs that end with a topic sentence are sometimes called "suspended paragraphs").

My first intention in composing this paper was to look at the various arguments advanced for and against the presentation of evolution. As I examined the evidence, I soon became aware that despite surface appearances, the "theory of evolution" is no homogeneous whole; rather, there are many theories of how species present on the earth today came to be and how earlier species, species that we are aware of only through the fossil record, became extinct. To truly address the issue of teaching evolution, one must come to grips with what evolution is.

Placement of the topic sentence early in the paragraph is the most common structure and should be given priority, although most good writers learn to place topic sentences throughout the paragraph. The appeal of placing the topic sentence early in the paragraph is clarity and straightforwardness.

The appeal of placing the topic sentence later in the paragraph, as in Kris's paragraph, is variety and suspense; the reader must wait to find out the point. The danger of waiting is that the reader must hold all the details or information until the end. This could be difficult for inexperienced readers or readers who do not fully understand the material. It is important to remember that suspended paragraphs require clear signals (usually in the form of transitional words and phrases) to let the reader know where you are going.

Ultimately, the placement of the topic sentence should be determined by considerations of audience and purpose. In other words, if your material is technical or difficult, or if your readers might be unfamiliar with the material, you should consider placing the topic sentence as close as possible to the beginning of the paragraph.

## Transitions

A topic sentence will not ensure that your paragraph is coherent and makes sense or that your readers will be able to follow your argument, your description, and your point. One immediately effective tool you can use to show the precise relationship between sentences is the use of transitional words and phrases. These are especially important at the beginning of those paragraphs that function as transitions from one topic to another. Some words and phrases move the paragraph in the same direction ("in addition," "also," etc.); some move it in the opposite or in another direction ("on the contrary," "however," etc.); and some move it toward the end ("and finally," "in conclusion," etc.). As you read the following paragraph, pay special attention to the words that signal the movement from one part of the paragraph to another—and note the direction the word or phrase takes you.

> There is no doubt that nicotine in cigarettes produces tranquilizing and relaxing effects. However, there is evidence that cigarette smoking decreases efficiency at work and in school. For example, a study done by the U.S. Public Health Service shows that males who never smoke miss 4.6 days of work per year, while males who smoke from one to two packs a day miss 6.5 days of work per year (Molotsky 1984). Similarly, another study revealed that while no difference has been found in intelligence between smokers and nonsmokers, younger smokers as a whole do not do as well in school as nonsmokers (Blamphin 1982).

Another effective tool that can help to establish a connection between your ideas is the repetition of keywords and key phrases. In the following paragraph, an excerpt from *A Nation at Risk*, note the pairing of such phrases as "the average citizen"/"the average graduate"; "better educated"/"not as well-educated"; "positive impact"/"negative impact").

> It is important, of course, to recognize that the average citizen today is better educated and more knowledgeable than the average citizen of a generation ago—more literate, and exposed to more mathematics, literature, and science. The positive impact of this fact on the well-being of our country and the lives of our people cannot be overstated. Nevertheless, the average graduate of our schools and colleges today is not as well-educated as the average graduate of 25 or 35 years ago, when a much smaller proportion of our population completed high school and college. The negative impact of this fact likewise cannot be overstated. (U.S. Dept. of Education 11)

## Count of Words in Paragraph

One of the most effective computer tools to help you achieve coherent paragraphs is a program that counts the number of words in a paragraph. The best of such programs will often graph out the length of each paragraph. The outline generator that David used for his paper on the stock market also counts the number of words in the paragraphs. The program graphs each paragraph that begins with a five-space indentation. The program numbers each paragraph, prints one asterisk for every five words in the paragraph, and then prints the total number of words in the paragraph. This particular program also notes any paragraphs that are shorter than 50 words or longer than 200 words. While there are often good reasons for short and long paragraphs, short paragraphs are sometimes an indication that the paragraph is underdeveloped, and long paragraphs are sometimes an indication that a paragraph has more than one topic in it and needs to be divided.

Here is an example from David's paper on the stock market. Note what the program did after David deleted the first sentence of the third paragraph.

```
Paragraph Graph

Paragraph 1: ********* 45
Paragraph 2: *************** 80
Paragraph 3: ***** 26
Paragraph 4: ********* 47
Paragraph 5: ************** 78
Paragraph 6: ********** 57
Paragraph 7: ************* 70
Paragraph 8: ********** 52

Total Words: 455
Paragraph Average: 56.9

Paragraph Graph

At least one of your paragraphs is very short.
If you aren't sure what to say in that
paragraph, you may want to run the paragraph
writing program in the first section of WRITER'S
HELPER to help you develop the paragraph.
```

As you can imagine, after looking at the results of the paragraph graph, David thought he'd better take a close look at that troublesome third paragraph. Here is what it looked like:

Stocks are a civilized, dignified way to make (or lose) money. But commodity trading is a brutal, frantic game. It is five hours of planned chaos.

Although not all short paragraphs are underdeveloped, this one clearly was. David developed the paragraph to fill it out. Here is what it looked like afterward:

> Stocks are a civilized, dignified way to make (or lose) money. The market usually moves slow and the holding of a stock is measured in weeks, months, or even years. Because of the time span involved and the slow movement of the market, stocks are a relatively safe investment. But commodity trading is a brutal, frantic game. Within the span of five short hours the entire trade day takes place. Five hours of screaming prices, getting conformation of a sell, and five minutes later a buy for the same customer. It is five hours of planned chaos.

Although there are still several errors (e.g., the word "slow" in the second sentence should be "slowly," and "conformation" is probably supposed to be "confirmation"), the added detail develops the paragraph so that the reader now has a much clearer picture of the difference between investing in stocks and investing in commodities.

## REVISING FOR CLARITY

Shortly after the release of yet another study that revealed American students to be weak in writing skills, the following editorial appeared in a local daily newspaper:

> Dere Students
>
> They say you cant rite so good nomore. Well, neither could we when we was students. Ever since they invented that dad-blamed telefone folks have sorta lost the art of putting words on paper in a way that makes much sense.
>
> Then came television and that didn't help neither.
>
> What you see now is a lot of run-on sentences that go in and out and on and on and don't seem to go nowhere and pretty soon the reader gets lost and by the time he comes to a period he is out of breath and has forgot what the sentence is all about.
>
> Also they use a lot of clichés which are no good because they are a dime a dozen.
>
> Speling mistakes are all over the place. Nobody seems to worry much nomore about punctuation which is very important and also about grammar which is also quite important although not as important as it used to be since people just seem to ignore the rules if they ever knew them in the first place.
>
> And about those incomplete sentences.
>
> All right, the state of writing isn't that bad, but it's not very good.
>
> We're not talking about spelling errors. The way the English language is constructed it's no wonder so many words come out wrong. Bad

spelling is not a sign of low intellect or of poor writing ability. The worst speller who ever worked for the *Stevens Point Journal* is now a columnist for one of the nation's largest and most prestigious newspapers.

We can even forgive grammatical errors.

What bothers us most is lack of clarity. We live in a complicated world where it's important to get your message across clearly.

Our impression is that people wrote better a century ago than they do today, even when they had little formal education. Probably it's because they couldn't pick up the phone when they needed to communicate. They wrote a lot more letters. Practice made perfect.

So sit down and write a letter today. And another one tomorrow. It'll hone your communication skills, and keep the Postal Service in the black. ("Improvement needed..." 4)

While we don't agree with everything in the editorial, we do agree that clarity is singularly important and a serious problem with much writing. Ultimately, the test of your writing lies in its effectiveness. Does it do what you want it to do? Have you done all you can so that your readers understand exactly what you are saying? In other words, have you been clear?

Once you are confident that your paragraphs are coherent and make the kinds of connections you want them to, your next task is to make sure that each sentence says what you want it to say. In this section we will present some strategies for achieving clear sentences.

## Readability Level

Reading experts have been trying for years to determine why certain types of writing are more difficult to read than others. They are still isolating the factors that make reading difficult, but one method they currently use is to count the lengths of sentences and the lengths of words. The longer the words and sentences, the harder the text is to read. Several formulas have been devised to compute the difficulty of text, and many of these formulas have now been programmed into computers. If you have one available on your computer, it will generally give your writing a rating of 1 to 16. This means that the writing is difficult enough to require from one to sixteen years of schooling to read comfortably.

The program adopted for this book uses a standard readability indicator called the FOGG INDEX. If you use this program, it will ask you what grade level you intend for your audience (from first grade to college senior) and will then let you know whether it rates your readability level too low or too high.

If your readability level is too high or too low for your readers, the program will suggest ways of revising to make your writing easier to follow. If your writing is too high, the program will suggest, for example, that your sentences might be too long and that you might want to break up some of the longer ones. You might also look for technical terms that you will have to explain before your readers will be able to understand you. If your writing level is too low, the program will suggest, for example, that your sentences might be too short and that you should consider combining some of them. A low readability level could also mean that your vocabulary is also not appropriate for your audience; look for vague words such as "nice," "lots," and "good."

## Count of Words in Sentences

Just as there are programs that will count the words in your paragraphs, there are also programs that will count the words in your sentences. They, too, will often graph out the length of each sentence. The program many of our students use prints a graph of each sentence; it prints one asterisk for every word and lets the students know the length of each sentence and the average length of their sentences.

If your sentences are almost of the same length, you should consider revising them to vary the length because sentences of the same length quickly bore readers, regardless of what these sentences say. One of your functions as a writer is to keep your readers awake long enough to get to the end of your writing.

If your sentences are generally short, you might not be getting your point across to your readers. After all, complex and difficult ideas often result in complex and difficult sentences. Similarly, if your sentences are too long, your reader, unless an expert, will probably not be able to follow the tortuous meandering of your thoughts.

When Frances ran a word count of the sentences in her research paper on the cost-effectiveness of acid rain control, one paragraph looked suspicious because there were too many short sentences. Here is what the graph looked like:

```
Sentence Graph

Sentence 16: ******** 8
Sentence 17: *************** 15
Sentence 18: ******** 8
Sentence 19: ******* 7
Sentence 20: ***** 5
Sentence 21: ****************** 18
Sentence 22: ******************* 19

Press ENTER to continue
```

When Frances checked the suspicious paragraph, she found that it was, indeed, unclear. The short sentences that were all of the same length indicated that the ideas were not clear and lacked emphasis. Here is what the paragraph looked like:

> One type of control method is the scrubber. Lime traps the sulfur dioxide that is part of the emissions of coal-burning plants. It is very successful in removing sulfur dioxide. It also produces large amounts of waste. Another disadvantage is its cost. Twenty-four utilities questioned in a study said that installation and maintenance would cost them over $15 billion (Remirez). *National Wildlife* estimates that a ten million ton reduction in sulfur dioxide would cost all polluting industries $2.4 billion (35).

As you can see, there is no clear emphasis in the paragraph, and the failure to link ideas has made the sentences difficult to follow. Had Frances been writing her paper for unskilled writers, she might have left the sentences short but worked on providing clearer transitions (not an easy task here). Because she was writing for a college audience, she chose to combine sentences using several rhetorical strategies. Here is what the paragraph looked like after Frances revised it:

> One type of control method is the scrubber. This device utilizes lime to trap the sulfur dioxide that is part of the emissions of coal-burning plants. This method's main advantage is that it is very successful in removing sulfur dioxide; however, one disadvantage is that it produces large amounts of waste. Another disadvantage of this method is its cost. Twenty-four utilities questioned in a study said that installation and maintenance of scrubbers would cost them over $15 billion (Remirez). However, *National Wildlife* estimates that a ten million ton reduction in sulfur dioxide would cost all polluting industries $2.4 billion (35).

Here is what the graph looked like after the paragraph was revised:

```
Sentence Graph

Sentence 16:  ******** 8
Sentence 17:  ****************** 19
Sentence 18:  ************************* 26
Sentence 19:  ******** 8
Sentence 20:  ******************* 20
Sentence 21:  ******************* 20

Press ENTER to continue
```

Frances did not have to do very much to make the paragraph easier to follow:

1. The phrase "This device utilizes" provides a link from the scrubber mentioned in the first sentence to the use of lime in the second sentence.

2. Beginning the third sentence with "This method's main advantage" offers a clearer reference to the previous sentence than the word "It" in the original.

3. Using a semicolon to link sentences 3 and 4 forces a stronger relationship between the ideas and ensures that readers will understand the emphatic shift from advantage to disadvantage.

4. The simple transition "however" in the third sentence provides a precise relationship between sentences 3 and 4 of the original paragraph.

5. The repetition of "method" in sentence 4 helps to move the paragraph and provides continuity from one idea to the next.

6. Inserting the word "scrubbers" in sentence 5 keeps the main idea of the paragraph on track for the reader.

7. Beginning the last sentence with "However" provides a clear and direct signal to the last sentence.

## REVISING FOR SUFFICIENCY

Computers can do many things. They can help you begin your writing. They can offer suggestions to get you started. They can help you find information. They can help you arrange that information in the most effective order. They can save you enormous amounts of time by keeping track of tedious chores, such as pagination, spacing, and formatting. They can even check your spelling. They can't do everything, however, and one of the most important things they can't do—*and that must be done*—is to make sure that your writing is sufficient.

### Adequate Support

"Sufficiency" means providing enough facts, details, examples, quotations from authorities, or reasons to support whatever point you are making. Although sufficiency can mean different things within different disciplines, there are some generally accepted notions of what constitutes *in*sufficiency. A piece of writing is insufficient if (1) it is based on misunderstanding of the material, (2) there is no logical connection between the support and the claim, (3) the writing is unclear, or (4) the support is inadequate.

If your writing is sufficient, you will have provided enough evidence to support your claims and the evidence you have offered will be reliable. The following paragraph is from a book report, written for a freshman history class, on A. T. Mahan's *The Influence of*

*Seapower Upon History*. The paragraph is insufficient because the writer has failed to adequately support any of the general statements that litter the paragraph:

> Many great leaders and countries have benefited from the information in this book, and the book itself has had a profound effect on history and world events. Mahan actually gives us the plans of twenty-four naval battles so we can see for ourselves exactly what the strategies were, and then he tells us what the outcome was, so that what strategies worked actually reveal why things are the way they are. This book is as useful today as it was when it was written. I think that if you really want to get a complete picture of the development of history and why things are the way they are today, you should read this book. Mahan does a wonderful job of making a complicated subject simple, direct, and to the point.

The paragraph makes a number of vague, general statements without supporting any of them. We have no idea of just what the great leaders and countries learned from the information in the book. We have no idea what profound effect the book had on history and world events. We have no idea in what way this book is useful today. We have no idea in what way it was useful when it was written.

This paragraph raises more questions than it answers—and while readers love good questions, they love good answers even more. As you revise your own writing, ask yourself whether you have answered the questions you ask, whether the information you have given your intended readers is accurate, and whether you have given your readers enough information so that they are either sufficiently informed or convinced.

Contrast the preceding paragraph (the report on Mahan's book ) with the following one. This paragraph is part of a research paper written for a freshman English class. The purpose of the paper was to evaluate the artificial heart program in terms of the unique moral and economic problems it presents. This paragraph is much more effective because it makes a point and supports that point with detailed examples.

> One argument in support of a redirection of funds currently spent on the artificial heart program is that the technology is too expensive to be considered a valid treatment option for cardiac disease. Barton Bernstein of Stanford University, who is part of an interdisciplinary group examining biomedical innovations and public policy, contends that the cost per patient could easily exceed $200,000. (2) (Expenses for the first artificial heart recipient, Barney Clark, exceeded $275,000 during the 112 days he survived with the device in place.) (3) If the device is made to work reliably, cardiologists estimate that as many as 50,000 a year "suffer heart disease so serious that they might benefit from artificial hearts.... Selling all of them could cost as much as $10 billion, in 1985

dollars." (4) Other guesses go as high as $40 billion! Our health care system is simply not able to absorb that expense. The government Medicare system is already straining under the burden of an estimated $85 billion in annual medical costs. (5) Private insurers are searching for ways in which they can limit health care cost increases and are, in many cases, curtailing subscriber benefits at the same time premiums are being raised.

## Logic

In the play "Rhinoceros," by Eugene Ionesco, a logician says to an old gentleman: "Here is an example of a syllogism. The cat has four paws. Isidore and Fricot both have four paws. Therefore, Isidore and Fricot are cats." The old man replies: "My dog has got four paws." To which the logician answers: "Then it's a cat." Although most of us are not logicians, we probably do not need formal training to recognize that the logic in the preceding exchange is faulty. However, much faulty logic is normally not quite as obvious. The purpose of this section is not to begin a formal study of logic, but rather to introduce you to some of the more common fallacies of logic. Your responsibility *to your readers* is to avoid faulty logic in your arguments; your responsibility *as a reader* is to recognize faulty logic in the arguments of others.

The most common fallacy is probably the *hasty generalization*. A hasty generalization is a generalization or conclusion based on insufficient or unrepresentative evidence. It is often recognizable in your own writing or in that of others through the use of such words as "all," "always," "everybody," and "most." It is usually necessary to qualify statements when you write and to be wary of unqualified statements when you read.

While most of us usually recognize the more obvious examples of hasty generalization (all young people are conformists; teachers like to give bad grades; jocks are dumb), it is the less obvious ones that give us the most trouble. Here are two hasty generalizations taken from student writing. These statements need to be severely qualified.

> Conformity is caused by many things, but the greatest cause is a lack of strong beliefs. (How could the writer possibly know this? Has she interviewed thousands of conformists?)

> It still amazes me to realize that the majority of people in the United States has no interest in sports. (How does one come to know anything about the majority of people in the United States?)

Another common fallacy is the *non sequitur*, a Latin phrase meaning "it does not follow." There are usually two parts to a non sequitur, an opening statement and a conclusion that is presented as a logical conclusion of that opening statement. A non sequitur occurs when one of the parts does not logically follow from the other, as in the statement "I'm old enough to fight for my country, therefore I'm old enough to drink."

*Begging the question* is a form of non sequitur. If you beg the question, you assume something that really needs to be proved first: "Since the traditional family is breaking up, surrogate mothering (bearing a child for another woman) should be legalized." Who says the traditional family is breaking up?

Although *analogies* can be dramatic and can often help to clarify and explain complex ideas, all the comparisons in analogies are limited and must be used carefully. Some analogies are more limited than others in that the points of similarity are very few. A great many analogies (unfortunately) fall apart before they begin. These analogies are called *false analogies*. Several years ago, a state senator, urging his colleagues to vote against legalizing bingo, based his entire argument on this analogy: "You can't eat without having dirty dishes, and you can't have bingo without corruption." While the sentence might have balance and a nice ring to it, it lacks the logic required of a reasonable analogy.

Similarly, it is fashionable among some child development specialists to explain the stages of development in terms of analogies. One popular explanation likens children to roses:

> Let's suppose you'd never seen a rose and you knew nothing about roses and how they grew. Then, one day, you saw a rose growing in a field. With your eyes only on the delicate and beautiful flower, you reach down and grasp the stem. What a shock! You jerk back your hand. You didn't know about the *thorns!*
>
> Children *are* like roses. *Much of their unpleasant ("thorny") behavior is normal.* When parents realize this, they are less apt to feel frustrated and inadequate. Furthermore, they can be consoled by the knowledge that pleasant stages of development come between the "thorny" periods.

This explanation goes on to name each thorn, beginning with colic at three to six weeks and running through each sharp and painful period until the bud is finally reached, by which time the thorns are gone and the child has reached "Sweet 16." Anyone who has reached the age of seventeen will recognize the falseness of the analogy.

To suggest that only two alternatives exist when, in fact, there are more, is to be guilty of the "either/or" fallacy. A teacher of children's literature recently asked students this question on an examination: "Is *Peter Pan* a whimsical fairy tale or a satire on religion?"

## Honesty

Although your writing might be sufficient in every respect, a piece of writing is, ultimately, insufficient if it is dishonest. And though computers can check for many things, no computer can check to make sure that you have been honest with yourself and with your readers. Have you exaggerated your position? Have you taken a quotation out of context to strengthen your argument? Do you believe what you have said? Remember that readers want to trust writers.

One of the most difficult problems facing writers of research papers is when to document. In order to avoid plagiarism, you must document another person's ideas or expressions. (This includes all direct quotations, paraphrases, and summaries.) All ideas that are not your own must be acknowledged. The following paragraph is taken from a research paper contrasting daily- and extended-wear contact lenses. The paper was returned to the writer for additional revising; one requirement was that the writer include any sources that should have been cited.

> Although there are advantages to extended-wear lenses, there are more advantages to daily-wear lenses. In fact, daily-wear lenses are recommended over extended-wear 80 percent of the time. This is because the eye is able to adapt to daily-wear lenses easier and faster than to the extended-wear lenses.

Here is the paragraph after it was revised. In addition to acknowledging the major source for her information, the writer made several other significant changes that improved the paragraph. The second sentence, for example, provides the reader with a sense of emphasis, and the addition of the writer's personal experience lends authenticity to the paper.

> Although there are advantages to extended-wear lenses, there are more advantages to daily-wear lenses. The most important of these advantages is adaptability. In fact, according to Kindy Optical of Stevens Point, daily-wear lenses are recommended over extended-wear lenses 80 percent of the time. This is because the eye is able to adapt more easily and rapidly to the lenses if they are kept in for only a few hours at a time. When I first started wearing extended-wear lenses my eyes were red all month long. My optometrist assured me this was normal. I did not think so. I switched to daily-wear lenses and my eyes were no longer irritated.

Just as you must acknowledge all ideas that are not your own, you must acknowledge all ideas that are not common knowledge. Admittedly, it is often difficult to know just what is common knowledge and what is not. For example, in a heavily documented article entitled "Summary of Scientific Evidence for Creation," the authors (Gish and Bliss) do not document this statement: "The First Law of Thermodynamics states that the total quantity of matter and energy in the universe is constant." (iii) Should that statement have been documented? Do you think that the writers assumed that their readers would know that the statement is common knowledge? Is the statement common knowledge to you?

Here are some questions to ask as you revise:

1. Have you documented all ideas not your own?

2. How much do you know about the person you are citing? Is the person an acknowledged authority? What are that person's credentials?

3. Have you been fair? Or have you chosen a quotation that casts someone in an unfavorable light?

4. Are your summaries accurate?

If you are one of the elect, revising will do little more than catch a few fuzzy transitions here, an awkwardly stated idea there. If you are, like us, one of the multitude, however, diligent revising will help you clarify your ideas and present those ideas coherently and sufficiently.

## ▬▬▬▬ EXERCISES

*1*. Here are two introductions to research papers written for a freshman English class. The audience for both papers was to have been the students in the class.

> South Africa is a nation in which a minority, some five million whites, deny voting and citizenship rights to the majority, some twenty-four million blacks. This practice, formally known as "separate development" but commonly called "apartheid" (the Afrikaans word for "apartness"), is the subject of intense international criticism. That apartheid is immoral is seldom questioned by Americans. What is being hotly debated, however, is the best way for the United States to encourage a reversal in this policy. Disinvestment, the complete withdrawal of American business, has a popular following who suggest it is the necessary catalyst. This has led many persons to pose the question: Should our nation advocate disinvestment?

> The National Council of Teachers of Mathematics (NCTM), in their unprecedented *An Agenda for Action*, has recommended that computers and calculators be used at all levels of mathematics education. They suggest three integral "actions" to support this proposition: (1) all students should have access to calculators and computers, (2) these tools should be integrated into the mathematics curriculum, and (3) integrated curriculum materials for calculators and computers should be developed and used. (Williams 4)

From what you have read from the two papers, do you think that the papers were, in fact, written to classmates? Why? Why not? How could the introductions have been stronger? If the writers of the two papers could revise their papers, what advice might you offer them?

**2.** Here is a paragraph written for a freshman English class. Can you find the topic sentence? Try rearranging the topic sentence elsewhere in the paragraph. Can you find a more effective place for it?

> You can watch a cup of coffee slowly give off thin wisps of steam that spiral upward and fade away about an inch above the coffee's surface. If you blow lightly at the steam, it vanishes like a handful of dandelion seeds before a gust of wind. If you tire of watching the steam, you can add cream to your coffee and watch the kaleidoscopic patterns of black and invading brown. Or, you can merely stir the coffee in time with the rhythm of your thoughts. Then, when the coffee finally cools, you can leisurely sip it. A well-managed cup of coffee can be a pleasant fifteen-minute study break.

**3.** From a topic sentence of your choice, write a fully developed paragraph using the topic sentence as the first sentence of your paragraph. Then rewrite the paragraph so that the topic sentence is the last sentence of the paragraph.

**4.** Read the following letter to *The Wall Street Journal* and summarize its main points; your summary should be about one-third the length of the original. (The original letter has 270 words.) Then compare your summary to those by your classmates. Discuss any differences. Consider the points you have either omitted or included; be prepared to discuss your rationale for your omissions or inclusions.

> Bruce Bartlett...argues that unemployment due to technological innovation is not a serious problem for the economy. He takes to task Wassily Leontief, Robert Kuttner and Tom Hayden for their pessimism and concern regarding future employment opportunities. They are charged with creating "unnecessary fear and anguish among workers" thereby "sowing seeds of discontent." I do not believe that workers need to rely on the words of economists and politicians to realize that jobs have been scarce and real income gains sluggish over the last decade. The recent experience of American labor at all levels of skill and training confirms the statistical evidence that the relationship between job seekers and employment opportunities is sadly distorted.
>
> Research indicates that high-level developments may not provide jobs in sufficient quantity and at high enough income levels to support a growing standard of living. The debate should not center on whether high-tech is the solution or the problem. The focus should be on how to provide job opportunities for all those who want to work and income maintenance for those who cannot find employment. These goals can be pursued regardless of the rate of technological change.

Finally, it is important to examine the chain of logic moving from high-tech to export expansion and economic recovery. One of Mr. Bartlett's sources, Adam Smith, discovered the mercantilist error in equating export sales with national prosperity. The primary benefit of foreign trade is improved efficiency through specialization and resources allocation, and imports are equal partners in that process. Overzealous export promotion intended to reduce unemployment is counterproductive and unsustainable in a world of flexible exchange rates.

5. Choose any page in this chapter and list all the transitions you can find. Do they provide coherence for the writing? Do they provide a clear signal to the reader? Can you think of any transitions that would improve the page?

6. Find, and bring to class, an example of one of the following:

   **a.** Hasty generalization

   **b.** Non sequitur

   **c.** Begging the question

   **d.** Analogy

   **e.** Either/or

## ▬▬▬▬▬PAPERS IN PROGRESS: REVISING

### Jonathan's paper on an Emily Dickinson poem

The first thing that Jonathan did after drafting his paper on Emily Dickinson's poem, "I Heard a Fly Buzz When I Died," was to make sure that his thesis was coherent, that there was a clear and logical connection between all the topics, and that each topic clearly related to his thesis. When he looked for the thesis, he found it in the conclusion:

> In conclusion, it appears that though there are many different interpretations of the meaning of the fly in Dickinson's "I Heard a Fly Buzz When I Died," most of them see the fly as a rather evil and pessimistic creature and the poem as a very pessimistic statement of the human condition.

Although the wording needs to be strengthened and the statement needs some editing, Jonathan was satisfied that the point he was trying to make was clear. Only after he was satisfied that the thesis was clear did he move on to what he considered the appropriate next step, generating an outline.

Jonathan used his outline generator to outline the first sentence of each paragraph. He felt that this would give him a good idea of the flow and development of the paper. Here is how the outline looked:

Emily Dickinson's poem "I Heard a Fly Buzz When I Died" was written about 1862.

Two early interpretations, both published in 1955, see the fly as representing negative and disagreeable things in life.

A year after Friedrich's article, John Ciardi also wrote an article in *The Explicator* in which he disagreed with Friedrich.

Also in 1956 was an article written by John Crowe Ransom.

In 1961 Caroline Hogue wrote an article in *The Explicator* in which she disagreed with Ciardi's interpretation.

The rest of the articles published in the 1960s also interpret the fly as a nasty, foul thing.

There were many other interpretations of the fly in the 1960s.

In 1979 Sharon Cameron offered one of the few hopeful interpretations of the poem.

The only interpretation of the fly in the 1980s I could find was just as pessimistic as the earlier ones.

In conclusion, it appears that although there are many different interpretations of the meaning of the fly in Dickinson's "I Heard a Fly Buzz When I Died," most of them see the fly as a rather evil and pessimistic creature and the poem as a very pessimistic statement of the human condition.

Because the paper is a chronological survey of critical interpretations of the poem, Jonathan looked for a sense of both chronology and critical interpretation in the outline. From the outline, it appeared to him that paragraphs 4 and 7 might be weak. When he looked at the paragraphs he found that, in fact, they were weak. Here is a revised version of the first sentences of paragraphs 4 and 7. While they are not yet polished, they do present a clearer picture of the organization and development of the essay.

Also in 1956, John Crowe Ransom wrote an article that appears to be somewhere between Friedrich and Ciardi.

All the other interpretations of the fly I found in the 1960s were equally pessimistic.

Once Jonathan felt comfortable with his outline, he began to work on his paragraphs. Because almost all the paragraphs began with a topic sentence, Jonathan's task was easier. All he had to do was to make sure that his paragraphs were adequately developed and that what he said in the paragraphs was, in fact, related to the topic sentence of the paragraph and to the thesis.

Because Jonathan had already checked to make sure that he had a clear thesis, checking his paragraphs went fairly smoothly. The thesis and topic sentences functioned as a template. At this point

Jonathan actually combined two tasks. Because his paragraphs were in such good shape, he started to work on refining his transitions. He knew that the paper was still not ready to be handed in, but he began to pay attention to the precise relationship between clauses, sentences, and paragraphs.

As Jonathan was working on transitions, he remembered that his freshman English teacher required the class to acknowledge the source of a quotation, a paraphrase, or a summary in the text of their papers. When he looked at his essay, Jonathan realized that sometimes he did that, but sometimes he didn't. Here is a reference that includes both a summary and a direct quotation:

> The rest of the articles published in the 1960s also interpret the fly as a nasty, foul thing. One critic said that because the fly is a feeder upon carrion the introduction of the fly in the poem at the moment of death means that there is no afterlife, that "stink and corruption are death's only legacies" (Griffith 136).

Here is how the same reference looked after Jonathan revised it to conform to what he knew would be expected of him:

> The rest of the articles published in the 1960s also interpret the fly as a nasty, foul thing. In *The Long Shadow: Emily Dickinson's Tragic Poetry* Clark Griffith says that because the fly is a feeder upon carrion the introduction of the fly in the poem at the moment of death means that there is no afterlife, that "stink and corruption are death's only legacies." (136)

After revising several other references, Jonathan felt comfortable enough with what he had written to move on to the next phase of his writing—editing.

## Jennifer's Paper on the Confederate Navy

Because her paper was relatively short, Jennifer was not too concerned about her ability to be coherent. She also planned to use graphs of her data for clarity.

A bigger revision concern for Jennifer was the area of sufficiency. She understood that her report was controversial. Officers switching sides during the war was a touchy subject. The fact that only a minority of officers from Southern states resigned to fight for the South could be very insulting to people from that part of the country. At the same time, the best reason she could find for the variation in resignation rates was the North's use of a promotion system that was strangling the Navy. What person from the North would want to read how poorly prepared the Navy was on the eve of war?

Jennifer decided that the best way she could defend her conclusion was to rely on the strength of her sources. She returned to the books in which she had found each of her major quotations and checked on the background of the author. It turned out that the chart on resignation rates came from a Southern historian writing only twenty-one years after the Civil War. This implied that the data was fairly reliable because it was relatively recent and probably accurate because it was presented by a Southerner yet was hardly complimentary to the South.

She decided to include a short description of the book with the chart, rather than merely use a standard reference. So prior to the first use of the chart she added, "According to the Southern historian Thomas Scharf, writing in 1886, there was a major difference in resignation rates for officers with homes in the South. Here are the resignation rates he presents:"

Now that readers would have a clear idea of the source for her information, she hoped that the chart will seem more accurate.

She now also checked on the source for her quotations about the deplorable condition of the U.S. Navy. She read that the author was a Northerner himself and wrote his description of the U.S. Navy in 1885, only twenty years after the Civil War. She decided to do two things to substantiate the quotations. First, she included a brief description of this source as she had the other. Second, she used longer quotations than she might normally. She used a ten-line quotation directly from her source, judging that if she were to put the ideas in her own words, readers might not trust her as much as an historian writing over a century ago.

Jennifer's next decision was to include the original charts in her paper rather than summarize them. She felt that a chart showing the wide variations in resignation rates would have more impact than a brief summary such as "resignation rates varied from 14 to 53 percent." Readers would want to see such data for themselves. So she transferred the data over to her word processing disk from her spreadsheet data disk.

As one final step to gather support for her conclusions, Jennifer decided to insert a graph in her paper. She generated a bar graph of the resignation rates of the top four ranks and inserted it into her word processing document after the chart. She felt that the chart would give visual support to her comments about the range of resignation rates and might reach some readers who were ill-disposed to numbers and charts.

## Kris's Paper on the Mechanism of Evolution

While she was drafting her paper, Kris realized that, just as her composition teacher had noticed in several earlier papers, she lacked a clear sense of audience in her writing. Some portions of the paper were very elementary and written with familiar words, while in others she had applied much of the technical vocabulary and sentence structures of the material she had been reading. In order to establish her own view of her audience, Kris turned to one of the electronic questioner programs available in her university's writing laboratory. Working through the first section of the program, she discovered that her two most important goals in writing were to demonstrate her knowledge on the subject of evolutionary mechanisms and persuade her reader that her thesis on the most likely of these mechanisms was correct.

Next the program led her through a discovery of her audience. As a result of this experience, Kris reached several important conclusions for revision of her paper:

1. Her audience was her biology instructor.
2. Not unexpectedly for this audience, Kris felt that her reader knew as much about the subject as she did.
3. Her reader would approach the paper with an interest in the subject.
4. Class lectures indicated that her professor tended to believe in the more recent theories of evolution.

With this clearer view of her reader in mind, Kris worked through the draft of the paper, bolstering the more elementary sections; since she was writing to an audience with considerable knowledge of the subject area, she felt that she could make extensive use of technical terminology and concepts. She was careful, however, to consider her own limitations. She knew that much of the material she had read during the course of her research was very complex, and she was not always sure that she fully understood many of the terms. In all such cases she avoided the use of the specialized term because she did not want to use it incorrectly; thus, much of her revision was devoted to paraphrasing quotations which she had originally used directly. By forcing herself to explain concepts in her own words, she came to grips with her own understanding of the topic.

Her instructor's apparent bias for the more recent explanations of evolution, such as that offered by Eldridge and Gould, meant that Kris had to be especially logical and convincing in supporting her thesis, which adopted a more traditional view of evolution.

Since her audience was the instructor, Kris realized that her paper would be read in conjunction with forty other papers submitted by other members of the class. She recognized that her original introduction was very conventional and mechanical and guessed that it was pretty much like the introductions of those forty other papers. Since her goal was, to a large degree, to impress her instructor, she revised her introduction to make it more forceful and unconventional, hoping that her reader would be attracted to a more novel approach to the assignment.

Finally, she used the computer to examine the lengths of her paragraphs and sentences. She found that with the exception of the first two paragraphs and her concluding paragraph, relatively lengthy sentences and paragraphs appeared throughout most of the paper. Given her audience, Kris believed that these structures were perfectly suitable and moved on to editing.

# Chapter 7

# *EDITING*

**W**hen you have revised your writing in accordance with the demands of audience and purpose and are comfortable with what you have written, you are ready to edit. "Editing" means making changes that do not substantively alter the content of your writing. Editing involves polishing the draft; clearing up matters of style and convention; and proofreading for spelling, grammar, and punctuation errors—ensuring that your writing is presentable to your readers. Careful editing eases the burden of the reader by making clear what you have to say. Editing ensures that words are used correctly; that sentences make sense; and that spelling, punctuation, and grammar are correct.

Because editing emphasizes choices, and because successful writers know that each choice a writer makes has an effect on a reader, effective editing makes sure that the effect on the reader is the one the writer intends.

Editing also includes a basic review of mechanics and spelling, rephrasing a thought or idea, and deciding which is the best possible word to use at certain strategic points. Several writing tools to help in the various editing tasks are described in this section. The aim of this chapter is to give you the tools to help you write clearly, logically, and imaginatively for different audiences.

Clearly, one of the strongest areas in computing is in the help available in editing. There are many programs available to help you polish your writing and clear up matters of style and convention. Which programs you use depends on the methods that work best for you. Just as you undoubtedly tried various methods of writing with pen and paper, we suggest that you experiment with various methods of writing using computer tools.

For many writers, probably the greatest benefit from the computer is the ease with which experimentation can be performed. Before the computer, when pencil, pen, or typewriter was used, experimentation was laborious and time-consuming. In order to make changes, one had to either rewrite or retype whole papers or at least large sections of them.

Now experimentation is simple, and because change is easy, writers are encouraged to experiment. The advantage of experimentation is that when you try different words, different sentence structures, and different paragraphs, you are actually testing and refining the expression of your ideas.

## THE WORD PROCESSOR

Although many programs are available that will make editing easier, faster, and more efficient, we suggest that you use your word processor before trying any of the many programs listed below. Many word processors have functions that can help in the editing process. Although you might never have occasion to use the full range of options offered by the word processor, you should be familiar with what it can do. When you have a clear notion of what your writing weaknesses are, you can use the power of the word processor to help in correcting those weaknesses. Also, using the full capabilities of the word processor will ensure that you get the right words before doing anything else. Most word processors have many of the features described in the following paragraphs.

What can the word processor do? It can make the task of adding and deleting letters, words, sentences, paragraphs, and entire sections as easy as a few keystrokes. You can move words around in a sentence to clarify ideas, refine word order, combine choppy sentences, and break up very long sentences.

You can move sentences around to give your paragraphs unity and coherence. If you prefer an inductive paragraph, you can have the sequence of sentences lead up to the main idea (or topic sentence). If you prefer a deductive paragraph, you can rearrange the order of the sentences so that the sequence of sentences develops from the main idea.

A typical word processor will allow you not only to add, delete, and move words around but also to copy text from one part of the paper to another while maintaining the original. It will allow you to change and justify margins and reformat part of a document or the entire text. It will allow you to change type and fonts, either for the requirements of a discipline or for aesthetic reasons.

## The Search Function

For editing purposes, the most significant function of the word processor is its search function. The search command allows you to move the cursor to the first instance of any word or phrase in your document that you might be unsure of or that is frequently troublesome. Because you will be able to see the word or phrase in the context of your writing, you will be able to choose whether to keep the word or replace it with a better choice. Moving to the next instance of the word or phrase usually requires only one or two keystrokes. Unless you have a very long piece of writing, you can usually move through an entire document very quickly. Our students have found the search function helpful in looking for some common grammatical errors and poor style practices such as those described in the following subsections.

**Pronouns** Check for "he," "she," "it," "they," "them," "this," and "whose" words. These pronouns can cause a multitude of problems. Carefully check all your pronouns: is it clear to what they refer? Or is a pronoun's antecedent (the word, phrase, or clause to which the pronoun refers) unclear? You should be able to find the antecedent for each pronoun. Here are two passages, one from a history paper and one from a literature paper. Both writers knew that they had problems with unclear pronoun references, so they used their word processor's search function to look for pronouns and found many errors and ambiguities in pronoun usage. The indiscriminate use of "it" in the first passage and "he" in the second passage make the passages difficult to follow.

> It is hard to know how pay in the U.S. Navy compared, so it may be that it was an inducement to some, but since there is only a $300 difference between the salaries of surgeons and lieutenants, yet there is a major difference between their resignation rates, money doesn't seem to be a major motivating factor.

> A year after Friedrich's article, John Ciardi also wrote an article in *The Explicator* in which he disagreed with Friedrich. He says that because Emily loved life and everything in it, even all the smallest creatures, she would have even loved the fly because the fly represents "The last kiss of the world, the last buzz from life."

Here are the same passages after the writers replaced just one unclear pronoun with a clear noun:

> It is hard to know how pay in the U.S. Navy compared, so it may be that these salaries were an inducement to some, but since there is only a $300 difference between the salaries of surgeons and lieutenants, yet there is a

major difference between their resignation rates, money doesn't seem to be a major motivating factor.

A year after Friedrich's article, John Ciardi also wrote an article in *The Explicator* in which he disagreed with Friedrich. Ciardi says that because Emily loved life and everything in it, even all the smallest creatures, she would have even loved the fly because the fly is representative of "the last kiss of the world, the last buzz from life."

**"And" Clauses** A clause is a group of words containing a subject and a predicate. Some clauses are independent clauses, which means that they contain a complete thought that can stand alone as a sentence; other clauses are dependent (or subordinate) clauses, which means that they do not contain a complete thought and cannot stand alone as a sentence.

The most common method of joining parts of sentences in order to show the relationship between them is coordination and subordination. Although the words might be unfamiliar, you have been coordinating and subordinating for most of your life. Words that coordinate ("and," "but," "for," "so," etc.) are used to show a more equal relationship between ideas. Words that subordinate ("although," "so that," "because," "unless," "until," etc.) are used to explain or modify an idea. Subordinating one idea to another does not necessarily mean that the subordinate idea is either inferior or less important; rather, it allows you to show the precise and logical relationship between one thought and another.

The following sentence is a good example of the confusion that can result from the failure to properly relate parts of a sentence:

As we have seen earlier, the Lamarckian theory of adaptive evolution appears to be refuted by everything we know of the hereditary process, and we must choose between Darwinian gradualism and the concept of abrupt steps.

When this student's teacher read her draft, he questioned her about this sentence. The student said she intended to emphasize the need to choose between Darwinian gradualism and the concept of abrupt steps. After her teacher pointed out that the need to choose was not clear, the writer tried several versions of the same sentence.

Because the Lamarckian theory of adaptive evolution appears to be refuted by everything we know of the hereditary process, we must choose between Darwinian gradualism and the concept of abrupt steps.

As we have seen earlier, the Lamarckian theory of adaptive evolution appears to be refuted by everything we know of the hereditary process; thus we must choose between Darwinian gradualism and the concept of abrupt steps.

As we have seen earlier, the Lamarckian theory of adaptive evolution appears to be refuted by everything we know of the hereditary process, so we must choose between Darwinian gradualism and the concept of abrupt steps.

Ultimately, the writer chose the last version above because she considered it the simplest and clearest one. Which do you prefer?

In addition to checking your sentences to make sure that each connection shows the precise relationship you intend, use your search function to check every "and" used to link clauses. Make sure that it is the precise connective you want.

**Negative Constructions** Even well-educated readers have trouble translating negative statements into positive ones. Although such constructions are grammatically not unacceptable, negative statements are more difficult to follow. If the previous sentence is a bit confusing, try rewriting it as a positive sentence. You might not catch all your negatives, but by using the search function to check for negatives ("not," "never," etc.), you can catch most.

**Contractions** We use contractions because they are informal, close to speech, and add a personal touch to what we are writing. If you are in Wisconsin in mid-January and are writing to a close friend in Arizona, you might not feel the need to say, "It is really cold here. I am going to visit you next week." You might feel more comfortable with the less formal, "It's really cold here. I'm going to visit you next week."

Of course, you might prefer to adopt a more formal tone with your friend. That is your choice. Normally we choose the tone that we think will be most effective. The problem is that it is often difficult to know exactly which tone to adopt when writing to professors or instructors. Some will appreciate a less formal tone; others will not. Our experience is that most college professors and instructors will expect you to use a more formal and less personal English. Ask them what they prefer. If in doubt, do not use contractions.

One easy way to check for contractions in your writing is to use the search function to look for all apostrophes. If you are writing for an audience that is expecting you to use formal English and you find a contraction, change it.

**Usage** Perhaps you or your professor or instructor have noted that you frequently misuse certain words. You can easily use a word processor to check for those words by using text search when you edit. The list could be maintained on a disk in a separate file. Here is a (admittedly lengthy) list of words many writers commonly misuse:

accept/except
adapt/adopt
advice/advise
affect/effect
aggravate/irritate
all ready/already
allude/refer
allusion/illusion
alot (should be "a lot")
alright (should be "all right")
among/between
amount/number
and etc. (should be "etc." only; "and" is redundant here)
anxious/eager
cite/site
conscience/conscious
could of (should be "could have")
criteria/criterion
data/datum
different from/different than
farther/further
good/well
imply/infer
in/into
in/within
incredible/incredulous
its/it's
lay/lie
loose/lose
may be/maybe
moral/morale
on to/onto

passed/past

precede/proceed

quote/quotation

suppose to (should be "supposed to")

their/there

to/too

use to (should be "used to")

use/utilize

How many words can you distinguish? Do you know the difference between "accept" and "except," "affect" and "effect," "quote" and "quotation"? Look up the words you don't know.

**Gender-Specific Language**   Gender-specific language which refers to a member of one sex in a hypothetical context (i.e., where a particular person is not being referred to) is acceptable in sex-specific medical usage ("her pregnancy," "his prostate gland," etc.) and in general reference to persons of certain historical eras or social groups where it is understood that one sex predominated (or predominates) within a particular capacity (e.g., all nurses in nineteenth-century England were female, all officers in the Confederate Navy were male, all kindergarten teachers in Japan are female, all Mexican laborers migrating to the United States under the Bracero Accord of 1942–1964 were male). In such cases it is safe to use male or female pronouns.

Gender-specific language becomes "sexist" language when it arbitrarily imposes sex stereotypes or employs sex-specific pronouns ("she," "he," "her," "his," etc.) when the reference is general (applying to both sexes equally). Sexist language in writing is poor style and invites the risk of offending readers. Admittedly, because the English language does not have a convenient set of neutral pronouns applicable to both sexes, it is often difficult or awkward to avoid sexism in writing. If you find that you have used gender-specific language indiscriminately, you can sometimes change to the plural ("they," "their," etc.) or use the pronoun "one" and its derivatives ("one's," "oneself," etc.; this is slightly awkward, though—try to avoid). Avoid "he or she" construction; this is awkward.

When changing to another pronoun (plural, etc.) is awkward or slightly alters the meaning, try to recast the sentence to avoid the use of pronouns entirely. This is the best solution, but it's often difficult. Consider the following example. A company has a job opening and is interviewing applicants for this one position, which can be filled by anyone (male or female) with the proper background and qualifications. Compare the following job description statements: (1) "the applicant must show that he has a working knowledge of . . . ," (2) "applicants must show that they have a working knowledge of . . . ," and (3) "the applicant must demonstrate a working knowledge of . . ." Which statement would you choose? Statement 1 is sex-specific, implying that the position is open only to men; statement 2 might lead prospective applicants to believe that there are several openings for this job description; whereas statement 3 refers to the applicant in the singular and without sex bias.

Consider the terms in the following list. If you are using any of these terms but are not referring to a specific person, try to use one of the alternatives suggested in the right-hand column.

| | |
|---|---|
| businessman | business executive; business manager |
| chairman | person chairing (or presiding at) a meeting; head |
| congressman | member of Congress; representative |
| craftsman | artisan |
| fireman | fire fighter |
| foreman | supervisor |
| handyman | maintenance person (in apartment complex, etc.) |
| landlady, landlord | property (apartment complex, etc.) manager or owner |
| lineman | line worker |
| mailman | mail carrier |
| man, mankind (as species, etc.) | human (noun), humanity, humankind |
| man-made | synthetic; artificial |
| manpower | work force; labor force |
| policeman | police officer |
| stewardess | flight attendant |
| workmanship | work; artisanship |

These are only a few examples; there are many gender-specific nouns in English.

One of the easiest ways of checking for sexist language is to use your word processor's search function for "man." If you do this, remember to tell the program not to search for the whole word; that way you will be able to find words such as "mailman" and "policeman." Not all gender-specific words are sexist, but doing a search will at least allow you to consider the implications of the words you have chosen.

**Punctuation** You can even use the search function to check for possible punctuation errors.

Surely one of the most troublesome pieces of punctuation is the *comma*. Even seasoned writers often have a difficult time determining just where all the various commas go. The papers of some unseasoned writers look as if they had commas thrown at them from afar. While we do not intend to offer you the rules for placing commas (any good handbook will do that for you), use the search function of your word processor to ensure that commas are in the right place. A related, and common, problem is the *comma splice*, which is an error caused by joining two or more main, or independent, clauses with a comma. Comma splices will either confuse readers or slow them down—or do both. Comma splices are corrected by either inserting an appropriate coordinating conjunction after the comma, substituting a semicolon for the comma, or removing the comma and making two separate sentences.

Below are three examples of comma splices. Find at least two ways of fixing the sentences.

Foreign visitors in China about the turn of the century were appalled by the crippling effect of footbinding and the untold suffering which it caused, they denounced the practice as barbaric.

No fossil remains of the land ancestors of the whales have been discovered as yet, blood tests indicate a relationship with the artiodactyls, the group to which cattle belong.

Hunting is good for animal populations, it thins them out so there isn't as much competition for food.

If your teacher has indicated that you have a problem with comma splices (also called *comma faults*), use the search function to locate every use of the comma. If, or when, you find a comma splice, determine the precise relationship between the clauses and correct the error.

If the comma is one of the most troublesome pieces of punctuation, the *semicolon* is surely one of the most misunderstood and misused pieces of punctuation. It is misunderstood because its role in the family of punctuation lies somewhere between the comma and the period; it is more forceful than a comma, but less forceful than a period.

Because it is misunderstood, it is misused. Some writers use semicolons between parts of a sentence of unequal rank: "Because it was hot and humid; they were in no hurry to move." The first part of this sentence is a subordinate clause. Do not use a semicolon to separate a subordinate clause from a main clause.

Although any good handbook on grammar and punctuation will gladly demonstrate the many uses of the semicolon, it is used primarily for two purposes. First, it is used to join closely related main clauses that are not already joined by a coordinating conjunction ("and," "but," "or," "nor," "for," "so," "yet"). In the following sentence, the semicolon emphasizes the close relationship between the three soliloquies discussed.

> The first of the soliloquies relates to Hamlet's parents and contains a note of dejection; the second is a reaction to the ghost and seals a vow; in the third, which is inspired by the players, Hamlet plans a test.

Second, it is used to separate items in a series already containing commas. Which of the following two sentences do you find easier to follow?

> My favorite new slang terms are "gork," a stuporous patient, "bogart," get something by intimidation, "knuckle dragger," a crude, somewhat stupid person, "puzzle palace," any higher headquarters, and "perk-meister," an official in charge of favors.

> My favorite new slang terms are "gork," a stuporous patient; "bogart," get something by intimidation; "knuckle dragger," a crude, somewhat stupid person; "puzzle palace," any higher headquarters; and "perk-meister," an official in charge of favors.

Although there are perfectly good reasons for using it, writers should be cautioned not to overuse the semicolon. Overusing it will lessen its impact and might cause the reader to wonder which of the relationships are the most significant.

If you have chronic problems with commas, semicolons, colons, apostrophes, question marks, and other punctuation elements, use your search function to root out these errors. In addition to irritating your readers, punctuation errors will often confuse them. If you are not sure how to use a particular piece of punctuation, check a handbook.

## The Search and Replace Function

If your word processor has a search and replace function, you can save yourself time by using it. Rather than having to use the search function to locate every instance of a misspelled word or every instance where you wanted to change the same word, the search and replace function will make it easy. Naturally you need to be careful here. Before you tell the computer to change all instances of "he" or "she," you should be sure that is really what you want to do.

Even if the only editing tool you have available is a word

processor, you will be able to make significant changes easily and efficiently. However, there are other kinds of editing tools that can increase the effectiveness of your writing. Basically, there are two kinds of editing programs available: one kind of program functions primarily as a proofreader, notifying you of potential errors in spelling, punctuation, and wrong words. The other kind of program helps to improve your writing by allowing you to analyze your style and to make changes that improve what you have written.

# THE PROOFREADER

Although there are occasions when even English teachers disagree over the spelling or punctuation of a word (Would you write "The movie was made in the *1950's*," or "The movie was made in the *1950s*"?), there is almost universal agreement about the conventions of spelling, punctuation, and certain word usages. Proofreading means checking your writing to make sure it conforms to those accepted conventions.

## Spelling Checkers

Those who study English as a foreign language usually find it difficult to learn. This is largely because many English verbs are irregular and many words are difficult to spell. This irregularity means that spelling rules are often of little use, even for a native speaker. For example, the often quoted rule "i before e except after c" works well when you are trying to remember how to spell words such as "believe" and "receive," but it doesn't work well for words like "eight," "weight," "sleigh," "weird," "either," and "seize." The only good spelling rule is "Spelling counts."

Misspelled words upset most readers, and the more misspelled words there are in a paper, the more upset readers become—and when readers are upset they tend to take you, your facts, and your ideas less seriously. This is something that every writer must contend with, sooner rather than later.

If you have difficulty in spelling, use a spelling checker. A spelling checker program checks each word in your document against a list of words in its dictionary. If a word in your document is not in the spelling checker's dictionary, the spelling checker will mark the word incorrect and, at your option, will even suggest alternative spellings. However, because dictionaries have limited numbers of words (ranging from as few as 20,000 to well over 100,000), they will question many of your correctly spelled words, including almost all of your proper names, abbreviations, and acronyms. For example, when we ran a spelling checker on the three papers at the end of this book, these words were among those flagged by the checker:

chronological

spiritual

Emily

Dickinson

John

Ciardi

homogeneous

giraffe

Dayton

Tennessee

Ernst

Mayr

chaplain

conspicuous

Soley

NY

asst

Because most style analyzers expect words to be spelled correctly and it is easier to use any of the many editing tools available when words are spelled correctly, you should correct spelling errors first.

We have tried some checkers that check your spelling as you write and let you know when you type a word not in the checker's dictionary. We find this a distraction and could not get used to it—you will have to experiment.

It is possible to add words to your spelling checker. As Jonathan was writing his paper on the poem "I Heard a Fly Buzz When I Died," he was having a hard time remembering how to spell the author's name (Dickenson, Dickinsen, or Dickinson?), so he simply added the name to his spelling checker (it's Dickinson, by the way), and the checker automatically checked it when he ran the program.

It is also possible to create multiple personal dictionaries for different purposes (e.g., a biology dictionary or an economics dictionary). Many students have found this very helpful, especially those taking classes in areas unfamiliar to them. Rather than always having to look up the spelling of exotic biology and astronomy terms or names (such as zygote, syzygy, or ascension), your biology or astronomy dictionary will provide the correct spelling for you.

It is important to remember that a spelling checker will not pick up all spelling errors; while the checker will flag all words not in its dictionary, it will not recognize homonyms ("to," "too," "two"; "their," "there," "they're"; "no," "know"; etc.), and it will not recognize words that are wrong but spelled correctly ("on" for "no"; "cot" for "cut," etc.). Too often, students feel that once the spelling checker has done its job, the paper is error-free. Unfortunately, just the reverse can be true. One study, done at a major state university by a well-respected composition researcher, demonstrated that students who relied on spelling checkers to catch errors turned in drafts with more mechanical errors than did those who had not used spelling checkers. While the students who used spelling checkers had fewer absolute spelling errors, they had more errors of the "cot" for "cut" type. One striking example of this kind of error is the following sentence, turned in by a young man who failed to proofread his final draft: "When I was seven my grandfather, who was eighty, seemed so old I thought he was immoral." Ultimately, checking the spelling is your responsibility. The spelling checker can help, but it is, after all, only a tool.

Of course, it would be best if writers did not have to spend time checking for spelling errors. One of the best methods of limiting, if not quite eliminating, the need to spend a lot of time checking for spelling errors is to be aware of just what causes spelling errors.

**Errors Due to Mispronunciation** Because some writers don't hear the "nun" in "mispronunciation," they spell it "mispronounciation." Because they don't hear the "r" in "February," they spell it "Febuary." For the same reason, teachers often find the word "jewelry" spelled "jewlery" or "jewlry." Other words often misspelled because of mispronunciation are "supposed to" (often spelled "suppose to"), "used to" (usually spelled "use to"), "government" (spelled "goverment"), and "congratulate" (spelled "congradulate"). These errors are rarely picked up during proofreading because writers think that they are spelled correctly.

**Punctuation and Typographical Errors** A student once complained: "I know the correct spelling, but my word processor doesn't." Punctuation and typographical errors (typos) come in a variety of forms: a letter might be missing ("goverment"), added ("arguement"), or transposed ("on" for "no"). Most of these errors can be caught by careful proofreading, especially with the use of a checker. Some errors in your writing might represent deliberate choices on your part; however, there are programs that will alert you to possible problems of punctuation and to typical typographical errors. If you have trouble with punctuation and typos, invest in one of these programs. Here is a brief list of some of the more common problems these programs will identify:

Doubled words

Incorrect, extra, or missing punctuation

Missing or extra space between punctuation

Incorrectly spaced ellipsis

Incorrect abbreviation

Doubled punctuation marks

Inconsistent capitalization

Missing capitalization at sentence beginning

Unbalanced quotation marks and parentheses

Placement of punctuation inside quotation marks

Incorrect form for numbers

Sometimes a transposed, dropped, or added letter results in a perfectly good word (drop the "l" in "complete" and you get "compete"; type in "e" to "can" and you get "cane"). Spelling checkers do not catch these errors; such typos are detected only through careful proofreading.

**Troublesome Words**  "Troublesome" words are words that are close in spelling but dissimilar in meaning ("principle," "principal"; "affect," "effect"; "stationary," "stationery"; "loose," "lose"). As you can imagine, spelling checkers will not catch such errors, but some checkers contain lists of the most troublesome errors that plague writers. If you have a problem with words like these, invest in one of these checkers. A less expensive method is to keep a list of problem words and make sure that you either check these words using the search and replace function of your word processor, include the problem words in your dictionary, or prepare a separate file of all the troublesome words to be checked when editing.

For successful editing, you will still need a "regular" dictionary, in addition to an electronic aid. We recommend a good, standard, desk-size "College" dictionary, such as *The Random House College Dictionary, Webster's Ninth New Collegiate Dictionary,* or *The American Heritage Dictionary of the English Language* (movie buffs will appreciate this dictionary's illustration for "décolletage").

You should also be familiar with unabridged dictionaries, such as

*The Random House Dictionary of the English Language, Webster's Third New International Dictionary of English,* and *The Oxford English Dictionary.* Most college libraries will have these and other dictionaries on hand. The library will also have specialized dictionaries that contain words peculiar to specialized disciplines, from art to zoology.

### Homonym Checkers

Homonyms are words that sound alike but are spelled differently ("to," "too," "two"; "bare," "bear"; "there," "their," "they're"; "piece," "peace"; "pare," "pear"; etc.). Normally, spelling checkers will not pick up such errors. If you are careful, many of these errors can be picked up during proofreading. However, if you *consistently* have difficulty with words that sound alike but are spelled differently, use a program that will check the more common occurrences. Remember, you can also use your word processor to catch frequent homonym errors.

## THE STYLE ANALYZER

The writing problems we have described so far are generally unambiguous. Unclear pronoun references, misplaced commas, misspelled words, and typographical errors need to be corrected. You can use your word processor and one of the various proofreading programs regardless of the paper, the class, the audience, the purpose, or the situation. The strategies we have presented are appropriate for almost any writing task.

The next set of strategies, however, are not as clear-cut. Problems of style often appear to be simply one person's opinion. There are few formal rules, but there are some generally accepted guidelines to help you edit for style. Just as we offered general and specialized guidelines for revising, we now offer general and specialized guidelines for editing.

"Style" refers to the way we choose to express ourselves to others. It is here that we make the choices that determine whether our ideas will be understood or persuasive. For example, which of the following two sentences do you prefer?

**1.** As a rule, the active voice is utilized by most writers.

**2.** Most writers use the active voice.

The question is not which sentence is more, or less, precise than the other. The question is which sentence is easier to read. We think that sentence 2 is easier to read and thus more concerned with the intended audience.

Concern for our reading audience is inherent in all phases of the writing process, and this concern is especially significant in the editing phase. It is here that you choose the words that will move your readers to accept what you have written. It is here that you organize combinations of those words into the sentences that ulti-mately will inform, persuade, or move your readers.

Computer programs do not actually analyze style; rather, they describe what you have written. This description can help you and your teachers evaluate your writing by telling you quite a bit about what you have done. Since style is often a matter of opinion and not rule, you must make the choice. No style analyzer program will make changes automatically, and most programs are limited to specific tas! s; however, because they can absorb great chunks of data rapidly, they can provide an immediate description of your prose and help you to discover things about your writing (and thus your ideas) that would ordinarily have taken literally hours of careful and tedious scrutiny.

## General Style Conventions

Just as there are general conventions of revising, there are general conventions of editing. General conventions are sometimes referred to as literary conventions because they make the writing more pleasing to read; writing that is more pleasing to read has what the economist John Kenneth Galbraith calls "grace." However, writing that is pleasing is also easier to read—and writing that is easier to read is easier to follow, is more precise, and is clearer. Writing that is easy to read, precise, and clear is also more likely to persuade, and most writing is persuasive. Several common stylistic problems for writers are described in the following subsections.

**Wordy, Redundant Phrases** Even a relatively simple train of thought becomes a nightmare for readers who have to wade through a sea of unnecessary words and phrases. We make sentences as economical as possible so that readers will be able to grasp our meaning quickly. Wordiness, needless repetition, and redundancy waste the reader's time and interfere with the clear communication of ideas. The quickest way to trim your prose is to cut out any word or phrase that contributes nothing worthwhile to the sentence.

wordy:     It is by gaining power that governments turn into being totalitarian.

improved: It is by gaining power that governments turn totalitarian.

better: By gaining power, governments turn totalitarian.

**Nominalization** *Nominalization* is the conversion of perfectly good verbs into nouns (such as the word "nominalization"). This conversion is almost always accompanied by the use of passive sentence structures rather than the more concise and effective active structures. Rather than "The new accounting system reduced overhead," the dedicated nominalizer will write "A reduction in overhead was achieved by adoption of the new accounting system." Instead of "The results were calculated in three months," we find "Calculation of the results was carried out over a three-month period."

Scientific, technical, and business writing are the natural habitats of nominalization, but like many species of pest, nominalization can find a home in any accommodating environment. Be aware of the problem, and scrutinize your writing for the telltale signs of general-purpose verbs such as "perform," "conduct," and "undertake" for the passive. When you see such constructions, locate the noun which identifies the activity being performed, conducted, or undertaken. Once you've found that noun, convert it into the main verb of the sentence. The nominalization will disappear. In its place you will find clear, concise, concrete expression.

Ultimately, nominalization can be traced to a common misperception of academic discourse. Students recognize that in an academic setting they are writing for an audience who already knows the subject matter. Knowing that their writing will be a factor in the evaluation of their work, they often immediately respond by attempting to impress with "professional" vocabulary. This approach misses an essential point: professors appreciate good, clear writing as much as anyone does. Unfortunately, the results of such attempts at "professional writing" are often based on an immature perception of professional vocabulary, a misperception which results in inflated, inaccurate word choices. It is far better to write at a level within your capabilities. Remember, if you know your subject, a straightforward, comprehensible choice of vocabulary will only serve to better reveal your knowledge; if you don't know your material, no amount of cosmetic inflation of vocabulary will disguise that fact.

**Usage Errors** While you can effectively use the word processor's search function to check for usage errors, there are style analyzer programs that will help you do this. Similar to spelling checkers, these programs contain a list of commonly misused words and phrases and check their list against your document. The words and phrases the program will display are not necessarily incorrect, but they are often overused or misused. If the usage checker lists a word or phrase, you should not automatically move to change it; rather, you will need to check your writing to see whether you have made the right choice.

Here are two excerpts from a student paper written for a class in international economics. Because the student had been having usage problems throughout the semester, she brought in this paper to have it checked. The first paragraph was written before it was audited by a program that checks usage.

There are several reasons why world trade is, in a very real sense, fundamental to central Wisconsin's economy. First, no progressive country or state is completely autonomous in the twentieth century. Because of the varied distribution of the earth's resources, many regions trade between each other to acquire the resources and/or manufactured goods which they lack. While central Wisconsin has an abundance of rich soil, quality water, and healthy forests, its mineral deposits are essentially limited. However, its plentiful resources are being utilized efficiently. Thus, trade is necessary to take advantage of the potential benefits available from the variation in the disbursement of nature's wealth.

The second factor which summons central Wisconsin to the world market is because of its climate and topography. Despite the fact that farmers grow cranberries and raise dairy cattle, our region obviously is not suitable for banana trees and coffee shrubs. Hence, world trade satisfies the large amount of consumer demands both here and elsewhere.

The following paragraph was written after the paper was checked by a usage checker program. While the ideas remain the same, they are easier to follow because the words are more accurate and the argument flows more smoothly.

There are several reasons why world trade is fundamental to central Wisconsin's economy. First, no progressive country or state is completely autonomous in the twentieth century. Because of the varied distribution of the earth's resources, many regions trade among each other to acquire the resources and/or manufactured goods which they lack. While central Wisconsin has an abundance of rich soil, quality water, and healthy forests, its mineral deposits are limited. However, its plentiful resources are being utilized efficiently. Thus, trade is necessary to take advantage of the potential benefits available from the variation in the disbursement of nature's wealth.

The second factor which summons central Wisconsin to the world market is its climate and topography. Although farmers grow cranberries and raise dairy cattle, our region obviously is not suitable for banana trees and coffee shrubs. Hence, world trade satisfies the large number of consumer demands both here and elsewhere.

While the second excerpt could still be improved, the usage checker made suggestions that the writer did not find on her own. Here are the changes the usage checker suggested and the reasons for them:

1. The phrase "in a very real sense" was deleted because it adds nothing to the sentence.

2. The phrase "between each other" was changed to "among each other" because "among" refers to three or more, while "between" refers to two. The writer agreed to the change because she admitted that she intended the sentence to refer to many regions.

3. The word "essentially" in the fourth sentence was deleted because it adds nothing to the sentence.

4. The usage checker flagged the word "utilize" in the fifth sentence. However, although the word is often misused, it is used correctly here.

5. The phrase "because of" in the first sentence of the second paragraph was deleted because it adds nothing to the sentence.

6. The phrase "Despite the fact that" is wordy and was changed to "Although."

7. In the last sentence, "large amount" was changed to "large number." Use "amount" to indicate things in bulk that are not considered as units; use "number" when the elements are countable.

**Passive Voice**   One of the most misunderstood matters of style is the "voice" of a verb. In the active voice the emphasis is on the subject. In the passive voice the emphasis is on the object.

>   active:   The customer should fill out the form.
>   passive:  The form should be filled out by the customer.

Many students taking science classes are under the impression that they should use the passive because science teachers require it for objectivity. This is not so. The major style publications for the sciences, the American Psychological Association's (APA's) *Publication Manual* and the Council of Biology Editors' (CBE's) *CBE Style Manual*, argue for the use of the active voice. The APA manual says, simply: "Use the active voice" (36). And the CBE manual, a bit wordier, says: "The active is the natural voice, the one in which people usually speak or write, and its use is less likely to lead to wordiness and ambiguity" (38).

As a rule, your writing will be more direct and vigorous if you write in the active voice. By writing in the passive you can often avoid saying who is responsible for an action.

However, sometimes the passive voice is necessary as well as preferable. Suppose that you are writing a paper for a political science class on farm subsidies and do not know who was responsible for a particular policy you are citing. Compare the active voice in a statement such as "I am not sure who, but someone established the policy in 1964" with the passive voice in a statement such as "The policy was established in 1964." The first sentence needlessly shifts the emphasis from the date the policy was established to the fact that you don't know who established it. In another example, you are preparing a biology report on a year-long fruit fly experiment. At one point in the report you want to tell the reader what the flies ate. You can use the active voice and try to list all forty or fifty people who fed the flies. Or you can use the passive voice and write: "The flies were fed a mixture of yeast, water, agar, and molasses."

**Clichés**  Some expressions have the power of originality when they are first coined, but as they are copied and overused they lose their punch and become trite. One good example of this is Harry Truman's famous line, commenting on those in power who find it difficult to make decisions and who can't take criticism: "If you can't stand the heat, get out of the kitchen." Any expression that, while once thought fresh and original, has been used so often that it has become dull and trite is considered a *cliché*. Here are just a few others. You can probably expand the list.

Busy as a bee
Dead as a doornail
Like water off a duck's back
Quick as a wink
Selling like hotcakes
Water over the dam
Went in one ear and out the other

Inexperienced writers often resort to using clichés because they are handy. Because readers quickly tire of the predictability of clichés, the expressions as well as the ideas in cliché-loaded writing will seem predictable.

**Jargon**  Jargon is the specialized language used by specific fields (medicine, computer science, etc.). Some professors claim that it is wrong to use jargon, but we see it as a kind of shorthand members of a discipline use when communicating to each other. If you are working in a travel agency, for example, and are writing to other travel agents, it would be entirely appropriate to use the terms "rack rate" and "shoulder" instead of "the official posted rate for a hotel room" and "the time between high (or peak) season and low (or off-peak) season." The specialized terms are more economical and just as accurate.

If you use jargon in writing to an audience that is not familiar with the specialized terminology you are using, however, you have failed to communicate. While there are no style checker programs that will flag jargon, it is your responsibility to make sure that no highly specialized language creeps into your writing when you are writing to a general audience or to readers not familiar with the language of your trade.

It is important to distinguish between slang and jargon. Slang is highly informal, nonstandard language that is rarely used in writing (except for the most familiar writing) and is limited almost solely to informal speech. Except in very specific situations (creative writing classes, etc.), do not use slang in writing.

**Pompous Phrases**   Occasionally, writers who are unsure of themselves or their ideas will attempt to impress their readers by using "big" words; Walker Gibson calls this style of writing "stuffy." Pompous, stuffy writing is rarely effective because most readers recognize the pretentiousness of inflated vocabulary. Which of the following two sentences is easier to read?

1. Readers who lack the ability to facilitate the understanding of the material generated by a writer generally get frustrated and angry with that writer.

2. Readers who can't understand what a writer is saying get frustrated and angry with the writer.

If we have done our job so far, you will have chosen the second sentence. The first sentence was actually written by a freshman English student on the topic, "How to write an 'A' paper."

Programs that check for pompous phrases will not accuse you of being pompous (after all, sometimes a "big" word is the most precise or descriptive word for the job), but they will draw your attention to words that might not be appropriate for the writing you are doing. In any case, you will have to make the decision to keep or to change the words.

**Sentence Fragments**   A *sentence fragment* is an incomplete sentence. It occurs when part of a sentence is punctuated as a complete sentence.

While skillful writers occasionally use fragments for emphasis, most fragments in student writing are unintentional. Although sentence fragments are a less common error than, say, a comma splice, they are potentially more disastrous. Here is an unintentional sentence fragment.

> Ants not only harvest the natural vegetation. Some species also plant and cultivate special crops.

To correct a fragment, a writer must either create two separate sentences:

> Ants harvest the natural vegetation. Some species also plant and cultivate special crops.

or link the fragment to the sentence before or after it:

> Ants not only harvest the natural vegetation, but some species also plant and cultivate special crops.

**Overused Words** Word frequency counter programs can give you an alphabetical list of all the words in your document and how often those words appear. The information can help you discover spelling errors and overworked vocabulary. These programs can also direct a writer to overused prepositional phrases.

While it should be apparent by now that editing programs can perform extensive analysis of a writer's style, alerting writers to real and potential hazards, writers should be cautioned that editing programs, such as word frequency counters, cannot do everything (yet). For example, since computers do not know anything about the meaning of words, an error that requires an understanding of the meaning of words, such as a fragment, cannot be detected.

**Vocabulary Problems—Thesaurus** If you consistently have trouble with the words you choose (too big, too small, slightly off the mark, etc.), you might consider using a thesaurus. You are probably familiar with a thesaurus and how it works. It is a collection of synonyms, words that are similar in meaning. The function of a thesaurus is twofold: (1) to help you discover a word more precise than the one you are using and (2) to suggest an alternative word in order to provide some variety in your writing.

There is no doubt that a thesaurus can be helpful if used with discretion. However, we believe that a warning label should be printed on the cover of every thesaurus: *"Warning:* Use of this thesaurus may be harmful to your writing." The reason is that many students think that synonyms are words that mean the same thing. A casual glance at a thesaurus will dispel that notion. If you look up the word "house" in the most popular thesaurus, *The New Roget's Thesaurus of the English Language*, you will find the following entry:

> house, n. mansion, castle, building, home

There are more words at "house," but you get the point. While one's home might be one's castle, a home and a castle are not interchangeable. Try it some time and see how strange your writing sounds. And while a house is a building, not all buildings are houses.

The problem is that while many words share the same broad, general meaning, the same words imply very different meanings. The difference between a large mouth and a big mouth may well be a punch in the mouth.

## Specialized Conventions of Style

As we pointed out in Chapter 6, "Revising," if you were to read examples of scientific or historical or literary or sociological writing, you would find that the writing within each discipline has certain characteristics in common. These common traits are the conventions of that particular discipline. Writing conventions are like social conventions. In some situations we dress one way; in other situations we dress another way. Successful writers understand that in order to be successful they must adhere not only to the general conventions of the language but also to the specialized conventions of the discipline they are writing for. Generally, the best advice we can offer is to find out what the conventions of your field are. You can find out in several ways: by (1) reading carefully and noting how successful writers in your field write, (2) asking your teachers, (3) reading the appropriate journals, or (4) checking the style manual appropriate to your field.

Generally speaking, we dress according to our audience. It is the same way with writing—we make choices according to our audience. Just as audience was important when we revised, audience is important when we edit. Here, for example, are the first two paragraphs of a 4000-word essay on the conservationist Aldo Leopold. The essay was written by the philosopher J. Baird Callicott and presented at a Multi-Disciplinary Conference on Agriculture, Change and Human Values at The University of Florida in October 1982.

> Aldo Leopold is, perhaps, America's most distinguished conservationist, especially renowned for his Land Ethic, and recognized as the seminal forerunner of contemporary environmental ethics.
>
> There is also present in Leopold's work a definite "Land Aesthetic" which has not enjoyed much attention, but which could prove more powerfully to inspire ecologically responsible behavior on the part of the private land owner than the Land Ethic. The Land Ethic (yet another set

of rules or limitations) may appear onerous and unwelcome to agrarian land owners especially now, in a time when agriculture is beset by economic hardship and bureaucratic interference. The Land Aesthetic, on the other hand, might be more palatable (while equally fostering conservancy) since it is based upon a mechanism of assets and rewards, rather than obligation, self-sacrifice, and restraint. "If the private owner," Leopold wrote, "were ecologically minded, he would be proud to be the custodian of a reasonable proportion of such areas [wetlands, woodlands, native prairies, etc.] which add diversity and beauty to his farm." (Callicott 1)

After having delivered the paper at the conference, professor Callicott submitted the paper to the *Journal of Soil and Water Conservation.* The editor and reviewers of the journal were impressed with the paper but asked professor Callicott to change the manuscript so that it would be more appropriate for the readers of the journal. According to the editor, Max Schnepf, "Our audience is multidisciplinary, and there is considerable variation in professional sophistication. A sizeable segment of our audience no doubt will look on the paper, as written, as pretty heavy reading. Anything we can do to improve readability, therefore, will be appreciated, I'm sure." Here are the same two paragraphs after having been edited for the readers of the journal:

Aldo Leopold is perhaps America's most distinguished conservationist. He is especially renowned for his "land ethic," which is recognized as the forerunner of all contemporary environmental ethics.

Leopold also expressed a definite "land aesthetic." Although his land aesthetic has not enjoyed as much attention as the land ethic, it could prove to be more inspirational to private landowners.

Leopold's land ethic is yet another set of rules or limitations. It calls for obligation, self-sacrifice, and restraint and thus could be unappealing to farmers and landowners. This is especially true at a time when agriculture is beset by economic hardship and bureaucratic interference.

The land aesthetic, on the other hand, might be more palatable since it emphasizes assets and rewards. Yet it also fosters conservation: "If the private owner," Leopold wrote, "were ecologically minded, he would be proud to be the custodian of a reasonable proportion of such areas [wetlands, woodlots, native prairies, etc.] which add diversity and beauty to his farm." (329)

Which version do you prefer? Which is easier to read? Why? Do you agree with the changes? For example, in addition to breaking two paragraphs into four short ones, the writer also broke five sentences into nine sentences. Why do you suppose he did that?

In addition to the structural changes, note the changes in word choice. For example, in the second sentence of the second paragraph the writer changed "onerous and unwelcome" to "unappealing" and "agrarian land owners" to "farmers and landowners." In the third sentence of the second paragraph the phrase "based upon a mechanism of assets and rewards" was changed to "emphasizes assets and rewards." Do you agree with the changes? Why? Do you understand why these changes, and many of the others, were made? What do the changes suggest to you about the writer's perception of his readers?

What is significant is that changes are not a matter of right or wrong, except for some obvious errors ("land owners" is one word). What is significant is that the writer revised the manuscript to conform to the conventions of a specific discipline and to the expectations of clearly defined readers.

Other journals and disciplines have similar conventions and expectations. There are too many specialized conventions to include here, but some of the more common (and a few less common) examples of specialized conventions of style are described in this section.

Because many of you will be reading and writing scientific writing and science writing, it is important that you understand the difference between them. Scientific writing is the writing scientists do for each other. Scientific writing assumes an audience of peers, an audience that understands the language of science. Science writing, on the other hand, is the writing that scientists do for nonscientists.

**Scientific Writing** In your classes you will be doing scientific writing if your audience consists of those knowledgeable about what you are writing. If you are writing for biology and the audience is the teacher, you will be doing scientific writing. If you are not sure what audience you are to address, ask your instructor.

If the audience consists of professionals in the discipline, the editing you will do will be different from that intended for laypersons. For example, professionals normally do not need terms explained. You can often use shortcuts with professionals that you could not use with laypersons.

**Science Writing** Science writing attempts to interpret scientific writing for the layperson. The science writer's obligation is to describe and discuss frequently difficult concepts in an understandable and clear manner. As with any type of writing, the material must be accurate and clear, but science writing demands that the material be precise and be presented in logical sequence.

While writing for other scientists is a relatively straightforward task, writing for laypersons is more difficult. With laypersons, the science writer must neither oversimplify nor represent science in a nonscientific manner. More importantly, the science writer must not represent nonscience in a scientific manner. These difficulties can be avoided by establishing the proper tone in the paper.

The tone of science writing must reflect the scientific method. Generally, the scientific method emphasizes relative truth (also known as "theory") rather than absolute truth. The scientific method demands a mechanistic tone, which supports the scientific view that the universe is governed and operates according to a set of natural laws. This does not mean that the tone must be stiff and formal— although it often is—but rather that the words, the sentence structure, and the meaning be consistent with the questioning process that characterizes scientific inquiry: observation, question, hypothesis, experimentation, and theory.

Here are some suggestions for maintaining a scientific tone in your writing. Use first person for what you did, second person for giving directions, and third person for what happened. Use the past tense for observations and completed procedures, and use present tense for directions and generalizations. Do not use informal language or jargon.

To illustrate some of the differences between scientific writing and science writing, we present the following excerpts from two articles on sex differences in mathematical reasoning ability. One (from *Science*) is the original scientific article written to scientists; the other (from *Newsweek*) is a science article explaining the original to an audience of educated nonscientists.

Sex Differences In Mathematical Ability: Fact or Artifact?

We favor the hypothesis that sex differences in achievement in and attitude toward mathematics result from superior male mathematical ability, which may in turn be related to greater male ability in spatial tasks (12). This male superiority is probably an expression of a combination of both endogenous and exogenous variables. We recognize, however, that our data are consistent with numerous alternative hypotheses. Nonetheless, the hypothesis of differential course-taking was not supported. It also seems likely that putting one's faith in boy-versus-girl socialization processes as the only permissible explanation of the sex difference in mathematics is premature. (Benbow and Stanley 1264)

Do Males Have a Math Gene?

Can girls do math as well as boys? All sorts of recent tests have shown that they cannot. Most educators and feminists have blamed this phenomenon on socialization—arguing that because girls are told they can't do well in math, they develop "math anxiety" and don't. But last week a new study appeared that explains the difference mainly in genetic terms. The authors' conclusion: "Sex differences in achievement in and attitude

toward mathematics result from superior male mathematical ability."
(Williams and King 73)

As you have undoubtedly noticed, there are a number of striking differences between the original report of the study published in *Science* and the *Newsweek* article. The differences help to illustrate the distinction between scientific writing and science writing, how successful writers pay careful attention to their audience, and at least one of the dangers of careless editing.

The original report is a good example of scientific writing. The writers are clearly writing to fellow scientists (a good example of a sexist slip—substitute "other" for "fellow"). References to other studies are liberally sprinkled throughout the report. The writers expect their readers to understand terms such as "endogenous" and "exogenous." And the tone of the writing is clearly scientific; that is, the writers are not suggesting that they have found an absolute truth, but rather they are supporting a hypothesis, a guess that can be rejected or not rejected only after repeated experimentation.

Note especially the tentative and conditional language used in the report: the writers "favor" the hypothesis; superior male mathematical ability "may" be related to greater male ability in spatial tasks; male superiority is "probably" an expression of endogenous and exogenous variables; it "seems likely" that believing in socialization as the only explanation of the sex difference in mathematics is "premature."

The writers of the scientific article are not hedging or being wishy-washy. Because they are scientists they know that much more experimentation is needed before their hypothesis can ever hope to become a theory. There are many variables to be considered and many other studies to be done.

Notice the attempts of the *Newsweek* writers to attract the reader's attention, beginning with the title and extending on down into the article. Here the writers apparently felt the need to cater to what they assumed were the sensibilities of their readers.

Besides the catchy title and the provocative introduction, note the language used by the authors of the *Newsweek* article. If you had read only the *Newsweek* article, you might have thought that the study proved that mathematical differences between boys and girls are genetic. The writers have taken out of context the quotation from Benbow and Stanley. The words left out are "favor" and "may," words that qualify.

When you edit your own writing, it is essential that you be honest, that you qualify what needs to be qualified, that you give accurate credit where credit belongs. The *Newsweek* writer failed to qualify what needed to be qualified, and look at the erroneous assumptions that resulted. Be careful.

**Humanities Writing**   In relation to style, few disciplines in the humanities require a rigidly detached, scientific tone. In fact, disciplines such as literature, history, and philosophy pride themselves on their literary tradition and their ability to reach a general audience. This means that, in order to be successful, students writing for any of the humanities should vary sentence length, vary the order of the words in their sentences, make sure that all paragraphs are unified and coherent, clearly signal all changes in argument or purpose, use clear transitions, and be imaginative in their choice of words.

However, we also advise students writing for the humanities to avoid a colloquial, or chatty, style, avoid using the first person, and avoid contractions.

The one exception to the above suggestions is the *personal essay*. The personal, or familiar, essay is common in several disciplines and has certain conventions all its own: the use of the first person, the use of colloquialisms, the use of contractions. In freshman English, for example, students are often encouraged to write familiar essays on a variety of topics. In courses such as sociology, home economics, and education, students are often asked to write short pieces reflecting their personal experience with a particular topic.

**Other Specific Conventions**   There are still even more specific conventions that writers need to be aware of in order to be successful. The list of highly exotic conventions is almost endless, but some of the more common conventions that trouble students are described here.

A difficult question for many writers is when to write out a number ("he bought four Ferraris") and when to use numerals ("he could have bought 127 Hondas"). The question is even more difficult when you consider all the different "rules" that exist. A cursory examination of a dozen English handbooks resulted in the following guidelines: one handbook says that, "Although usage varies, writers tend to spell out numbers that can be expressed in one word or two; they regularly use figures for other numbers" (Hodges and Whitten 124). Another handbook says: "In general, books and magazines write out all numbers through one hundred and also larger numbers that can be written in two words (six thousand, three million). This style is usually appropriate for college papers and for most other kinds of general and formal writing" (Corder 191).

The problem with these guidelines is that they are wrong. In preparing this book we asked faculty from various disciplines about writing conventions specific to their disciplines and what they *required* of students. To the question "What is your rule for writing out numbers?" faculty in psychology, history, and many of the physical sciences replied that they *required* students to adhere rigorously to the *Publication Manual of the American Psychological Association*. That manual is very clear. It says: "The general rule governing APA style on the use of numbers is to use figures to express numbers 10 and above and words to express numbers below 10" (71). Faculty in the biological sciences said that they required their students to adhere to the rules outlined in the *CBE Style Manual*. That manual also says to "use words for numbers one through nine and numerals for larger numbers" (146).

When we asked English teachers what they required of students, many said that they adhered to the *MLA Handbook for Writers of Research Papers*. That handbook, surprisingly, recommends the same style as APA and CBE: "In general, write as words all numbers from one to nine and write as numerals all numbers 10 and over (about 500 years ago)" (Gibaldi and Achtert 40).

The problem is that not all teachers agree. If you are writing a paper for psychology, biology, physics, or home economics, we can almost guarantee that you will be required to write out numbers below ten. However, if you are writing a paper for freshman English, you will have to adhere to whatever handbook your teacher is using. If there is no handbook, ask the teacher. The editors at McGraw-Hill, publisher of this book, prefer that their authors spell numbers under 100.

*Should a capital letter appear after a colon?* This is a stylistic matter that can cause a writer a small amount of grief. It will not cause your paper to fail, but failing to follow the particular convention of the field you are writing for could be distracting at least.

If you are writing for humanities (English, philosophy, foreign languages, history) or fine arts (theater, art, music), the general rule is *not* to capitalize the first letter following a colon; if you do, you run the risk of calling attention to a stylistic infelicity and away from the content of your writing.

If you are writing for social sciences (psychology, sociology, political science, economics, etc.) or physical and natural sciences (physics, geology, chemistry, biology, etc.), the general rule is to capitalize the first word after a colon; if you do not, you run the risk of calling attention to a stylistic infelicity and away from the content of your writing.

*Eponyms* are terms derived from the names of persons (e.g., "Krebs cycle," "Paget's disease"). The Council of Biology Editors recommends that for scientific writing, "Standard, descriptive, equivalent terms are preferable to eponymous terms . . . when they are available" (43). For the above examples, the council suggests that "citric acid cycle" is preferable to "Krebs cycle," and "osteitis deformans" is preferable to "Paget's disease."

*Typographic conventions* pertain to the use of capital, small capital, and lowercase letters and italic, roman, and boldface type. These conventions have special meanings especially in science. For specific applications of typographic conventions, you should check with the discipline you are writing for. With the availability of a wide variety of computers, programs, and printers, the ability to change characters and typefaces makes it easy to adhere to almost any typographic requirement.

# CONCLUSION

Although editing programs have great capabilities, each document should still be carefully checked by a human. We recommend that you enlist the aid of a friend to help you edit. We have found that the following questions are usually better answered by someone other than the writer. Most of us feel that we write clearly, use words correctly, and have a pretty good sense of language—that is, until someone (or something) points out that we have been unclear here, wordy there, or simply wrong. Here are some questions we and our students have found helpful:

1. Are the vocabulary, the explanations, and the tone of the writing appropriate for the knowledge and the experience of the readers?
2. Are the vocabulary, the explanations, and the tone of the writing appropriate for the purpose?
3. Are the sentences clear? Has the writer tried to vary sentence length?
4. Does it appear that each word is used correctly? Does it appear that each word means what the writer wants it to mean?
5. Are any words repetitious or unnecessary?
6. Are there any awkward, unclear, or vague phrases?
7. Check all "which" clauses. Are they necessary?
8. Are the passive constructions necessary?
9. Does the punctuation (commas, periods, colons, semicolons, etc.) help you read the paper more clearly? Or are the sentences more difficult to read because of the punctuation?
10. Is it clear to what specific idea, person, or thing each pronoun

refers? Or are you unclear about what it is "he," "she," "it," "that," or "this idea" refers to?

11. Has the writer used standard forms of spelling, punctuation, and grammar?

12. Have any words been left out?

13. Are there any fragments?

14. Are there any typographical errors?

15. Is the writer's name on the paper?

## ▬▬▬▬▬ EXERCISES

1. Can you determine the antecedent for the underlined pronouns?

> Chancellor Stevens called Mayor Adams to discuss a strategy for improving the image of the university. *He* said it would be a difficult task, at least until the debate team had a better season. (Does the "he" refer to Chancellor Stevens or to Mayor Adams? Is there any way to tell? How can the second sentence be clarified?)

> Relying on state and national statistics, he presented his radical theory on animal rights, *whose* effects are felt by everyone. (To what does "whose" refer: the writer's radical theory? animal rights? statistics?)

2. Many beginning writers tend to connect clauses with "and." The following sentence is from a policy manual on personal loans. The manual is intended to offer guidance to managers and loan officers.

> This is a convenience loan to a good Second City Savings and Loan customer, and we must recognize the impracticality of making this small personal loan.

One purpose of a policy is to help people make decisions. Note the confusion caused by the failure of the writer to relate two different ideas clearly. Does the company want to emphasize the convenience to a good customer or the impracticality of making the loan? How is a manager or loan officer to decide? The problem with the sentence above is that the coordinating conjunction "and" suggests a balance of convenience and impracticality. Using subordination, revise the sentence twice, once to emphasize the convenience to a good customer, and once to emphasize the impracticality of making the loan.

3. To demonstrate the extremes to which use of the thesaurus can be carried, try your hand at deciphering the following passage from a student autobiography:

On my fourteenth natal anniversary, I, in conjunction with my familial personages, made an egress from the shores of Balboa's discovery, to establish our domicile beside a sylvan lagoon in the Gopher state.

**4**. Here are some exercises in spelling:

　**a.** Make a list of troublesome words in a course you are taking. Try writing a sentence using these words.

　**b.** For all your courses, keep a list of words your instructor has indicated are errors on papers, exams, and so on.

**5**. Improve these wordy sentences.

　wordy:　　Take the paintbrush and dip it in the glass of water until the bristles are saturated.

　improved:

　wordy:　　The owner of Samsa's pest control was found to be suspect of a murder.

　improved:

**6**. Below are ten unfinished clichés. How many can you complete? Give yourself ten points for each correct answer. What does your score tell you about the predictability of clichés?

　At the drop of a . . .

　Flat as a . . .

　Last but not . . .

　Like a needle in a . . .

　More fun than a . . .

　It's no use crying over . . .

　Sly as a . . .

　Stubborn as a . . .

　My new car will stop on a . . .

　The bigger they are the . . .

**7**. Fragments that work are sometimes called "The English minor sentence." Here is a fragment that does not work. Using either of the strategies recommended in the chapter, correct the error.

　The sun was setting. Which was very beautiful.

## ▰▰▰▰▰▰▰PAPERS IN PROGRESS: EDITING

### Jonathan's Paper on an Emily Dickinson Poem

Because Jonathan intended to use a style analyzer, the first thing he did when he started to edit was to use his spell checker. Having the words spelled correctly would allow the various style analyzers to give Jonathan a more accurate description of his writing.

Because Jonathan knew that he had a tendency to overuse certain words, the first thing he did after correcting his spelling was to use a program listing all the words in a document and how often those words appear. When Jonathan ran a word frequency count of his paper, one section of it looked like this:

```
Word Frequency Count
THAT         38    THINKS    1    TOUCH        1
THE          96    THIS      2    TOUCHES      1
THEM          2    THOMAS    2    TRADITION    1
THEN          1    THOSE     2    TRAGIC       1
THERE         3    THOUGH    1    TRIVIAL      1
THEREFORE     1    THUS      1    TRUTH        1
THING         3    TIMELY    1
THINGS        2    TO       13
```

Some words go unnoticed despite repeated checking. Jonathan had gone over his paper carefully, a friend of his had looked at it, and Jonathan's teacher had scrutinized it. And somehow they had missed all the "that's." One reason they missed them, of course, is that the thirty-eight "that's" are spread out over five pages. When Jonathan saw the thirty-eight "that's" he became suspicious and checked his essay. Here is just one example of what he found:

> Ronald Beck says that he agrees with Friedrich and Hogue that the "small, ugly, unpleasant, and, in the context, rather sinister" fly represents putrefaction and decay.

Jonathan decided to edit out the first "that" in the sentence, leaving the sentence looking like this:

> Ronald Beck agrees with Friedrich and Hogue that the "small, ugly, unpleasant, and, in the context, rather sinister" fly represents putrefaction and decay.

In the process of editing the sentence for wordiness, an interesting thing happened. Jonathan noticed that he had managed to get rid of not only the "that" but also two other unnecessary words, "he" and "says." That prompted him to check his word frequency counter for "says." He found that he had used the word "says" seventeen times in the essay. After auditing his use of "says," Jonathan changed many of them for variety and precision.

Jonathan made many small, and a few large, editing changes. In addition to using his word processor's search function to check for "that" and "say," he used it to check for those items he knew he had

had trouble with: pronoun references, "and" clauses, and commas. He changed a few words, found one (unintentional) sentence fragment, rearranged several sentences, and agonized over whether the period goes before or after a quotation mark.

## Jennifer's Paper on the Confederate Navy

Jennifer was well aware of spelling errors she usually made, so one of the first things she did as she proofread a late version of her paper was to use the search and replace function of her word processor to seek out the kinds of mistakes she normally makes. She began with "alot." She was proud to find that she had only misused the word once, and she automatically changed it to "a lot." She was also slightly concerned that she might have dropped a letter or two in "Confederate," so she used the search and replace function for this word too but searched only for the first three letters: "Con." She found one typo this way and corrected it.

Her next use of the search and replace function was with contractions. Her professor had cautioned her against using them in formal writing, and she was sure that she had let one or two slip. So she did a search and replace for the apostrophe and found five cases of contractions such as "wasn't" and "couldn't." She spelled out each of the five words fully.

She next ran a spelling checker program over her writing. The first time she ran it she looked for misspelled words and found three. Then she ran it again because it had a word frequency counter. She looked at her frequencies and tried to identify words she had overworked. Several were obvious; one was "resigned." She looked for synonyms in her dictionary and found "submit, accept, quit." She decided that none of these alternatives would work, so she left "resigned" untouched.

Another problem word was "so." She had used it nine times in six pages. When she looked back she saw that she had begun sentences with it seven times. She decided to drop two of the "so"s and replace two others with "as a result." The paper seemed to be less redundant as a result.

## Kris's Paper on the Mechanism of Evolution

Kris began editing her papers by reviewing the file CHKLIST. She had created this file with the word processor and stored it on disk; it listed all the mistakes that she made frequently and needed to check before submitting any paper. Using the word processor, she could call up the file and use it as a checklist for the editing process. If she discovered she was making a new error frequently, she added it to the list; she could also add special check-off areas for individual papers (such as the need to check documentation accuracy for a research paper).

Even though Kris prided herself on her good spelling (giving thanks to Mrs. Mumphrey at Millard Fillmore Elementary School), she ran her word processor's spelling checker to ensure that her paper was ready for the rest of the editing process. She created a special dictionary for this purpose since she didn't want the process to be interrupted by frequently used names such as "Mayr" and "Gould" and specialized biological terminology not in the general dictionary. After running the spelling checker she didn't locate any actual spelling errors, but did find a significant number of typing mistakes (at least Kris assumed the appearance of "hteories" rather than "theories" to be a typing error).

Next, she used her word processor's search function to locate contractions by finding all occurrences of "n't"; since this was a formal paper for biology, Kris recognized that contractions were inappropriate, and as the word processor found them, she replaced each with its full form. She again used the search function to locate and eliminate use of "alot," a word that was number 1 on her CHKLIST. Recently, Kris had noticed that she was using "there" when she meant "their" so she used the word processor's search and replace to make the necessary adjustments; since she wasn't sure that she should make the replacement in every case, she had the word processor ask her to verify every replacement.

Having completed her electronic review of the manuscript, Kris printed out a copy for final proofreading. Some students can proof-read directly on the screen, but Kris felt more comfortable working with a hard copy on this last, crucial step; she made final correction notes on the draft copy and later returned to the word processor to make the corrections permanent. It is fortunate that she did, for she discovered several errors that none of the electronic aids were capable of catching: "on" for "one," "if" for "is," and "no" for "not."

# Chapter 8

# PRESENTATION

You might believe that once your paper has been researched, written, and revised, you can simply print or type a final copy and hand it to your instructor. However, if you wish to be fully successful in your writing, before that final printing and presentation, there is still work to be done and decisions to be made. The paper must be put in acceptable final presentation form. This means that you must decide—or adhere to disciplinary conventions in such matters—how you want your work to appear on the paper, what any graphic aids will look like, and what final form your documentation will take.

## FORMAT CONSIDERATIONS

### Sizing the Text

First, you must determine the appearance of your pages. This means that you must establish the margins, paragraph form, line spacing, and the use of headings and titles. While these might appear to be matters of little consequence, you should stop to consider that the overall layout and design dictates the reader's first impression of your paper. If readers see dense, black, edge-to-edge text with no helpful title or headings, they are prepared for a difficult reading job, one they are likely to approach with some frustration. However, if you have provided ample white space in the form of intersection spacing and ample margins, if readers find natural pause points in the form of section headings, and if graphics are clearly labeled, your paper will create a positive first impression.

Figures 8-1 and 8-2 present the same text; the only difference is in the manner in which the material is presented on the page. Notice

As Ernst Mayr (1982) points out in his major history of the discipline, The Growth of Biological Thought, six major theories have been put forward to explain the mechanism of evolution. One theory holds that living organisms have a built-in drive to increase their level of perfection; this theory was expressed in one form or another by Jean Baptiste Lamarck in the late 18th century, Robert Chambers in the mid-nineteenth and Teilhard de Chardin in our century. A second view that as organisms use various bodily features to cope with their environment and make less use of others, these organs develop or atrophy and these changes are passed along to descendents. This theory, often called "soft inheritance" is most closely associated with Lamarck.   Another view holds that organic change is directly induced by the environment and transmitted to succeeding generations. Yet another view is that evolution is a process of Saltation, the development of species in large, abrupt, changes. The theory of stochastic (random) differentiation (also called 'non-Darwinian' evolution) holds that the environment does not, either directly or through selection, shape the direction of variation and evolution.   Finally, there is the classic "Darwinian" view that direction is given to random variation by natural selection

These theories can be divided into three general categories: inheritance theories, gradualist theories, and stepped theories.

Inheritance theories (Mayr's theories 1,2 and 3) explain evolution in terms of changes effected in a parent which are passed genetically to succeeding generations.   This theory is most closely identified with the eighteenth century natural historian Jean Baptiste Lamarck who, in the Philosophie zoologique (Burkhardt, 1977), stated, as an organism uses a part of its body to meet the needs of its surroundings, it causes changes in that pert which are passed along, genetically, to its children (Eisley 1961).   In Lamarck's famous example, the giraffe which stretched its neck to reach leaves on branches above its head caused a gradual increase in its neck length and, finally, a generally longer and longer neck in the species.

This theory, popular into well into the present century, has been generally discredited by the discoveries of genetics. There is no denying that use or disuse of a bodily organ by an individual may no result in changes in that organ in that individual.   But all experimental evidence seems to demonstrate that changes in an organism's exterior form  cannot be transmitted to that individual's genes; the genes are set at birth and do not alter (Mayr 1982; Provine 1982; Gould 1983). As Steven Jay Gould (1983) points out

> . . . we have found nothing in the workings of Mendelism or in the biochemistry of DNA to encourage a belief that environments or acquired adaptations can direct sex cells to mutate in specific directions.  How could colder weather "tell" the chromosomes of a sperm or egg to produce mutations for longer hair? . . . . It would be nice.  It would be simple. . . . But it is not nature's way . . . .

Gradualism is the Darwinian view of the evolutionary process.  This explanation asserts that changes take place over very long periods of time, that new species arise from old as a result of a series of very small changes following one after another.  The changes occur as a result of random changes in the genetic makeup of individuals. Sometimes such change is a result of a mutation, a sudden, drastic change in the genes:

> Every lifeform on Earth has a different set of instructions, written out in essentially the same language.  The reason organisms are different is the difference in their nucleic instructions.  A mutation is a change in a nucleotide, copied in the next generation, which breeds true.  Since mutations are

**Figure 8-1.** *Poorly formatted page.*

how increased margins at top, bottom, and side and a change from single to double spacing make Figure 8-2 more visually attractive and easier to follow. If you knew you were going to be reading ten or more pages of text presented in either fashion, which would you prefer? Increasing the indentation of the inset quotation further separates it from the author's own words, making the nature of content easier to identify. Finally, by incorporating a section heading and an indented and enumerated list, the author has made it easier for the reader to locate specific items of information and to keep abreast of changes in the flow of ideas. All this through simple changes in formatting.

Fortunately, electronic text manipulation makes page layout and spacing a matter of utmost simplicity. Any word processor you are likely to encounter will allow you to set both right and left margins,

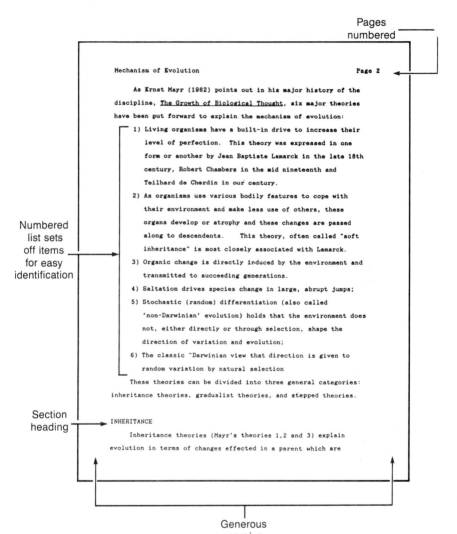

Pages
numbered

Numbered
list sets
off items
for easy
identification

Section
heading

Generous
margins

**Figure 8-2**. *Effective page formatting.*

single or double spacing, and additional presentation features such as boldface printing for titles and headers, with just a few keystrokes. Once you have examined the layout of your page, you can use the word processor to alter the shape of the entire document or just selected portions. Thus, it is a simple matter to create indented, single-spaced blocks for lengthy direct quotation and return to full-width, double-spaced text.

First, and most importantly, consult with your instructor for course requirements on page design. For example, many instructors insist on specific margins and line spacing.

If the choice is up to you, set the margins left at 7 or 8 and the right at 72. Since most printers produce eighty characters across the page (about ten per inch), this allows equal left and right margins of just under 1 inch. With 66 lines on a standard page, set top margin at 6 lines and bottom margin at 5, allowing a maximum of 55 text lines.

Generally, double-spaced text is preferred except in special circumstances such as tables. Set your word processor's line spacing to 2. By the way, your word processor will probably ask you at this time if you wish to right-justify your text. Many students are impressed by the sight of a straight right margin, believing it to look more professional. We strongly recommend against this choice. Current word processing and printer technology generally carries out right justification by adding spaces between words to fill out the line; the resulting gaps are distracting and disconcerting to a majority of readers and are best avoided.

## Titles

Although they are often overlooked or written in haste, titles can be important to your paper's success because they can tell the reader not only what the paper is about but in what direction the paper will move: a title helps the reader anticipate an attitude and a direction. For example, a business student might submit a paper with the title "An Economic Analysis of the Textile Industry." What does this title tell the reader? Will the paper be a review of wages, material costs, and growth of markets for cotton mills in the southern United States? Might it address the same issues for batik makers in Sri Lanka? Certainly it could withstand revision. With the improved title, "Apparel Imports Pose a Threat to the American Textile Industry," readers have a good idea of what to expect and will find the paper easier to read.

Titles, whether they appear at the top of the first page of text or on a separate title page, should be centered. If the title is on the first page of text, place two or three blank lines before and after the title to isolate it visually.

## Section Headings

Section headings serve three purposes. As papers become longer and more complex, as they attempt to communicate large amounts of specific and often quite complex detail, their readers become more and more subject to fatigue. The sheer mass of information requires some break. While proper paragraphing helps to meet this need, section headings are an important component in assisting the reader. In addition, section headings highlight changes in direction and emphasis in the paper, allowing readers to concentrate on the material they find most interesting and important. Finally, the conventions of certain disciplines require their use. For example, as we have discussed earlier, reports of research results in the physical and biological sciences fall into specific patterns with a background section followed by a summary of experimental procedures, report of results, analysis of results, and a conclusion. In almost every circumstance, these required sections should be clearly identified with headings.

Begin headings flush with the left margin, preceding them with twice the space you allow between lines; for instance, put four blank lines before a heading in double-spaced text. Print the headings in boldface type, if this is available on your printer. If your paper contains subheadings within a section, underline the main headings for added emphasis. If a heading will end a page without a line or two of the following text, stop the page before the heading and place it at the top of the next page.

## Appendixes

You may elect to place one or more appendixes at the end of your paper. An appendix contains supporting material not essential to the paper, material which may interest some readers but which any reader can ignore without damaging the ultimate success of your presentation.

If you have lengthy, complex tables filled with data which you discuss and interpret in the paper, ask yourself if every reader will need to examine the tables in detail. If your answer is "No," place those tables in an appendix to avoid interrupting the flow of the paper itself. If you have a large number of graphics scattered throughout your paper, you may wish to place them in an appendix so readers can locate them easily.

If you do elect to use appendixes, be sure that they are clearly identified and clearly referenced in the body of your text. For example, "Test results (Appendix A) revealed a strong correlation. . . ." Note that a paper can contain several appendixes to serve different purposes, each identified with a letter and a descriptive title. (See Figure 8-3.) Place appendixes after the "Works Cited"; precede them by a title page which identifies what follows as "Appendixes."

```
                        APPENDIX C
            Observed Melting Point of Water/Alcohol
              Mixtures at Increasing Pressures


                              % Alcohol in Mixture
           Pressure (cm./Hg)    5%   10%   25%   50%   95%
```

**Figure 8-3**. *Identifying an appendix.*

# GRAPHICS

As a writer, your primary goal is communication. While you may think that this means communication through the written word, there are many occasions when the effectiveness of your words can be significantly enhanced if you add nonverbal weapons to your communication arsenal. A graph displaying the rise and fall of imports and exports over the last century clarifies a discussion of protectionist economic policy. A table showing the lengths of the monthly installments of Dickens's novels reveals patterns in this large and complex body of information far more quickly and clearly than words in normal paragraph structure ever could.

Graphic aids should be part of your presentation whenever their use would enable you to make your point more concisely and effectively. When your subject involves numerical, relational, or visual concepts, consider the possibility for graphic support for your writing.

Keep in mind that graphic aids and the written word work in tandem. For the presentations we discuss in this book, graphics cannot replace the clearly written work; graphics do, however, serve as a useful adjunct by

1. *Condensing the text.* By assigning the presentation of data to a graphic, you can often avoid the dense and complex passages of prose which would be required to convey the same information as part of the text. Compare the following paragraph as a means of presenting the results of a survey to the visual aid, a table, in Figure 8-4.

   An in-home survey of adults in Louisville, Kentucky revealed public perception of the relative influence of twelve community groups. Television and radio stations were identified as having the greatest influence by 29.7 percent of those responding and as having the least influence by 1.7 percent. Daily newspapers were credited with the greatest influence by 20.8 percent and with the least influence by 3.6

percent. Utilities had greatest influence to 5.3 percent and least influence to 4.6 percent. Industries and manufacturers were identified as the greatest influence by 6.3 percent and as the least by 6.1 percent. Banking and financial institutions were seen as the greatest influence by 7.2 percent, with 8.3 percent seeing them as the least influential. While 9.4 percent saw churches and synagogues as the greatest influence, 11.0 percent saw these institutions as having the least influence. (The paragraph goes on to list the greatest and least influential statistics for an additional 6 community groups.)

2. *Emphasizing patterns.* Graphics are especially useful in stressing changes and patterns in those changes. A line graph displaying the grams of a salt which dissolve in water as the temperature rises shows the reader much more effectively that solubility increases with temperature than would the same relationship expressed in a textual recitation of the weight of salt dissolving at each temperature. A pie graph of the national budget stresses the large chunk that military spending takes out of each tax dollar.

3. *Clarifying relationships.* Presenting a clear impression of the spatial or organizational relationships between all but the simplest subjects is often difficult using text alone. The appearance of a complex mechanism, the relationships between various departments in an organization, and the flow of information through a computer program are all likely candidates for visual aids.

## General Considerations

The text of your paper and its graphics work together and support each other. The graphic reveals relationships that you wish the

---

TABLE I
**Perceived Influence of Community Groups**
**N = 430**

| Ranking | Group | % Greatest Nominations | % Least Nominations |
|---------|-------|------------------------|---------------------|
| 1 | Television/Radio | 29.7% | 1.7% |
| 2 | Daily Newspapers | 20.8 | 3.6 |
| 3 | Utilities | 5.3 | 4.6 |
| 4 | Industries/Manufacturers | 6.3 | 6.1 |
| 5 | Banking/Financial Institutions | 7.2 | 8.3 |
| 6 | Churches/Synagogues | 9.4 | 11.0 |

Source: Kim A. Smith, "Perceived Influence of Media On What Goes on in a Community," *Journalism Quarterly*, 61 (1984): 262)

**Figure 8-4.** *A formal table.*

audience to take note of, but it should not be expected to do this on its own. Don't depend on the reader to draw the conclusion you want from visual evidence alone. The relationship you want the reader to notice should be clearly discussed in the text, with specific reference to the relevant graphic support. However, don't repeat the entire data of the graphic in the text. Highpoints of the data may, of course, be singled out for special attention ("The interest rate rose throughout the year to reach a high of 18.6 percent in December" rather than "The interest rate began the year at 14.3 percent, rose to 14.8 percent in February. In March it reached. . . .")

**Integrating Graphics and Text** You should always keep in mind that any graphic is an aid to the communication of the ideas which are principally being developed through your words. Text and graphics must work together to make your point. Neither one should simply repeat the other nor should graphics seem simply to stand alone as extraneous material, unintegrated with the text. Students generally make one of two errors in the area of text-graphic integration.

1. Often, students make the mistake of creating a graphic, or photocopying one from a source, and then simply sticking it into their paper without any text reference to the graphic. Readers are left wondering why the graphic has been included, what point it is trying to make, or if it is really important to try to understand the relationship between words and graphics. At best this puzzlement disrupts the flow of ideas; at worst, it may lead the reader into mistaken assumptions. Always reference a graphic in the text, with some comment as to the reason readers should examine it and the message they should receive from that examination: "Figure 1 shows that increased life expectancy leads to increased medical costs. . . ." Under no circumstances assume that a relationship that you feel is obvious in a chart or table will be as obvious to the reader; always state such relationships clearly in your text reference to the graphic.

2. Equally unwise is the student's tendency to repeat, verbatim, the content of a graphic in words. If a table displays a series of temperatures over a period of time, don't repeat these same figures in your text. Such repetition makes the graphic superfluous and fails to recognize the graphic's power to condense information. Instead, as noted above, use the text to emphasize the relationships that the graphic displays.

**Labels and Titles** If your graphic is to be truly effective, your readers must be able to interpret it; thus, it must be clearly titled and labeled. A main title which indicates the basic content of the graphic must be prepared, as well as labels for each axis. Simply numbering an axis is not sufficient unless those numbers are self-explanatory: if the axis is divided into 1970, 1975, 1980, and so on, the label "Years" would be superfluous.

If possible, labels should be positioned so that they can be read without rotating the page. You may also wish to label specific data points on the graph itself; do so if such labeling will not create a confused and crowded graphic.

Another important element of labeling is the acknowledgment of sources. Even though you created your own graph or table, if the information was located in your reading, be certain to indicate this. See for examples of such crediting.

**Placing the Graphic in the Paper** Where, in relation to the text of your paper should you place the graphic? You have three choices:

1. *In the body of the text.* If the graphic is small and closely linked to the text, it may be inset directly into the text. If your presentation is relatively informal, a table presented in this manner will not need a title or number; other graphics should still include a title and figure number.

2. *On a separate page.* Larger, more complex graphics should be placed on a separate page following the passage in the text which first references them. Such text references can take the form of direct reference: "See Figure 5" or of parenthetical reference "The browsing habits of moose at several locations (Table 12) reveal. . . ." In any event, be certain that all but the most informal graphics are clearly referenced in the text.

3. *In an appendix.* In longer, more formal presentations containing several graphics, the visual aids will often be placed in an appendix. This placement is especially appropriate for complex tables since these are often included as supporting data that won't always be read with the paper but might be checked only by those readers with a special interest in the subject. As always, be certain to provide references to appendix material in your text and include the appendix in the table of contents.

In terms of location, there is one essential rule: always place the graphic *after* the text which first references, explains, or discusses that graphic. Since graphics are visually arresting, they are certain to attract reader attention. Imagine the consternation of readers who first encounter a graph or table without any idea of how it relates to their reading. Almost certainly they will interrupt their reading to search the text for reference to the graphic. To keep the flow of thought moving, simply be sure that no graphic will appear before the reader has an idea of what it is intended to convey.

**Selecting Size and Scales** Select size and scales. How large should your graphic be? The answer, while obvious, bears repeating: large enough to do the job. A graphic should be large enough to present the information you wish to convey clearly and effectively. It should not be so crowded that your reader will lose the important points in a maze of confused lines or figures. In preparing your graphic, go as large as you feel comfortable with; remember, you can always reduce the graphic through photocopying or insert the graphic as a foldout.

**The Danger of Novelty** One of the major dangers in integrating visuals in your presentation is the possibility of getting carried away with enhancements. Don't give in to the temptation to show off all the "bells and whistles" in your graphic bag. It is especially tempting to overpower the reader with graphic glitz if you are creating your graphics using a computer program which offers a variety of options, simply because it's so easy. If you give in to these temptations, you will focus attention on what Edward Tufte, in his book *The Visual Display of Quantitative Information* calls "chartjunk."

Showing off every possible type style, all the shading patterns, and three-dimensional enhancements of bar and pie graphs can only lead to confusing presentations which fail to communicate with the reader. When you compound this by adding more data elements than the reader can easily grasp from a single chart, you have assured a failure to communicate. Which of the two graphs shown in Figures 8-5 and 8-6 conveys the message most clearly?

**Conventions for Graphic Presentation** The discipline you are writing for will determine several elements of your presentation. While the humanities are usually quite liberal about the presentation of graphics material (probably because such presentation was infrequent in the past), the social and natural sciences are quite specific about the details of graphic presentation. The Council of Biology Editors *CBE Style Manual* includes fourteen pages of discussion of the proper use and form of graphic aids. The American Psychological Association's *Publication Manual* calls these displays "figures" and devotes eleven pages to the proper presentation of such material. (In contrast, the *MLA Handbook* devotes just over one page to graphic presentation.) We clearly do not have the space available to deal with all these

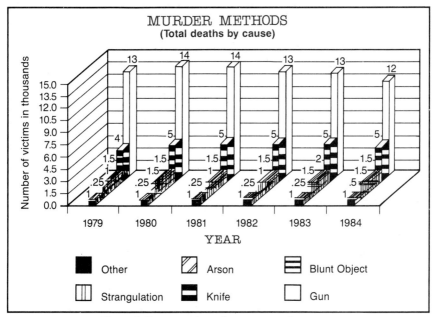

**Figure 8-5**. *A graph with too many features.*

conventions in detail, and in many respects they are quite similar. For further information, consult the appropriate style manual available in the reference room of your library.

   If you elect to create your graphic using a computerized charting package, it is possible that you will not be able to adhere to all the conventions of the discipline. For example, conventionally, the starting point of a pie chart is placed at 3 o'clock with the pie slices being added clockwise. Some packages do not allow such placements. If you were preparing your paper for publication, these restrictions would preclude use of certain computerized packages, but for most university work, the deviation from convention is almost certainly acceptable.

**Producing Graphics** Once you have determined that some form of graphic aid can assist you in conveying your message and have selected the most appropriate form, it is time to prepare your graphic presentation. Several choices await you. You must determine whether you must create your own visual or whether one from one of your research sources is suitable for your purposes. Frequently, you will decide that you need to prepare your own graphic in order to effectively focus the reader's attention on the specific information

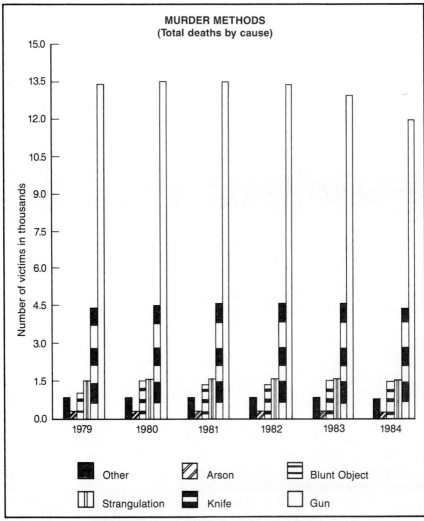

**Figure 8-6**. *Restrained use of graph features.*

your presentation requires. Once you have made this decision, several additional decisions remain.

Obviously, you can create your graphic using the standard tools of manual preparation: pencil and pen, ruler, compass, and paper. (For many projects the use of graph paper can make the task easier.) You need not have artistic talent to prepare acceptable graphics; careful work and attention to detail will see you through the job. For a more professional look, you can make use of transfer letters and shading patterns. (If you select this option, submit a photocopy of your graphic as the transfer letters are apt to be damaged by frequent handling of the paper.) Another option which may be available to you is computerized preparation.

If your graphic concerns numerical data which you wish to display in a bar, line, or pie graph, you can use any of a number of computer programs to create the graphic. Computerized graphics have the advantage of easy preparation: the program prompts you to make necessary decisions and then creates the graph and prints it out. Computerized graphics also suffer from certain drawbacks. Unless you use a specialized (and, generally, expensive) software package, your choices for graph type, label placement and style, number of shading patterns, and so on are limited. As already noted above, although these limitations often prevent strict adherence to some conventions found in various disciplines, graphs produced in this way are generally acceptable for student work.

More importantly, quality from the dot matrix printers usually available to students is often less than ideal. The quality issue can often be resolved by photocopying the computer graphic in reduced size. As laser printers—with their exceptional reproduction ability— become more accessible, this issue will, no doubt, cease to be a consideration.

For students the spreadsheet is the most effective means of producing graphics for their papers. It's relatively easy to produce basic graphics, and unlike manual preparation methods, the spreadsheet allows you to revise a graphic once you have viewed it. If you have used the spreadsheet as part of the analysis process (see Chapter 4), you will find that it offers additional benefits for the production of your paper's graphics. Most importantly, the data has already been entered. In fact, you may have begun the preparation of your graphics, at least in rough form, as part of the analysis process. All that remains to be done is simple refinement. Generally, this includes adding titles, legends, and labels; selecting shading and line patterns and type styles; and determining proper axis scales. To finalize these determinations, simply make the appropriate selections from the graphing package's menu.

**Graphics from Sources** If you don't have access to a computer graphing program and don't feel confident in your own drawing skills, you can often use photocopies of source graphics. Successfully duplicated, (i.e., sharp and with contrast properly set) source copies can often be inserted into your paper with good effect.

Remember, however, that a graphic used in a source may not be suitable for your purposes. A published photograph of a timber wolf (*Canis lupus*) in its natural habitat may contain confusing, irrelevant details such as shadows and underbrush if you attempt to use it to illustrate the animal's size and shape; it would, however, be an excellent choice if your point is related to the manner in which the animal fits into its natural surroundings. A table from a source may contain more information than your presentation requires, information that might distract the reader from the trends and relationships important to your point. In such cases you are well advised to construct your own graphic.

If a suitable photograph, graph, or table is found in one of your sources, be certain to credit that source when you make use of the graphic. Note how we have acknowledged the sources of the graphics used in the examples earlier in this chapter; in each case, the citation contains all necessary information for your readers to locate the original, in case they wish to examine the source further. For graphs and illustrations the citation is provided as part of the caption of the graphic. In the case of tables, source information is provided as a note keyed to the title of the table. If the original included source information, you should duplicate that as well.

## Tables

Tables are a systematic presentation of information, either numbers or words, in horizontal rows and vertical columns. In this arrangement items are grouped so that comparisons and relationships can be determined. Tables are especially useful when a large body of discrete items of information needs to be presented with greater precision than a graph would allow. Since tables often present a sizable body of specific facts, any relationships you wish to emphasize should be pointed out in the body of your text; be careful to reference the table which contains the specific items of information.

For example, the same article which contained the table displaying public perceptions of the influence of community organizations presented at the beginning of this chapter emphasized the important relationships with the following textual discussion:

> Table 1 below shows the ranking of the perceived influence of the twelve groups on community life. As hypothesized, television-radio and daily newspapers both ranked far above the other groups in terms of their perceived influence on the community. In fact, except for utilities and industries-manufacturers, the remaining eight groups were judged to be of least influence more often than they were considered of greatest influence. (Smith 262)

Tables can appear in your paper in one of two forms: formal or informal. If your table is brief and not too complex (two or three columns and no more than five or six rows) and you want your readers to treat it as part of the text, use an *informal* table. While such tables fit directly into the body of the paper, they retain the space-saving advantages of a table and focus the reader's attention on the information they provide. Because of their informality, such tables are not provided with a table number and are not enclosed in a frame; in fact, they best suit their purpose when they contain no internal ruling whatsoever. Remember, their purpose is to provide tabular information with as little interruption to the flow of the text as possible. The following paragraph from Jennifer's paper demonstrates how an informal table can contribute to the efficiency of expression.

> Another figure which shows how unusual resignation was comes from the number of nonofficers who resigned. As the figures below show, almost all Southern seamen stayed with the North.
>
> | | From the South | Number Resigning | Percent Resigning |
> |---|---|---|---|
> | Gunners | 11 | 2 | 18.18 |
> | Carpenters | 20 | 1 | 5.00 |
> | Sailmakers | 14 | 3 | 21.43 |
>
> This helps to explain why the Confederacy had such a continuing shortage of seamen.

There are times when an informal table just won't do the job: for example, it may not provide enough space to include all the data you wish to present, or the conventions of the discipline you are writing for may require the use of a formal table structure. Formal tables contain several standard parts:

1. *A table number.* This allows you to reference the table in the text and makes it easy for the reader to locate the table. Conventionally, the table number is placed at the top of the table, centered or left-justified (flush left). Tables are numbered consecutively throughout the paper.

2. *A title.* The title should briefly, but clearly, identify the purpose and content of the table. The title should be complete rather than cryptically telegraphic but should not repeat information to be found in the column and line headings.

3. *Column and line headings.* Headings should make the logic and plan of your table clear. Each column should be clearly labeled and can be subdivided using "stub" headings. Formal tables should include a descriptive label for the column containing the line labels. Column heads should be centered in the column and should be no more than four characters longer than the longest

data item in their column. To reduce the length of headings, you may use standard abbreviations for nontechnical terms (e.g., % for percent, "hr" for hour), but abbreviations for specialized terms should be explained in a note at the bottom of the table. You may divide rows and columns with lines, as in the table shown in Figure 8-7, or omit such divisions.

Since tables are simply rows of letters and numbers, they can be constructed manually, but—as anyone who has ever constructed a table using a typewriter can attest to—the task is a difficult one. Making certain that the columns line up properly, especially when they contain decimal numbers, takes time and great care. The word processor simplifies the task immensely, especially if it contains a decimal tabulator option which automatically aligns columns of numbers relative to the decimal point. The word processor is the only tool to consider for creating informal tables in the body of your text; its simplicity makes importing data from the spreadsheet more bother than it is worth.

To create a word processor table, all that is required is to set up the multiple tabs for each row and type away. Set the tab for each column at the position to be taken by the leftmost digit in the largest number to be entered. When you tab to a column, use the space bar to properly align the first digit of smaller numbers. An entire row can be moved or deleted, if necessary, without disrupting the rest of the table; on many word processors, moving or deleting a column is a more cumbersome job. One word of caution: remember, partial deletions of a line will affect all characters in that line to the right of the deletion, so insert spaces to realign your columns.

For more complex tables, consider using a spreadsheet as Jennifer

| TABLE NUMBER TITLE OF THE TABLE | | | | |
|---|---|---|---|---|
| (Optional) Label for Lines | Main Column Head | | Main Column Head | |
| | Stub Head | Stub Head | Stub Head | Stub Head |
| Line Heading (Subhead) (Subhead) (Subhead) | | | | |
| Line Heading (Subhead) (Subhead) | | | | |
| SOURCE: | | | | |

**Figure 8-7**. *Table format.*

did in creating her paper. It will automatically justify either right or left or center columns, allow different column widths, and save you the trouble of performing calculations. Unlike word processors, spreadsheets allow rearranging and deleting columns without disrupting the remainder of the table. When the spreadsheet table is completed to your satisfaction, it can be saved to a separate file in a form that can be read by your word processor and thus incorporated into your paper. Remember that even though spreadsheets are designed to work with numbers, they can handle text data for tables as well.

## Graphs

Graphs (also called *charts*) display relationships which can be expressed in terms of numerical quantities. The change in the volume of a solid as its temperature is decreased, the populations of several species in a sample environment, the occurrence of religious images in Wordsworth's poetry as the years passed—all these relationships can be effectively conveyed to your readers through graphs. Sophisticated graph users are aware of a wide range of graph types, including scatter graphs, area graphs, histograms, and Gnatt charts; most of these require a more sophisticated graphing package than most students will have available. Undergraduate research writers can add effective clarification to their presentations with an understanding of three basic graph forms, all of which can be generated by any spreadsheet program which includes graphing capability.

You should exercise both care and honesty in selecting the scales for line and bar graphs. The scale of a graph is determined by the starting and ending points of the values on each of its axes. Readers generally expect the scales in a graph to begin at zero and continue in logical, even increments to some value slightly higher than the largest value to be plotted. Deviations from this practice can lead to distorted impressions.

Consider the following enrollment statistics for new freshmen at Millard Filmore State University:

| Year | Number of Freshmen |
|------|--------------------|
| 1970 | 1675 |
| 1972 | 1678 |
| 1974 | 1695 |
| 1976 | 1700 |
| 1978 | 1704 |
| 1980 | 1710 |
| 1982 | 1700 |
| 1984 | 1654 |
| 1986 | 1503 |

The expected graph of this information would have a base value of 0, and a maximum *y*-axis value of 1800, with the axis divided into increments of 100. (See Figure 8-8.)

Note how this scale tends to minimize any fluctuations in freshman enrollment at MFSU. One could, however, present two quite different views using the same data. On one hand, beginning the scale near the minimum enrollment and suppressing the zero make it appear as if the period 1972–1982 were a time of significant growth (Figure 8-9); on the other hand, expanding the scale by using the total MFSU enrollment of 6,000 as the maximum *y*-axis value effectively hides the recent, rather substantial drop in freshman enrollments (Figure 8-10).

Both of the latter graphing techniques should be avoided. Your reader has a right to expect "truth in packaging"; just as you can lie with statistics, you can distort impressions with poorly scaled graphics. If your writing is clear and logical and your data accurate, you will not need to resort to such ploys.

**Line Graphs** Whenever you need to display a pattern of trends or

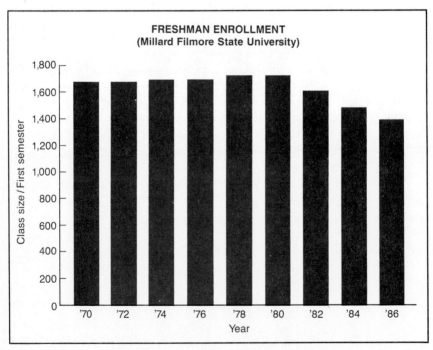

**Figure 8-8**. *Bar graph—standard scaling.*

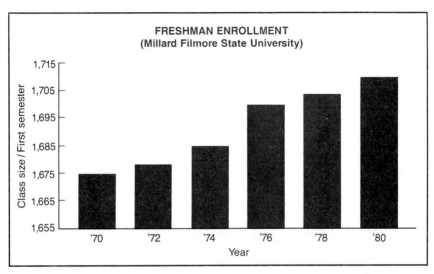

**Figure 8-9**. *Bar graph—suppressed zero.*

relationships involving a large number of comparisons, a line graph is the most appropriate choice since readers instinctively recognize the trends illustrated in a line graph. In addition, the use of color or different line construction (e.g., dotted, dashed, or mixed dotted-dashed construction lines) allow the display of multiple relationships. Be aware, however, that the line graph does not allow the reader to accurately identify precise data values; if this is important to your presentation, use another form of visual, such as the table, which presents precise data points.

The line graph deserves special attention because it is probably the most useful of our graph types for use as a means of analyzing data during the preparation of your paper. Just as readers respond quickly to the relationships displayed in line graph form, you can often profit from looking at your data in the same way. Additionally, line graphs are easily and quickly generated, making them even more valuable as an analysis tool. When using graphs for personal analysis, you are free to disregard the conventions of construction, but be sure to revise your graph to meet such standards before including it in your final presentation. (See Figure 8-11.)

When preparing a line graph for formal presentation, consider the following conventions:

1. Use line graphs when you have continuous data. In continuous data every value within a range is possible, and to move from one

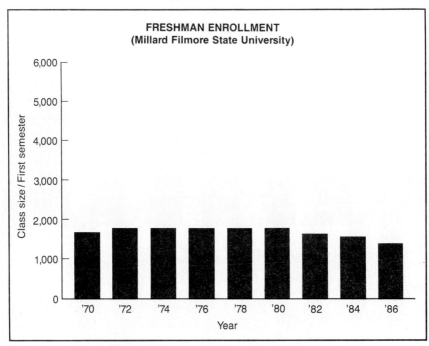

**Figure 8-10**. *Bar graph—expanded scale.*

value to another, you must pass through all the intermediate points. For example, in measuring temperature you know that if there is a rise from 50 degrees to 80 degrees, at some time you could have measured 70 degrees. Thus, your data collection may not have measured every possible point, since it is continuous, and the reader can estimate values between the measured and plotted points. Noncontinuous data is by nature composed of separate and distinct values, and moving from a higher value to a lower one does not mean that you must touch any intermediate point. For example, if we wished to graph the number of words in several plays by the same playwright, we could not assume that if the first play contained 5,000 words and the last play 7,500, then some play written in between these two extremes would have contained 6,000 words. For such noncontinuous data, a line graph is inappropriate since it implies that intermediate points have meaning.

2. Maximize the clarity of your line graphs by minimizing the number of lines on each graph, and be especially careful to avoid, when possible, graphing lines with multiple intersections.

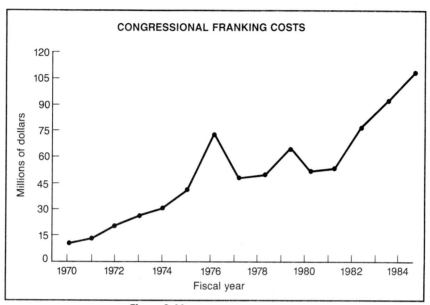

**Figure 8-11.** *Typical line graph.*

3. Make use of different line types (e.g., solid, dotted, dashed) and varying symbols for the plotted data points to avoid confusion between lines. Be certain to provide a legend or key to your use of such uses. Although your computer may allow the use of color to distinguish lines, remember that your printer very likely won't, so depend on other means to make such distinctions.

**Bar Graphs** Use a bar graph to display comparisons between a relatively small number of discrete data items. Bar graphs are especially effective in stressing relative quantities. Properly labeled bar graphs allow the reader to see the trends and the precise value of specific points in a graph. For example, annual totals over a span of years are effectively displayed in bar graph form. Using a multiple bar graph—that is, by combining several bars at each point in the bar graph by either stacking or grouping—several comparisons can be made at the same time. Be careful, however, not to group so much data in the same graph that the entire graphic becomes confusing.

Bar graphs most often are oriented with vertical bars. This places the *dependent variable* on the vertical, or y, axis. The dependent variable is the measured or counted quantity. For example, in a graph plotting maximum temperature against date, the temperature is the dependent variable. On some occasions, however, a horizontal

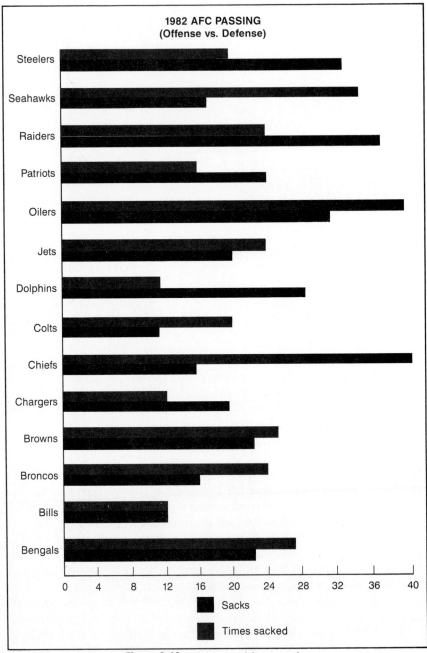

**Figure 8-12**. *Horizontal bar graph.*

orientation is best. For example, if the dependent variable is a distance, the reader will naturally identify a horizontal bar best. The sample (Figure 8-12) uses horizontal bars since it displays distance.

**Pie Graphs** The pie graph (sometimes called a *circle graph*) stresses the relative proportions of several items which combine to make a whole. You have probably seen this graph used to display how a budget is broken down—for example, with the relative portion of each tax dollar spent on defense, social welfare, agricultural support, and so on. It can just as effectively display relative importance of various food sources in the diet of the black bear, or the portion of a day spent in various activities; the only restriction is that the items graphed can logically be considered to combine to form a whole. Thus, the number of students receiving A's in biology, history, and English literature classes would not constitute a reasonable pie graph since (we hope) these do not combine to represent *all* the A's awarded on campus.

Effective pie graphs follow several conventions. In general, you should order the segments from large to small moving clockwise from 3 o'clock; an exception to this rule is that a "catch-all" segment (often labeled "Other") is usually the last item in the clockwise order. Remember to shade the segments to make each easy to identify; it is best to shade the segments from light to dark, with the smallest segment receiving the darkest shading. (See Figure 8-13.)

## ▤▤▤ ILLUSTRATIONS

In terms of everyday experience, the most familiar graphic presentations are those which depict the actual visual appearance of their subjects. Photographs and drawings show the viewer the appearance of things pretty much as we would see them in life. While such "literal" depictions of reality are obviously classified as illustrations, other, more diagrammatic presentations are also included in this category. The essential quality shared by the members of this group is that they all emulate to some degree the physical appearance and relationships inherent in their subjects.

### Photographs

Photographs are the most literal and "realistic" of all illustrations. They contain every detail that readers might be able to observe if they observed the subject in person. By specialized techniques such as x-ray photography, photomicroscopy, and infrared technology,

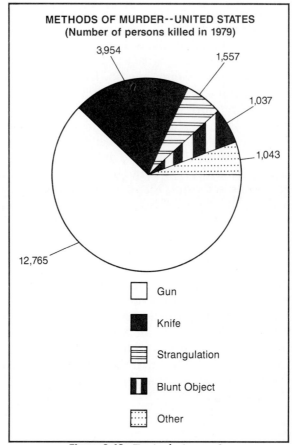

METHODS OF MURDER--UNITED STATES
(Number of persons killed in 1979)

3,954

1,557

1,037

1,043

12,765

☐ Gun

■ Knife

▤ Strangulation

▮ Blunt Object

▦ Other

**Figure 8-13**. *Typical pie graph.*

photographs can capture images not available to the human eye. In fact, high level of detail and literalism of a photograph may be so great that a more selective form of graphic aid may be appropriate.

If you feel that a photograph is suitable in your presentation, you may, of course, take your own. This is especially attractive if the photograph will represent an aspect of your own laboratory or field research. Preparing your own photographs has a distinct advantage: you have a high degree of control over the photograph; lighting, location, background can all be manipulated when you are the photographer. However, many of us have neither the skill nor the resources to prepare our own photography. If this is the case, a clearly duplicated and properly credited photograph from an outside source can be included to support your writing.

## Drawings

Drawings offer almost the same level of realism as photographs; they also allow you to stress aspects of your subject by eliminating irrelevant and distracting details and effects of lighting. For example, a line drawing of the tail assembly of an airplane designed to illustrate the location and design of the elevator, horizontal stabilizer, and rudder is almost certainly clearer than a photograph containing the distracting details of hundreds of rivets, identification markings, and the patterns of light and shade which would be part of a photograph.

Again, properly acknowledged drawings from published sources may be found to support your writing, but often a carefully prepared original which emphasizes the details important to your particular presentation is the best choice.

## Diagrams

Our final category of illustrations do not, at first glance, appear to be literal depictions of reality; they do, however, have the essential quality of displaying actual physical relationships. Just as a photograph or drawing of a laboratory setup shows the relative locations of the beakers, flasks, burners, and connecting tubing, the flowchart of a computer program shows the order in which the segments of the program operates. A map of the Western Front during the First World War, with its political boundaries and lines indicating the ebb and flow of battle, also represents diagrammatically a series of physical and chronological relationships. A genealogical chart such as Figure 8-14 can help the reader understand the often complex relationships between family members.

Many forms of diagrams, such as electronic circuit diagrams and engineering blueprints, depend on the reader's ability to interpret the stylized symbols conventionally used, but are, nevertheless, appropriate and effective when presented to a knowledgeable reader. Consider Figure 8-14. The reader must understand that the symbol "===" represents a marriage and the lines connect descendents with their ancestors.

## DOCUMENTATION

Before you can present your paper to your readers, you must document your sources and your use of those sources in your writing. Documentation consists of a listing of your sources, "Works Cited," at the end of the paper and, when the occasion demands, as noted above, reference to the specific sources of information in the body of

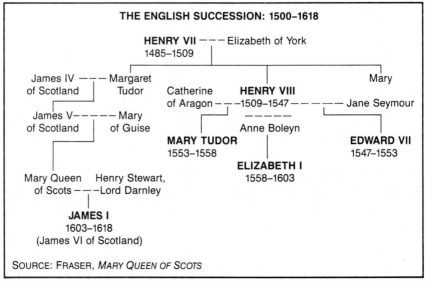

**THE ENGLISH SUCCESSION: 1500–1618**

HENRY VII – – – Elizabeth of York
1485–1509

James IV – – – Margaret
of Scotland   Tudor

Catherine    **HENRY VIII**
of Aragon – – –1509–1547– – – – – Jane Seymour

Mary

James V– – – – –Mary
of Scotland    of Guise

Anne Boleyn

**MARY TUDOR**
1553–1558

**EDWARD VII**
1547–1553

**ELIZABETH I**
1558–1603

Mary Queen    Henry Stewart,
of Scots – – –Lord Darnley

**JAMES I**
1603–1618
(James VI of Scotland)

SOURCE: FRASER, *MARY QUEEN OF SCOTS*

**Figure 8-14**. *Diagram showing genealogy.*

the text. Papers which make use of sources, either primary or secondary, need to provide documentation for a variety of reasons.

1. Documentation allows readers to examine your sources further. They may wish to learn more about the subject you have elected to cover in your paper, and documentation provides them with the information they need for additional reading. Using your documentation, readers can verify the accuracy of your use of sources to assure themselves that you have not quoted out of context or misinterpreted information. (You certainly made no such errors, but some readers may still want to check.)

2. Documentation displays the extent of your research. It reveals not only the breadth of your research but also the currency and scope of that research. It allows readers to know whether your sources are recent, whether they come from technical or general readership sources, and whether the writers you rely on are acknowledged experts.

3. Documentation gives credit to those whose ideas and information you have used in formulating your own presentation.

## When to Document

Another problem faced by writers of research papers is deciding when to document. Although the forms of documentation might differ widely, in order to avoid plagiarism you must document your use of another person's ideas or words. This includes all direct quotations, paraphrases, and summaries. All ideas that are not your own or that are not common knowledge must be acknowledged.

The form of documentation used depends on the academic discipline for which it is prepared. In most cases your instructors will stipulate the form to use; if in doubt, be sure to ask your instructor.

It is not our purpose in this book to provide comprehensive instructions for the forms of documentation in all the disciplines. Rather, we consider the logic that lies behind all documentation. Once you understand that logic, learning the details of the various forms is a relatively simple matter.

All documentation is based on the needs of the reader as outlined above. The principal uses of both the textual notes and the list of works cited require that readers be able to obtain the resource material. Thus, the documentation should provide basic publication information: author, title, publisher, date, and place of publication, for books; author, title, name of journal, and the specific issue in which the material is to be found for periodical resources. The need for the author's name and the titles of book, article, and periodical, as well as the periodical issue, are obvious; you made use of this information in carrying out your own research. The need for the publication date, publisher, or place of publication is less obvious. Nevertheless, this information is an important aid if the reader is to locate precisely the source you used. Remember that books may be published in several editions over a span of years, sometimes with different publishers for different editions; such changes may be accompanied by changes in content. It is important that you identify your sources as fully as possible. For example, Charles Dickens's *Oliver Twist* appeared in numerous versions during the nineteenth century; some versions included changes made by Dickens himself, some were authorized reprints which introduced relatively inconsequential errors, and others were pirated versions which often contained significant alterations. It may very well be important for your reader to distinguish which version you reference in your paper; without adequate documentation, such identification would be impossible.

The logic of documentation can be seen in *The American National Standard for Bibliographic References* (New York: American National Standards Institute, 1977). This important reference tool to disciplinary conventions classifies documentation elements into three classes:

*Essential data.* This information is required to provide unique identification of a work (e.g., author, title, volume number of periodical, year of publication). The most abbreviated documentation style contains only essential data, but this data is fully present.

*Recommended data.* This provides information to make identification of the specific work easier (e.g., issue number, page numbers). The interested reader could find an article given only the volume number and author's name, but providing some additional information, such as the page reference, eliminates the need to search the table of contents for the volume. Additionally, most interlibrary loan services require much of this recommended information before they can fill a request to obtain material from another library.

*Optional data.* This aids the reader by providing additional information. For example, many professional journal articles include the affiliation of author; optional documentation might include this information to allow readers to write directly to the author of the article. Student papers generally do not include such optional information unless specifically dictated by the instructor.

The "Works Cited" list provides the necessary information required to locate the source; the textual notes allow readers to locate the appropriate publication in the "Works Cited" list. Thus, far less information is required in the text references. Most commonly, text references contain the author's name (since the "Works Cited" list is usually arranged in alphabetical order by author's name) accompanied by adequate information to distinguish the specific reference from other works by the same author. For the humanities, this additional information consists of the title of the work in question; for the sciences, where the currency of information is of great interest to readers in the discipline, the distinguishing information is most frequently the year of publication.

The "Works Cited" list should be exactly that: an accounting of the works that are actually referenced in the body of the paper. Too often students seem to believe that a lengthy bibliography, one containing many titles that are not mentioned in the text, is impressive. Actually, quite the contrary is true for most readers; "padded" bibliographies often give the impression that their authors are attempting to gain more credit than they really deserve. If you have researched your topic thoroughly and supported your point adequately using relevant resources, a simple listing of works cited will do the job.

Finally, disciplinary conventions and concerns shape the text references. Since the humanities characteristically make use of relatively lengthy sources, readers are well served by a reference to the specific page on which the material is located. (Consider the difficulty in determining the accuracy of a quotation from *Oliver Twist* if all you are told is that it appeared somewhere in the 1833 edition.) In the sciences, where most referencing is to the current research as reported in journal articles a few pages in length, no page reference is necessary and the year of publication is, as noted above, of far greater interest. Keep these concepts in mind, and you will understand the fuller descriptions of documentation forms as detailed in the following resources, available in your school's library.

## Specific Forms of Documentation

*Note:* As we examine the three major forms of documentation, we will use the same sources to illustrate the differences between the forms. It is unlikely that the same material would be a useful reference in fields as different as those governed by the *MLA Handbook* and *The CBE Manual;* remember, these are examples only.

**MLA Style**   For the humanities and history, the most widely used form is that advocated by the Modern Language Association in the *MLA Handbook for Writers of Research Papers* (2nd ed. New York: Modern Language Association, 1984). References in the text include author and page within the source. The MLA recommends that in order to lend authority and improve readability and sentence structure, authors should remove authors' names from the parenthesis and cite them within the idea structure of the sentence whenever possible. Text references in MLA style take the following forms:

> Bates argues that Arizona Cranes are best approached when bathing (99).

> The most appropriate time to approach an Arizona Crane for close observation is during bathing activity (Bates 99).

Note the absence of a comma in the second example and the "p." abbreviation in both.

The "Works Cited" list in MLA form is relatively familiar and complete. It includes the author's full name (naturally in inverted order for alphabetizing) and conventional use of quotation marks and underlining for article, book, and periodical titles.

> Bates, Norman. "The Social Life of the Arizona Crane." *Journal of Avian Psychology* 12 (1960): 96–102.

Note the absence of punctuation following the journal title and of "pp." at the page reference; also notice that the year of publication is enclosed in parenthesis. If the monthly or bimonthly journal begins each issue with page 1, the form is changed slightly:

Baggins, Bilbo. "The Care and Feeding of the Great Bronze Dragon" *Mirkwood Monthly* May 1939: 12–20.

**APA Style** Commonly, research in the social sciences makes use of the form detailed in the American Psychological Association, *Publication Manual of the American Psychological Association.* (3rd ed. Washington: American Psychological Association, 1983). The focus of the text references is on currency; the reference provides the author's name and the year of publication. As in the MLA form, the author's name can appear either inside parenthesis or be merged into the structure of the sentence.

Bates (1960) argues that Arizona Cranes are best approached when bathing.

The most appropriate time to approach an Arizona Crane for close observation is during bathing activity (Bates 1960).

In the "Works Cited" list, APA form is more heavily abbreviated than the MLA form.

Bates, N. (1960). The social life of the Arizona crane. *Journal of Avian Psychology 12* (1960): 96–102.

Note that titles of periodical articles use uppercase only for the first word and proper nouns, but that journal titles are fully spelled out and retain normal capitalization and underlining. For magazines which begin each issue with page 1, APA includes the issue number. Magazine references but not those for professional journals add "pp."

Baggins, B. (1939). The care and feeding of the great bronze dragon. *Mirkwood Monthly 17(5):* pp. 12–20.

**CBE Style** The physical and biological sciences are the most widely variant in their documentation conventions. For biology and other life sciences, the basic documentation reference is found in the *CBE Style Manual: A Guide for Authors, Editors, and Publishers in the Biological Sciences* (5th ed. Bethesda: Council of Biology Editors, 1983). The physical sciences frequently use a form such as that found in the *American Chemical Society Style Guide and Handbook* (Washington: American Chemical Society, 1985). Generally speaking, the natural sciences demand the most condensed documentation forms of all.

Within the text, references take two forms: author-year similar to the APA, but without the intervening comma, and a number referring to a list of references found at the end of the article. Those references may be arranged alphabetically by author's name or in order of the first appearance in the body of the text.

Bates (9) argues that Arizona Cranes are best approached when bathing.

The "Works Cited" list contains very little capitalization and does not use underlining. Abbreviations are used whenever possible; journal titles are abbreviated according to a standard listing which you can find in any bibliography in the field.

> 9. Bates, N. 1960. The care and feeding of Arizona Cranes. J. Av. Psy. 12:96–102

Given these variations between scientific fields and the subtle differences in detail imposed by specializations within disciplinary areas, the best course is to check the requirements of the specific discipline with your instructor, and then turn to the appropriate style manual for the details and examples.

# ABSTRACTS

One last presentation element may remain. In many situations you will be asked for an abstract preceding your paper. Many professional journals, in all disciplines, require that papers submitted for publication consideration be accompanied by an abstract which will be included with the article, either in the table of contents or immediately preceding the article, at the time of publication. In preparation for this professional requirement, instructors in a range of disciplines, but most frequently in the natural and physical sciences, will require students to submit abstracts along with their papers. Thus, in both your academic and later professional career, you will be well served by the ability to write clear, concise abstracts in a minimum amount of time.

An abstract is a very brief (often limited to 100 words) condensation of the essence of a longer piece of writing. Even more than in the summary, in the abstract you must seek to make every word work efficiently to convey the content of the original. Unlike your summaries of research information, which serve in lieu of the full source, your abstract will come to the reader as a companion to the full work. Thus, your abstract should be written to help readers decide if the information they are seeking is likely to be found in the paper.

Some abstracts are written by persons other than the authors of the original work; such abstracts can be found in specialized reference works, such as *Historical Abstracts, Abstracts of English Studies,* and *Chemical Abstracts,* which cover articles relevant to a single discipline or specialized area of study within a discipline, e.g., *Pollution Control Abstracts.* You might turn to such professional journals in the field you are researching for additional models for your own abstract.

Abstracts can be classified as either descriptive or informative. While the two forms differ significantly, they share certain conventions: generally the first person should be avoided, and references to the work of other authors need not be documented in the abstract since such information will be found in the work itself.

The descriptive abstract, as its name implies, describes the content of the full-length material; it tells readers what type of information they will find but does not summarize the information itself. It helps its readers decide whether they should read the full-length presentation. Since the descriptive abstract need not convey the information or conclusions contained in the original, it can and should be quite condensed; in fact, greater length in the original will add little length to a descriptive abstract. There is little reason to write a descriptive abstract of more than 100 words. Remember also that the longer work is itself the subject of the descriptive abstract; in fact, the work being abstracted is the subject of most of, if not all, the sentences in a descriptive abstract. Frequently, descriptive abstracts adopt a "telegraphic style" to further condense length: the subject of sentences in the abstract is understood to be the larger work, and therefore all sentences begin with an active verb.

Consider the following abstract describing an article entitled "The Asymmetry of the Human Brain":

> Discusses the role of the two hemispheres of the human brain in hearing, vision, and hand movement. Tests of aural discrimination, visual perception, and depth perception are described. The specialized role of the right hemisphere is targeted for analysis.

This abstract contains forty words presented in the telegraphic style; it is important to recognize what these forty words tell us about the original article and what they do not tell us. We do not learn what the results of the tests were, but only that such tests were conducted and that results are presented. If we wish to learn what role the right hemisphere plays in perception, we need to read the full article.

Descriptive abstracts, especially those devoted to works in the physical and social sciences, are often quite heavily prescribed. They must contain bibliographic information as well as a description of the work:

> *The atmosphere.* A.P. Ingersoll. *Sci. Am.* (USA). vol. 249, no. 3, p. 114–30 (Sept. 1983.) A summary is given of the present state of knowledge about the Earth's atmosphere. The heat balance and optical properties of the atmosphere are described. A large part of the article describes the large scale circulation of the atmosphere and the attempts by meteorologists to make computer models of this circulation. Climate

modeling and weather forecasting are also considered. (no refs.)
[*Physics Abstracts*]

Informative abstracts convey the essence of the information of their original; this form of abstract is actually a heavily condensed summary. Your main goal in writing an informative abstract is to balance the need for detailed information with the goal of brevity. This can be especially tricky when abstracting your own work; we all feel the urge to tell "just this one more detail" as we recognize the role that detail plays in the totality of our writing. We caution you to resist that urge. Convey only key information in your abstract. Your readers want to know the results and conclusions of your article; if they are interested in the details of your methodology, they will consult the full-length article.

The following abstract appeared at the start of the article it covers. It is essentially informative; it gives the reader the results of the examination of snow goose productivity and offers a statement of the authors' explanation of the reason for the variation. In its final sentence, the abstract describes some of the article's content since a full summary of these additional materials would stretch the abstract beyond appropriate limits; the description informs readers that material of possible interest is available in the article.

Abstract: Two factors about annual productivity in the lesser snow goose (*Chen caerulescens caerulescens*) are considered. First, annual productivity in years of spring prairie drought was lower due to reduced clutch size and lower numbers of successful breeders. Second, a strong negative correlation was found between average date of egg laying and average clutch size. This suggests that when snow geese are forced to delay breeding because of late arctic snow melt, less nutrient is available for egg production. A general explanation in terms of annual variation in the stored nutrient status of females is presented and relevance to management is discussed.

Your abstract should be placed either on a separate page following the title page or at the top of the first text page; check with your instructor for the requirements in this matter. Abstracts are usually single-spaced and use margins reduced from the body of the paper at both the left and the right.

# FINAL PRESENTATION

All that remains now is putting your manuscript in the hands of its intended audience. Of course, for the college writer, that audience is usually a faculty member. Before presenting the results of a sustained period of carefully conducted research to your instructor, spend a few more moments on those final details of packaging which, although they are your last efforts, will create a first impression for good or ill with your audience. The final packaging of the paper should reflect the care which went into its construction.

It goes without saying that the final submitted draft of the paper should be mechanically produced. If you are using a word processor to prepare your paper, the printer output will take care of that concern, otherwise, you must prepare the manuscript on a type-writer. This does not mean, however, that you should not make manual corrections if you become aware of errors after you have produced the final copy. Neat and legible corrections of minor errors such as misspellings, faulty punctuation, and omitted words or brief phrases should be inserted in ink before you submit the paper. Remember that while the word processor should allow for the elimination of such mistakes, a few are bound to slip in, and therefore careful final proofreading and manual correction are necessary. When you submit a paper, you are, in effect, stating that you have examined your paper and stand behind its correctness in every detail. Thus, the excuse "it's only a typographical error" is pointless. All errors should be corrected.

If you have produced your paper on a printer connected to your word processor, it is likely that it will come out on fanfold paper with tractor-fed strips along both edges. Before submitting the paper, be sure to separate (in computer jargon, "burst") the individual pages and remove the strips along both sides. For a really polished presentation, one where you feel the slightly ragged appearance of perfo-rated edges is inappropriate, you may wish to feed single sheets of bond typewriter paper through the printer. This will usually require an adjustment of both the printer and the word processor's printing sequence, but it may be appropriate in some situations. Check with your instructor.

Once the paper has been produced, you should provide some means of keeping the entire document together with its pages in order. There are several ways to accomplish this: binders, paperclips, and staples come most easily to mind. Under no circumstances should you allow a set of loose pages to reach your reader. Even if you have included your name and the page number on every page using the word processor's heading capability (something you should do no matter how firmly you fasten the pages together), you must join the pages somehow. Imagine the frustration of a reader who has dropped a paper or stack of papers (such things do happen, you know) and has to separate and reorder the pages. It is true that instructors have different preferences concerning this aspect of submission. Some, like one of the authors of this book, absolutely hate binders with slip-on spines (they are always getting separated in one's briefcase); others prefer paperclips since they allow easy separation of pages; others want a staple placed in the upper left corner of the manuscript. Again, the best course is to check with your instructor for the class requirements in this area. One thing we can say is that you are unlikely to be told that an acceptable method of presentation is to fold over the upper left corner and make a small tear to hold the thing together. Don't you think that the time you spent preparing your work deserves more than this?

# EXERCISES

**1**. For each of the following situations, indicate which type of graphic aid would be most appropriate. In all cases, assume that any data you need in order to prepare your graphic, photographs, or drawings is available. Justify your choice of graphic.

   **a.** You have collected information, using a survey, on students' preferences for new degree requirements for your university. You asked each student surveyed to indicate which of four possible degree plans was best. After two weeks, during which time the student newspaper presented several articles debating the issue, you surveyed the same students again.

   **b.** You wish to show the effect of protective colorations on the survival of young animals of several species.

   **c.** You have data showing the total production of radioactive waste during each of the last ten years for each of the five major producers of nuclear electric power.

   **d.** You wish to show your audience what you believe to be is a relationship between the length of the hemlines of women's dresses and economic conditions over the last eighty years.

   **e.** You wish to display the development of the modern electronic computer from its earliest ancestors to the present day.

**2**. For each of the situations above, sketch (or describe in detail) the graphic you would use. Include titles and axis labels and scales where appropriate.

**3**. Prepare an abstract for each of the three sample papers contained in Appendix A. For Jonathan's paper, "A Chronological Survey of Critical Interpretations of Emily Dickinson's 'I Heard a Fly Buzz When I Died'," prepare a descriptive abstract in the telegraphic style. For Jennifer's "Officers in the Confederate Navy" and Kris's "The Mechanism of Evolution," write informative abstracts.

# ▓▓▓▓▓▓▓*PAPERS IN PROGRESS: PRESENTATION*

## Jonathan's Paper on an Emily Dickinson Poem

Since Jonathan was not using any graphics, he did not have to be concerned with choosing or placing tables or graphs. At this final step in the preparation of his paper, Jonathan's concerns were making sure that he was documenting his sources properly, determining an accurate title for his paper, and sizing his text.

Before he began to add the formal documentation, Jonathan asked his teacher what form he should use. His teacher told him to adhere to the 1984 *MLA Handbook for Writers of Research Papers.* Jonathan was used to using external documentation with numbers in the text that corresponded to endnotes. The *MLA Handbook* recommends using internal documentation, similar to the APA method. Jonathan found many differences between the method of documentation he had learned in high school and the method advocated in the *MLA Handbook.* For example, in addition to using internal documentation, the MLA recommends a "Works Cited" page, an alphabetical list of those works actually used in the text, rather than the standard "Bibliography" listing all the works consulted.

After he finished documenting his paper, Jonathan turned his attention to something he had been avoiding, the title. Jonathan had always had difficulty in writing effective titles. Most of the time he simply omitted the title from the paper. This time, his teacher told him he had to have one. After a friend suggested that Jonathan simply use a title that was an accurate description of his paper, Jonathan decided to title the paper "A Chronological Survey of Critical Interpretations of Emily Dickinson's 'I Heard a Fly Buzz When I Died'." It's not fancy or catchy, but at least his readers will have some idea of what the paper is about before they read it.

Jonathan's final concern was with sizing his text: what kind of paper to use, where to place margins, whether to double-space, and where to put the page numbers. It did not take him long to find the answers to these (and other similar) questions. Jonathan's teacher told him that most literature papers followed roughly the same mechanics for preparing manuscripts, and the mechanics were described in any comprehensive handbook. However, Jonathan's teacher had some additional suggestions for him: "Use good-quality bond paper, not erasable or onionskin paper, make sure to leave a 1-inch margin around each page [for the inevitable comments], and put your last name on each page just before the page number" (in case pages get misplaced).

## Jennifer's Paper on the Confederate Navy

Jennifer was concerned about clarity. Most of her paper relied on tables of figures. She was worried that these tables might be confusing for most people. Therefore, one of her steps was to modify the tables so that they contained only essential information. The first of her tables originally looked like this:

|  | Total | Total South | Resigned | Stayed | Resigned, % |
|---|---|---|---|---|---|
| Captains | 93 | 38 | 16 | 22 | 42.11 |
| Commanders | 127 | 64 | 34 | 30 | 53.13 |
| Lieutenants | 351 | 151 | 76 | 75 | 50.33 |
| Surgeons | 43 | 31 | 11 | 20 | 35.48 |
| Principal Assistant Surgeons | 43 | 21 | 10 | 11 | 47.62 |
| Assistant Surgeons | 36 | 18 | 7 | 11 | 38.89 |
| Paymasters | 64 | 27 | 10 | 17 | 37.04 |

She decided to remove the first column since it didn't refer directly to the number of officers choosing to resign. She also thought the two sets of figures on assistant surgeons could be combined. Finally, she decided not to use abbreviations in the column titles. This was the result:

|  | Number of Southerners | Number Who Resigned | Number Who Stayed | Percent Resigned |
|---|---|---|---|---|
| Captains | 38 | 16 | 22 | 42 |
| Commanders | 64 | 34 | 30 | 53 |
| Lieutenants | 151 | 76 | 75 | 50 |
| Surgeons | 31 | 11 | 20 | 35 |
| Assistant Surgeons | 39 | 17 | 22 | 44 |
| Assistant Paymasters | 27 | 10 | 17 | 37 |

Jennifer also took another look at the graph she was using to emphasize the differences in resignation rates for different ranks. She thought that a bar graph did a good job of making the distinctions clear, but she added labels at the top of each bar so that numerical information would also be available for those who wanted it.

She was tempted to adjust the scaling of the graph so that differences between ranks looked even more impressive. With each bar starting at zero, they all seemed relatively high on the graph. She thought if she used 30 as a base, the differences between the ranks would be even more obvious, with surgeons having a very short bar and commanders seeming gigantic by comparison. Ultimately, she thought that approach would be misleading, so she left the original scale.

Since her paper involved history, Jennifer used MLA-style documentation.

## *Kris's Paper on the Mechanism of Evolution*

Since her paper was essentially an analysis of the opinions of experts, containing little numerical evidence in support of its thesis, Kris did not feel that there was any way to appropriately use a graph or tables in her final presentation. Thus, the last stage in her preparation was to determine the proper format and documentation of the paper.

First, she turned to completing the documentation. She had collected her working bibliography in her database, so she moved through the entries, using the manual selection feature to create a list of those she had actually cited in the paper. After sorting by author's name, she wrote the list, complete with all the necessary publication information, to a word processing file and appended that file to her paper.

Because she had never used the CBE style before, she did need to use her word processor to change capitalization and underlining as well as moving some items, such as the date, within each entry. After completing this, she reviewed the paper to see that references in the text contained author and year of publication and that each was represented in the "Works Cited" list.

Her instructor had dictated margin widths and double spacing, so after making one final review of the draft for mechanical correctness, Kris set her word processor's print options to put a heading with her name and the page number at the top of each page, placed her title neatly centered on a title page with her name and class, and started the printer.

# Appendix A

## EXAMPLES OF STUDENT PAPERS

A CHRONOLOGICAL SURVEY OF CRITICAL INTERPRETATIONS OF EMILY
DICKINSON'S POEM ''I HEARD A FLY BUZZ WHEN I DIED''

    I heard a Fly buzz—when I died—
    The Stillness in the Room
    Was like the Stillness in the Air—
    Between the Heaves of Storm—

    The Eyes around—had wrung them dry—
    And Breaths were gathering firm
    For that last Onset—when the King
    Be witnessed—in the Room—

    I willed my Keepsakes—Signed away
    What portion of me be
    Assignable—and then it was
    There interposed a Fly—

    With Blue—uncertain stumbling Buzz—
    Between the light—and me—
    And then the Windows failed—and then
    I could not see to see—

Emily Dickinson's poem ''I Heard a Fly Buzz When I Died''
was written around 1862. Since then there have been many
different interpretations of the poem. This paper offers a
chronological survey of those interpretations that focus on
the significance of the fly in the poem.

Two early interpretations, both published in 1955, see
the fly as representing negative and disagreeable things in
life. Thomas Johnson, in An Interpretative Biography, says
that the fly is just one of those nasty things that are always around the house and that Dickinson used it ''to give

the touch of petty irritabilities that are concomitant with living—and indeed—with dying'' (214). Similarly, Gerhard Friedrich, in an article in The Explicator, says that the fly represents ''a distraction from a momentous issue.'' He states that when the dying person sees the fly, it prevents the dying person from seeing ''the light'' or spiritual awareness. Friedrich says that ''To the dying person the buzzing fly would thus become a timely, untimely reminder of man's final, cadaverous condition and putrefaction.''

A yearafter Friedrich's article, John Ciardi also wrote an article in The Explicator in which he disagreed with Friedrich. Ciardi claims that because Emily loved life and everything in it, even all the smallest creatures, she would have even loved the fly because the fly is representative of ''the last kiss of the world, the last buzz from life.''

Also in 1956, John Crowe Ransom published an article that appears to be somewhere between Friedrich and Ciardi. He says that the fly is neither a nasty thing nor a lovely thing. He sees the fly as not very significant. To Ransom, the fly is ''one of those homely inconsequences which may

be observed in fact to attend even upon desperate human occasions'' (90).

In 1961 Caroline Hogue wrote an article in The Explicator
in which she agreed with Friedrich's interpretation and
disagreed with Ciardi's interpretation. Hogue says that because we know that Dickinson was a practical housewife, she
would have hated a blowfly: ''It pollutes everything it
touches. Its eggs are maggots. It is as carrion as a
buzzard.'' Hogue goes on to say that ''just as she would
abhor the blowfly she would abhor the deathbed scene.''

The rest of the articles published in the 1960s also interpret the fly as a nasty, foul thing. In The Long Shadow:
Emily Dickinson's Tragic Poetry, Clark Griffith says that
because the fly feeds on carrion the introduction of the
fly in the poem at the moment of death means that there is
no afterlife, that ''stink and corruption are death's only
legacies'' (136). And James Connelly bases his interpretation on the fact that Dickinson knew Shakespeare. Connelly
says that Dickinson was familiar with Shakespeare, who uses
the superstition of a candle burning blue as an omen of
death. In the poem, it is only after the fly appears that

the speaker becomes aware of the color blue and the speaker dies. According to Connelly, ''Emily Dickinson was employing this same superstition to identify the fly, the corrupter of dead flesh, with Death itself.''

All the other interpretations of the fly published in the 1960s were equally pessimistic. Thomas Ford says that because flies are associated with carrion, ''The inescapable fact is that the dying one will soon be a corpse'' (114). Ronald Beck agrees with Friedrich and Hogue that the ''small, ugly, unpleasant, and, in the context, rather sinister'' fly represents putrefaction and decay. And Eugene Hollahan, who bases his interpretation on the fact that Dickinson was brought up in a Puritan tradition, says that the fly is ''an agent or emissary of Satan, the Satan Puritans would expect to be present at the death of an individual possibly or certainly damned to Hell.'' Hollahan supports his interpretation by saying that Dickinson believed, with other Puritans, that at the moment of death some sign would be given to the dying person. Because Beelzebub was the Lord of the Insects, the fly, therefore, is ''the sign of damnation.''

In 1979 Sharon Cameron offered one of the few hopeful interpretations of the poem. In Lyric Time: Dickinson and the Limits of Genre, Cameron says that the appearance of the fly allows the dying person to perceive the truth of death. She feels that the fly ''obliterates the speaker's false notions of death, for it is with his coming that she realizes that she is the witness and he the king, that the ceremony is a 'stumbling' one'' (114).

The only interpretation of the fly in the 1980s I could find was just as pessimistic as the earlier ones. In Dickinson: The Anxiety of Gender, Vivian Pollak agrees with most of the earlier critics that the fly is negative and disagreeable, but she seems to disagree with many of them when she says that the fly is not a messenger from another world. The fly, to her, ''represents nature in its most trivial, demeaning, and least glorious manifestation'' (196). She says that the fly represents ''banality,'' and that the ''incoherent'' death of the fly represents the equally incoherent life of the speaker.

In conclusion, it appears that although critics have presented many different interpretations of the meaning of the fly in Dickinson's ''I Heard a Fly Buzz When I Died,'' most of them see the fly as disagreeable, foul, and evil, and the poem itself as a very pessimistic statement of the human condition.

7

Works CitedWorks Cited

Beck, Ronald. '' Dickinson's 'I Heard a Fly Buzz When IBeck, Ronald. ''Dickinson's 'I Heard a Fly Buzz When I
   Died'.'' The Explicator December 1967: Item 31.

Cameron, Sharon. Lyric Time: Dickinson and the Limits of
   Genre. Baltimore: The Johns Hopkins University Press,
   1979.

Ciardi, John. ''Dickinson's 'I Heard a Fly Buzz When I
   Died'.'' The Explicator January 1956: Item 22.

Connelly, James T. ''Dickinson's 'I Heard a Fly Buzz When I
   Died'.'' The Explicator December 1966: Item 34.

Ford, Thomas W. Heaven Beguiles the Tired: Death in the Poetry of Emily Dickinson. University, Alabama: University of Alabama Press, 1966.

Friedrich, Gerhard. ''Dickinson's 'I Heard a Fly Buzz When
   I Died'.'' The Explicator April 1955: Item 35.

Griffith, Clark. The Long Shadow: Emily Dickinson's Tragic
   Poetry. Princeton, NJ: Princeton University Press,
   1964.

Hogue, Caroline. ''Dickinson's 'I Heard a Fly Buzz When I
   Died'.'' The Explicator November 1961: Item 26.

Hollahan, Eugene. ''Dickinson's 'I Heard a Fly Buzz When I

262

Died'.'' The Explicator September 1966: Item 6.

Johnson, Thomas. An Interpretative Biography. Cambridge,

MA: Harvard University Press, 1955.

Pollak, Vivian R. Dickinson: The Anxiety of Gender. Ithaca:

Cornell University Press, 1984.

Ransom, John Crowe. ''Emily Dickinson: A Poet Restored.''

Perspectives USA Spring 1956: 5–20.

OFFICERS OF THE CONFEDERATE NAVY

When the Civil War began, the South had to establish its own army and navy. One primary source was the officers and men of the U.S. Army and the U.S. Navy, especially those from Southern states. Already by March 4, 1861, 259 officers of the U.S. Navy had resigned or were dismissed from the service (Cochran 17). As each of the Southern states seceded, special efforts were made to induce those U.S. forces within the state to enter the forces of the Confederacy. One captured Colonel reported:

> Great exertions were made and the most flattering inducements were held out by agents of the Confederate States for them to resign and enter that service. These officers having resisted these temptations, to which so many others have yielded, is strong proof of their devotion to their country. (War of the Rebellion 553)

At one point even Jefferson Davis was involved in such efforts, appointing a particular officer to a post in Texas on the belief that this officer would be able to persuade members of the Second Cavalry to join the Confederate Army. Records of the time reveal that the effort didn't work, but the fact that the effort was made by people at that level shows how important such recruits were to the Confederacy.

Even while he made these efforts, Jefferson Davis knew

there were many difficulties in recruiting members of the regular U.S. forces. In 1861 one of his officers wrote to him explaining that the problem wasn't just one of loyalty. Also involved were the attitudes any professional soldier would feel for the very unprofessional army being created in the South. ''I am sure that our State service can afford no inducements, not only on account of a lack of permanency, but really the want of respect and antagonism they feel to militia, volunteers, and uneducated officers'' (War of the Rebellion).

Clearly, inducing members of the U.S. military to resign and join the Confederacy was no easy matter. The South's relative lack of success makes that very clear.

Despite the difficulties, a special effort was made to recruit members of the U.S. Navy, and already by April 17, 1861, the Governor of Virginia issued Ordinance No. 9, which included his wishes to

> immediately invite all efficient and worthy Virginians and residents of Virginia in the army and navy of the United States to retire therefrom, and enter the service of Virginia, assigning them to such rank as will not reverse the relative rank held by them in the United States service, and will at least be equivalent thereto. (Scharf 38)

He additionally established ''the pay, rations, and al-
lowances, which were to be the same in all respects as
those then in the U.S. Navy'' (Scharf 39).

This invitation seemed insufficient to draw many recruits
from the ranks of enlisted men. The Confederate Navy was
perenially short of seamen. Naval officers were sent to
military training camps to recruit sailors for the navy but
had very little luck. ''Recruiting for the navy was barely
sufficient to supply the deficiencies occasioned by deaths,
discharges, and desertions'' (Scharf 41). Even in 1864 the
total number of enlisted men in the Confederate Navy was
3,674 (Scharf).

But recruiting naval officers went much better. This
seemed to be one major area of success for the South. In
fact, at one point, the South had such a surplus of naval
officers that it put them to work manning shore batteries,
getting supplies, and refitting captured ships (Cochran).

While many Southern officers left the North for the
South, not all did, and the number who left the U.S. Navy
varied considerably by rank. Here is a breakdown by rank of
the officers who joined the southern Navy:

|  | Southern Officers | Number Who Resigned | Percent Resigned |
|---|---|---|---|
| Captains | 38 | 16 | 42 |
| Commanders | 64 | 34 | 53 |
| Lieutenants | 151 | 76 | 50 |
| Surgeons | 31 | 11 | 35 |
| Paymasters | 27 | 10 | 37 |
| Chaplains | 6 | 1 | 16 |
| Mathematicians | 7 | 1 | 14 |
| Masters | 16 | 6 | 37 |
| Midshipmen | 20 | 5 | 25 |

The percentage of Southern officers who resigned ranged between 14 and 53 percent. Only one chaplain and one mathematician from Southern states resigned, while over half the Southern commanders did so.

What would cause such a variation? Why wouldn't a similar percentage of officers leave? One explanation might be that resignation was a normal thing to do, and only unusual individuals such as mathematicians would remain with the North. But the vast majority of Southern midshipmen stayed on, as did most paymasters. Another figure which shows how unusual resignation was comes from the number of nonofficers who resigned. As the figures below show, almost all Southern seamen stayed with the North.

|  | Number | Resigned | Percent |
|---|---|---|---|
| Gunners | 11 | 2 | 18.18 |
| Carpenters | 20 | 1 | 5.00 |
| Sailmakers | 14 | 3 | 21.43 |

Only two out of eleven gunners, one out of twenty carpenters, and three out of fourteen Southern sailmakers resigned from the U.S. Navy to fight for the South. This helps to explain why the Confederacy had such a continuing shortage of seamen.

While recruiting naval officers seemed more successful than recruiting seamen, there were only two ranks where a slight majority resigned their commissions and joined the Confederate Navy: commanders and lieutenants. Why would these two ranks resign at a level substantially higher than any of the others? It is almost impossible to determine such reasons 100 years after the war, but there are two explanations that are worth examining.

The first possible explanation is money. The South, trying to build a navy from scratch, might have offered special inducements to senior officers. A report of Southern payments per rank shows specific earnings officers could expect.

|  | Stayed | Resigned, % |
|---|---|---|
| Captains | 5000 | 42.11 |
| Commander | 2825 | 53.13 |
| Lieutenants | 2550 | 50.33 |
| Surgeons | 2200 | 35.48 |

Yet we know that at least in Virginia, pay was initially identical to that of the U.S. Navy, besides which, the most attractive salaries were for captains, and the number of captains who resigned was less than that in the next two ranks. In addition, there is only a $300 difference between the salaries of surgeons and lieutenants, yet there is a major difference between their resignation rates. Money doesn't seem to be a major motivating factor.

What else would explain the high resignation rates among commanders and lieutenants? One possible explanation is found in a description of navy life just prior to the Civil War. According to that report, advancement through the ranks was impossible since the navy had adopted a strict seniority system for promotion. Here is one description of the effect of this approach:

> The excessive accumulation of older officers at the head of the list was felt as a heavy drag all the way down to the foot. Promotion was blocked, as there was no provision for retirement; and the commanders and lieutenants, many of whom were conspicuous for ability and energy, were stagnating in subordinate positions. The commanders at the list were between fifty-eight and sixty years of age—a time of life at which few men are useful for active service. The upper lieutenants were forty-eight or fifty—some indeed were past fifty—and very few were in command of vessels, as there were 200 officers above them. (Soley 5)

Clearly the navy just prior to the Civil War was a home for frustration. Men had no opportunity to advance their careers or develop to the extent of their potential. Given this situation, it might be possible that officers of a junior grade would be more likely to resign as they had little chance of promotion in the U.S. Navy and better chances in the Confederate Navy. In fact one of the pronouncements of the governor of Virginia guaranteed that if officers joined the Confederate Navy, their rank would ''at least be equivalent'' to the rank they had formerly held. As a result, they were guaranteed a chance to start a new career with all their current status and an improved chance for promotion.

Attempting to determine the causes for individual men's actions more than 100 years after the fact is, of course, very dangerous. Each man no doubt acted according to his own conscience after examining his individual situation, but it does seem at least possible that so many officers of specific ranks left the service of the North partly because they wanted to finally be free of a seniority system that had crippled their careers for decades. There were other reasons, of course, but for at least some men, the senior-

ity system may have been the extra reason to leave.

Such resignations were no doubt still very difficult. As

one cadet at the Naval Academy expressed it:

> Then followed the news of the firing on Fort Sumter. The
> rest of the lads from the South resigned as rapidly as
> they could get permission from home to do so—I among the
> rest. I passed over the side of the old Constitution and
> out of the United States Navy with a big lump in my throat
> which I vainly endeavored to swallow. (Morgan 33)

Hundreds of men and boys no doubt experienced the same

kind of lump in their throats. But they went back to the

South anyway, quite possibly as much because of the fail-

ings of the North as the inducements of the South.

## Works Cited

Cochran, Hamilton. *Blockade Runners of the Confederacy*. New

    York: Bobbs Merrill, 1958.

Morgan, James Morris. *Recollections of a Rebel Reefer*.

    Boston: Houghton Mifflin, 1917.

Scharf, Thomas. *History of the Confederate Navy*. 1887; rpt.

    Freeport, NY: Books for Libraries Press, 1969.

Soley, James Russell. *Campaign of the Civil War, Volume*

    *VII*. New York: Thomas Yoseloff, 1885.

*War of the Rebellion: A Compilation of the Official Records*

    *of the Union and Confederate Armies*. Washington, DC:

    U.S. Government Printing Office, 1880.

THE MECHANISM OF EVOLUTION

1986. Forces again seem to be marshaling for a renewal of the battle begun sixty years ago in Dayton, Tennessee. The object of the conflict: the role of evolution in American education. Most participants—parents, teachers, students, and advocates for various points of view—seem to have one thing in common. All <u>know</u> what the heart of the battle entails; each <u>knows</u> what ''evolution'' is. Their only quarrel would seem to be whether or not <u>the</u> theory of evolution should be taught in our public schools.

My first intention in composing this paper was to look at the various arguments advanced for and against the presentation of evolution. As I examined the evidence, I soon became aware that despite surface appearances, the ''theory of evolution'' is no homogeneous whole; rather, there are many theories of how species present on the earth today came to be and how earlier species, species that we are aware of only through the fossil record, came to become extinct. Before anyone can truly address the issue of teaching evolution, they must come to grips with what evolution is.

As Ernst Mayr (1982) points out in his major history of

the discipline, <u>The Growth of Biological Thought,</u> six major
theories have been put forward to explain the mechanism of
evolution:

> 1)Living organisms have a built-in drive to increase
> their level of perfection. This theory was expressed in
> one form or another by Jean Baptiste Lamarck in the late
> eighteenth century, Robert Chambers in the mid-
> nineteenth century, and Teilhard de Chardin in our
> century.
>
> 2)As organisms use various bodily features to cope with
> their environment and make less use of others, these
> organs develop or atrophy and these changes are passed
> along to descendants. This theory, often called ''soft
> inheritance,'' is most closely associated with Lamarck.
>
> 3)Organic change is directly induced by the environment
> and transmitted to succeeding generations.
>
> 4)Saltationism.
>
> 5)In random (stochastic) differentiation, environment
> does not (directly or through selection) shape the
> direction of variation and evolution (often called
> ''non-Darwinian'' evolution).
>
> 6)Direction is given to random variation by natural
> selection.

These theories can be divided into three general categories: inheritance theories, gradualist theories, and
stepped theories.

Inheritance

Inheritance theories (Mayr's theories 1, 2, and 3) explain evolution in terms of changes effected in a parent
which are passed genetically to succeeding generations.
This theory is most closely identified with the eighteenth-
century natural historian Jean-Baptiste Lamarck, who, in
the Philosophie zoologique (Burkhardt 1977), stated, as an
organism uses a part of its body to meet the needs of its
surroundings, it causes changes in that part which are
passed along, genetically, to its children (Eiseley 1961).
In Lamarck's famous example, the giraffe which stretched
its neck to reach leaves on branches above its head caused
a gradual increase in its neck length and, finally, a generally longer neck in the species.

This theory, popular well into the present century, has
been generally discredited by the discoveries of genetics.
There is no denying that use or disuse of a bodily organ by
an individual may result in changes in that organ in that
individual. But all experimental evidence seems to demonstrate that changes in an organism's exterior form cannot
be transmitted to that individual's genes; the genes are

set at birth and do not alter (Mayr 1982, Provine 1982,

Gould 1983). As Steven Jay Gould (1983) points out:

> we have found nothing in the workings of Mendelism or in the biochemistry of DNA to encourage a belief that environments or acquired adaptations can direct sex cells to mutate in specific directions. How could colder weather ''tell'' the chromosomes of a sperm or egg to produce mutations for longer hair?...It would be nice. It would be simple....But it is not nature's way....

## Gradualism

This is the Darwinian view of the evolutionary process. This explanation asserts that changes take place over very long periods of time, that new species arise from old as a result of a series of very small changes following one after another. The changes occur as a result of random changes in the genetic makeup of individuals. Sometimes such change is a result of a mutation, a sudden, drastic change in the genes:

> Every lifeform on earth has a different set of instructions, written out in essentially the same language. The reason organisms are different is the difference in their nucleic instructions. A mutation is a change in a nucleotide, copied in the next generation, which breeds true. Since mutations are random nucleotide changes, most of them are harmful or lethal, coding into existence non-functional enzymes. It is a long wait before a mutation makes an organism work better. And yet it is

that improbable event, a small beneficial mutation in a nucleotide a ten-millionth of a centimeter across, that makes evolution work. (Sagan 1984)

Changes also occur as a result of new genetic combinations created through the sexual process:

Sex seems to have been invented around two thousand million years ago. Before then new varieties of organisms could arise only from the accumulation of random mutations—the selection of changes, letter by letter, in the genetic instructions. Evolution must have been agonizingly slow. With the invention of sex, two organisms could exchange whole paragraphs, pages and books of their DNA code, producing new varieties ready for the sieve of selection. (Sagan 1984)

Such genetic changes become permanent only in so far as they allow the creature to fit into its environment as well or better than its predecessors (Provine 1982, Thuiller 1982, Wickramsinge 1982). Only changes which are superior will cause species change--Darwin's ''survival of the fittest.'' As might be expected, such ''fortunate changes'' are infrequent, accounting for the slowness of evolutionary change:

In strict neo-Darwinism, species track shifts in their environment through the selection of heritable adapta- tions: at its simplest, four-toed Eohippus became single-toed Equus through a series of equally adapted intermediates, each merging gradually, imperceptibly into the other. (Lewin 1985)

Stepped Theories

A final view is that evolution takes place as a result of inherited genetic changes brought about by mutation and sexual combinations but takes place in rapid, drastic changes. In other words, change does not occur in tiny, almost imperceptible steps, but in great leaps and bounds. This theory is prompted in large measure by gaps in the fossil record, the fact that for most large evolutionary changes, no intermediate species are to be found; if the process were truly gradual, ''we would find, despite the discontinuous nature of fossilization, mixture of ancestor and close descendents'': but we don't (Eldridge and Gould 1972). Those who subscribe to the stepped theory believe that species evolve as a result of abrupt genetic changes—but only when outside factors such as large-scale extinction or geographic isolation of the new species reduce competition and possibilities for breeding with a more numerous parent population. Eldridge and Gould (1972), the leading advocates of this view, suggest that new species come into being only when a small local population is isolated on the extreme edge of its parent species range.

Thus, new fossil species do not originate in the areas where their ancestors lived, and, naturally, we won't be able to trace evolution of species in the fossil record. Change of descendant species will follow the same pattern; thus full fossil record of Darwinian gradual change is not to be expected.

Conclusion

Which of the theories are we to accept as the most likely mechanism for evolution? As we have seen earlier, the Lamarckian theory of adaptive evolution appears to be refuted by everything we know of the hereditary process, so we must choose between Darwinian gradualism and the concept of abrupt steps. Logically, we must believe that the large steps which must occur for the latter theory to operate must be few and far between. To expect such leaps to be accompanied by the isolation required for the fixation of a new species is to expect a very unlikely series of events. It has also been pointed out by a series of computer simulations that the complexity of the step theory is not required to explain the development of current life forms

(Mednikov 1982, Chesser and Baker 1986).

Thus, applying Occam's razor, the explanation of the evolutionary process offered by the ''modern synthesis'' of Charles Darwin's views and modern genetics, the process of gradual change over vast periods of time, seems most satisfactory.

## 9

Works Cited

Burkhardt, R. W., Jr. The spirit of system: Lamarck and evolutionary theory. Cambridge, MA: Harvard University
Press; 1977.

Chesser, R. K.; Baker, R. J. On factors affecting the fixation of chromosonal rearrangements. Evolution
40:625–632; 1986.

Eiseley, L. Darwin's century. Garden City, NY: Doubleday &
Co.; 1958. Garden City, NY: Anchor Books; 1961.

Eldridge, N.; Gould, S. J. Punctuated equilibria: an alter-
native to phyletic gradualism. Schopf, T. J. M., ed.
Models in paleobiology. San Francisco: Freeman, Cooper
& Co. 1972: 82–115.

Gould, S. J. Hen's teeth and horses' toes. New York: Norton
& Co.; 1983.

Lewin, R. Pattern and process in life's history. Science
9:151–153; 1985.

Mayr, E. The growth of biological thought: diversity, evolution and inheritance. Cambridge, MA: The Belknap
Press of Harvard University Press; 1982.

Mednikov, B. Computer confirms Darwin was right. UNESCO

courrier 35(5):33–35; 1982.

Provine, W. B. Influence of Darwin's ideas on the study of
    evolution. Bioscience 32:501–506; 1982.

Sagan, C. The mystery of life. UNESCO courrier 37(9):31–35;
    1984.

Thuillier, P. The evolution of evolution. UNESCO courrier
    35(5):29–32; 1982.

Wickramsinge, C. An astronomer reflects: was Darwin wrong?
    UNESCO courrier 35(5):36–38; 1982.

# Appendix B

# MLA AND APA DOCUMENTATION FORMATS

As was noted in Chapter 8, documentation format varies. There are a number of documentation formats; the two most common ones are based on the style sheets published by the Modern Language Association (MLA) and the American Psychological Association (APA). You should ask your instructor which form you will be expected to follow.

## Modern Language Association (MLA)

### INTERNAL DOCUMENTATION

In the body of your paper you will want to acknowledge your sources for particular pieces of information and make reference to the exact pages from which your information came. The Modern Language Association accomplishes this type of documentation through the convention of parenthetical references. Their parenthetical references involve two sets of rules: contents of the references and punctuation of the references.

**Contents** You are expected to identify the source of your information and the page number or numbers which directly apply. In general, this will be the name of the author followed by a page number. Here is an example:

```
    One major problem with the navy was the seniority sys-

    tem. As a result, most of the captains ''had reached an

    age that unfitted them for active service afloat''

    (Soley 5).
```

The author was Soley, and the quotation came from page 5 of the source. The same form would be used if there were no direct quotation, but you wanted to acknowledge the source of your information. Here is an example:

```
One major problem with the navy was the seniority sys-

tem. It created a whole generation of aging captains who

were too old for active duty (Soley 5).
```

**Exceptions**  If you have already mentioned the author in the text, it is sufficient to just note the page number. Here is an example:

```
James Soley is among many historians who note the damag-

ing effects of the seniority system on the Navy (5).
```

Another exception occurs when you don't know the author of a work, as in a newspaper article. In this case, use an abbreviated version of the title.

```
The crash of the airliner followed a history of mainten-

ence failures (''Airliner Crashes'' 33).
```

Another exception comes if there is more than one author of a work. If there are two authors, cite both (Smith and Jones 123). If there are more than two authors, name the first and add "et al." to indicate that there are additional authors (Martin et al. 56).

**Punctuation**  In the preceding examples, note that the parenthetical reference is included before the period. It should also follow any quotation marks. There should be one space before the parenthesis and two spaces after the final period.

**Long Quotations**  If you are quoting something longer than four lines, indent the entire quotation an extra ten spaces on the left. Here is an example:

```
Soley's description of the effects of the seniority sys-

tem shows just how bad things had become.

          Promotion was blocked, as there was no provision
          for retirement; and the commanders and lieuten-
```

```
ants, many of whom were conspicuous for ability
and  energy,  were  stagnating  in  subordinate
positions.(5)
```

# THE BIBLIOGRAPHY

The purpose of the bibliography is to give complete publication information about each of the sources you used in creating your paper. In general, you will supply the author, the title, and then other publication information such as the name of the publisher and the date. Each of those three sections is separated by a period and two spaces. We will look at specific instances of bibliographic reference in a moment, but first study the required arrangement of references.

The Modern Language Association requires that references be placed on a separate page at the end of your paper, that the page begin with the heading "Works Cited," that all references be double-spaced, and that if a reference is longer than one line, all additional lines be indented five spaces. Here is a brief example:

```
                Works Cited

Cochran, Hamilton. Blockade Runners of the Confederacy.

   New York: Bobbs Merrill, 1958.

Morgan, James Morris. Recollections of a Rebel Reefer.

   Boston: Houghton Mifflin, 1917.

Scharf, J. Thomas. History of the Confederate States Navy.

   Freeport, NY: Books for Libraries Press, 1969.
```

Note that the references are listed in alphabetical order according to the author's last name. If the name of the author is unknown, the title of the work is used, placed in order according to the first word of the title other than an article ("a," "an," "the").

# BOOK CITATIONS

The general form for book citations is author (last name first), book title (underlined), place of publication (followed by a colon), publisher, and year of publication. In the following example note also that a period is used to separate each of the three major sections of the citation.

Morgan, James Morris. <u>Recollections of a Rebel Reefer</u>.

Boston: Houghton Mifflin, 1917.

The following examples illustrate some of the most frequently used forms for book citations.

**An Anthology**   Add "ed." after the name of the editor.

Richter, David H., ed. <u>Forms of the Novella</u>. New York:

Alfred Knopf, 1981.

**Multiple Authors**   Name the first three authors; use "et al." if there are more than three.

Young, Richard E., Alton L. Becker, and Kenneth L. Pike.

<u>Rhetoric: Discovery and Change</u>. New York: Harcourt,

Brace, Jovanovich, 1970.

Coburn, Peter, et al. <u>Practical Guide to Computers in Edu-</u>

<u>cation</u>. Reading, MA: Addison Wesley, 1982.

**Multiple Books by the Same Author**   Only spell out the name the first time. In subsequent citations substitute "———" for the name. Alphabetize entries by title.

Salinger, J. D. <u>Catcher in the Rye</u>. New York: Bantam

Books, 1951.

——— . <u>Nine Stories</u>. New York: Bantam Books, 1953.

**A Work in an Anthology**   Refer to the author and title of the work you are citing first, then give information about the book in which it can be found.

Murray, Donald M. ''Internal Revision: A Process of Dis-

covery.'' <u>Research on Composing: Points of Departure</u>.

Eds. Charles R. Cooper and Lee Odell. Urbana, IL: Na-

tional Council of Teachers of English, 1978.

# PERIODICAL CITATIONS

The standard form for journal article citations is the author (last name first), title (in quotation marks), title of the journal (underlined), volume number (no punctuation before or after the number), year of publication (in parentheses and followed by a colon), and the pages of the article.

> Daiute, Colette. ''The Computer and Stylus as Audience.''
>
> College Composition and Communication 34 (1983):
>
> 134–145.

If the periodical is published daily, weekly, or monthly, give the complete date instead of the volume number and year.

> Daiute, Colette. ''The Computer as Stylus and Audience.''
>
> Newsweek 19 Feb. 1984: 23–25.

# CITATION OF MATERIAL FROM A DATABASE OR OTHER INFORMATION SERVICE

In general, give the same bibliographic information you have given with other sources, but then add the name of the information service and any record numbers attached.

> Daiute, Colette. ''The Computer as Stylus and Audience.''
>
> Newsweek 19 Feb. 1984: 23–25. DIALOG file 234, item
>
> 3345234.
>
> Marcus, Stephen. Preliminary Report on the Effect of Com-
>
> puters on Writing Abilities. South Coast Writing
>
> Project, 1985. ERIC ED 391 456.

# American Pyschological Association (APA)

# INTERNAL DOCUMENTATION

The American Psychological Association also uses parenthetical references within the body of a text to acknowledge sources. The primary difference is that rather than give the author and page, APA prefers the author and year with a comma separating the two.

```
One major problem with the navy was the seniority sys-

tem. It created a whole generation of aging captains who

were too old for active duty (Soley, 1885).
```

## Exceptions

If you are including a direct quotation, give the page number of the source as well as the author and year.

```
One major problem with the navy was the seniority sys-

tem. As a result, most of the captains ''had reached an

age that unfitted them for active service afloat'' (Soley,

1885, p. 5).
```

Note that each part of the reference is separated by commas, and the page reference begins with "p." followed by a single space.

Another exception occurs if you have already mentioned the author in the text. It is then sufficient to just note the year of publication (and page if applicable). Here is an example:

```
James Soley is among many historians who note the damag-

ing effects of the seniority system on the Navy (1885).
```

An additional exception occurs when you don't know the author of a work, as in a newspaper article. In this case you use an abbreviated version of the title.

```
The crash of the airliner followed a history of mainten-

ence failures (''Airliner Crashes,'' 1979).
```

Multiple authors are another exception. If there are fewer than six authors, cite all of them the first time, and only the first author plus "et al." after that (Smith, Polaski, Brown, and Jones, 1984), (Smith et al., 1984). If there are more than five authors, name the first and add "et al." to indicate that there are additional authors (Martin et al., 1987).

## Punctuation

In the preceding examples, note that the parenthetical reference is included before the period. It should also follow any quotation marks. There should be one space before the parenthesis and two spaces after the final period.

## Long Quotations

If you are quoting something longer than four lines, indent the entire quotation an extra five spaces on the left. You will also place the parenthetical reference *after* the final punctuation. Your quotation will be double-spaced, and there will be no punctuation following the parenthetical reference. Here is an example:

```
Soley's description of the effects of the seniority sys-

tem shows just how bad things had become.


    The excessive accumulation of older officers at the

    head of the list was felt as a heavy drag all the

    way down to the foot. Promotion was blocked, as

    there was no provision for retirement; and the com-

    manders and lieutenants, many of whom were conspicu-

    ous for ability and energy, were stagnating in sub-

    ordinate positions. (1885, p. 5)
```

## ▬▬▬THE REFERENCE LIST

The purpose of the reference list is to give complete publication information about each source you used in creating your paper. In general, you will supply the author, the year of publication, the title, and then other publication information such as the name of the publisher. Each of those four sections is separated by a period and two spaces. We will look at specific instances of bibliographic reference in a moment, but first a look at the required arrangement of references.

The American Psychological Association requires that references be placed on a separate page at the end of your paper, that the page begin with the heading "References," that all references be double-spaced, and that if a reference is longer than one line, all additional lines be indented three spaces. Here is a brief example:

References

Cochran, H. (1958). Blockade runners of the confederacy.

   New York: Bobbs Merrill.

Morgan, J. M. (1917). Recollections of a rebel reefer.

   Boston: Houghton Mifflin.

Scharf, J. T. (1969). History of the confederate states

   navy. Freeport, NY: Books for Libraries Press.

Note that the references are listed in alphabetical order according to the author's last name. If the name of the author is unknown, the title of the work is used, placed in order according to the first word of the title other than an article ("a," "an," "the").

## Book Citations

The general form for book citations is author (last name first, followed by initials), year of publication (in parentheses), book title (underlined and lowercase other than first word), place of publication (followed by a colon), and publisher. In the following example, note also that a period is used to separate each of the four major sections of the citation.

Morgan, J. M. (1917). Recollections of a rebel reefer.

    Boston: Houghton Mifflin.

The following examples illustrate some of the most frequently used forms for book citations.

**An Anthology**  Add "Ed." in parentheses after the name of the editor.

Richter, D. H. (Ed.). (1981). Forms of the novella. New

   York: Alfred Knopf.

**Same Book by Multiple Authors**  Name all the authors.

Young, R. E., Becker, A. L., & Pike, K. L. (1970). Rheto-

   ric: Discovery and change. New York: Harcourt, Brace,

Jovanovich.

**A Work in an Anthology** Refer to the author and title of the work you are citing first, then give information about the book in which it can be found. In the following example, note that the editor's name is given with first initials before the last name, the word "In" is added before the name of the editors, and the actual page numbers of the article are included in parentheses.

```
Murray, D. M. (1978). Internal revision: A process of dis-

    covery. In C. R. Cooper & L. Odell (Eds.), Research

    on composing: Points of departure (pp. 85–104). Ur-

    bana, IL: National Council of Teachers of English.
```

## Periodical Citations

The standard form for journal articles is the author (last name first, initials following), year of publication (in parentheses), title (*no* quotation marks, and only the first word capitalized), title of the journal (underlined), volume number (underlined and followed by a comma), and the pages of the article.

```
Daiute, C. (1983). The computer and stylus as audience.

    College Composition and Communication, 34, 134–145.
```

If the periodical is published daily, weekly, or monthly, substitute the complete date and delete the volume number. Note that the date is given with the year followed by complete month and year, and now the page numbers are preceded by "pp.".

```
Daiute, C. (1984, February 19). The computer as stylus and

    audience. Newsweek, pp. 23–25.
```

## Citation of Material from a Database or Other Information Service

In general, give the same bibliographic information you have with other sources, but then add the name of the information service and any record numbers attached in parentheses.

Daiute, C. (1984, February 19). The computer as stylus and audience. Newsweek, pp. 23–25. (DIALOG file 234, item 3345234).

Marcus, S. (1985). Preliminary report on the effect of computers on writing abilities. South Coast Writing Project. (ERIC Document Reproduction Service No. ED 391 456).

# Appendix C

# GLOSSARY OF
# COMPUTER WRITING TERMS

**Block move**. The process of taking a section of text and moving it to another location.

**Boolean logic**. Logic named for mathematician George Boole. Two of its functions, AND and OR gates, are used to select database records for retrieval.

**Buffer**. A place in the computer's memory where information can be held temporarily during such actions as block move and delete.

**Byte**. A unit of measurement for memory. Generally enough memory to hold a single character.

**Catalog**. A listing of the contents of a disk.

**CPU: Central Processing Unit**. The part of the computer that performs all calculations.

**Daisy Wheel**. A printer which generates characters from a spinning head, or daisy wheel. Generally considered "letter-quality."

**Database**. A program which collects, orders, and retrieves textual information. May be either .mdul/personal.mdnm/ (small user-created database) or .mdul/online.mdnm/ (large commercial database holding millions of records).

**Directory**. A listing of the contents of a disk.

**Disk Drive**. A device for storing computer information in a magnetic medium. Used to permanently hold the contents of a computer.

**Dot matrix**. A printer which generates characters from a set of pins. Useful for generating graphics. Inexpensive and fast. Generally considered "draft-quality" because the characters are often slightly blurred.

**Editor**. A computer program that allows manipulation of text. Often allows manipulation of only a single line at a time. Increasingly similar to word processors.

**Electronic mail**. A system of creating and retrieving pieces of text stored in public files. Requires the interconnection of computers to some common storage facility.

**Field**. A category of information held in a database, such as book names or author's names.

**File**. A related collection of information stored on a disk.

**Floppy disk**. A medium for storing computer information. Usually 5¼-inch. Newer disks are 3½-inch. Information is stored in the magnetic surface of the disk.

**Format**. (1) A program which prepares new disks to hold information; (2) word processing features which allow for the adjustment of text margins and spacing.

**Function keys**. Special-purpose keys that can be programmed to carry out a unique purpose, such as printing text or deleting blocks of text.

**Hard disk**. A disk capable of storing much more information than less expensive floppy disks. Generally hold 10 to 200 million characters of information.

**K**. The abbreviation for kilo, or 1,000. Used primarily as a unit of measurement for computer memory. The expression "256K RAM" means that a computer can hold 256,000 characters in its memory.

**Laser printer**. A form of printer that uses a laser to create an image. Is equally adept at text and graphics. Quality is generally high. Often very fast, but still relatively expensive.

**Load**. The process of transferring information from a disk to the computer's internal memory (RAM).

**Memory**. Structure built into a computer to store information typed in from the keyboard or loaded in from a disk. Ranges considerably in size, from 64K in home computers, to 512K in microcomputers for business, to millions of bytes in commercial computer installations.

**Menu**. Selections available for use with a particular computer program. Word processors often have a menu for activities such as inserting, deleting, and moving text.

**Modem**. A device for changing the signals of a computer so that they can be sent through telephone lines to remote computers. They make it possible for one computer to "speak" to another.

**Monitor**. The screen which displays the output of a computer. Vary widely in the ability to display color and in degree of resolution.

**Network**. The physical and program linkages between computers. Allow computers in close proximity to each other to share information or devices such as printers.

**Online**. To connect a computer to another computer through wires or phone lines.

**Program**. A set of instructions to a computer.

**RAM**. Random-access memory. The internal memory of the computer.

**Record**. A set of information held in a database about a specific individual, book, article.

**Save**. The process of preserving information in a computer by sending it to some form of secondary memory where it can be stored with more stability.

**Search and replace**. The ability of a word processing program to find specific words or phrases in text and replace them with another set of words or phrases. Abbreviated SAR.

**Secondary memory**. Disk or tape drives which use magnetic processes to hold computer information over long periods of time.

**Software**. Computer programs.

**Spelling checker**. A program which matches words in text against words in its own "dictionary." Any word not found is marked as "suspect." Some can suggest corrections.

**Spreadsheet**. A computer program designed to hold information in rows and columns similar to an accountant's ledger. Generally used for numeric calculations.

**Style analyzer**. A program which checks text for certain words or phrases. May also perform counts of different word types.

**Text editor**. An early version of modern word processor programs.

**Window**. A section of a computer screen.

**Word processor**. A computer program that allows easy manipulation and formatting of text. Standard features include the ability to insert, delete, move blocks, do search and replace, format, store, and print.

**Word-wrap**. The ability of a word processor to automatically carry over any part of a word that might be split between lines.

# WORKS CITED

*American Chemical Society Style Guide and Handbook.* Washington: American Chemical Society, 1985.

*American National Standards for Bibliographic Reference.* New York: American National Standards Institute, 1977.

BENBOW, CAMILLA PERSSON, and JULIAN C. STANLEY. "Sex Differences in Mathematical Ability: Fact or Artifact?" *Science.* 210 (1980): 1262–1264.

BRADDOCK, RICHARD. "The Frequency and Placement of Topic Sentences in Expository Prose." *Research in the Teaching of English* 8 (1974): 287–302.

BRIDWELL, LILLIAN, and DONALD ROSS. "Integrating Computers into a Writing Curriculum." *The Computer in Composition Instruction: A Writer's Tool.* Ed. William Wresch. Urbana: National Council of Teachers of English, 1984.

BURNS, HUGH. "Recollections of First-Generation Computer-Assisted Prewriting." *The Computer in Composition Instruction: A Writer's Tool.* Ed. William Wresch. Urbana: National Council of Teachers of English, 1984.

CALLICOTT, J. BAIRD. "Aldo Leopold's Land Aesthetic and Agrarian Land Use Values." Unpublished paper, 1982.

———. "Leopold's Land Aesthetic." *Journal of Soil and Water Conservation* 38 (1983): 329–332.

CARSON, RACHEL. *Silent Spring.* New York: Crest, 1962.

*CBE Style Manual.* Bethesda: Council of Biology Editors, 1983.

CORDER, JIM W. *Handbook of Current English.* 5th ed. Glenview: Scott Foresman, 1978.

D'ANGELO, FRANK. *A Conceptual Theory of Rhetoric.* Cambridge: Winthrop Publishers.

ELBOW, PETER. *Writing with Power.* New York: Oxford UP, 1981.

EMIG, JANET. "Writing as a Mode of Learning." *College Composition and Communication* 28 (1977): 122.

FRASER, ANTONIA. *Mary Queen of Scots.* New York: Delacorte Press, 1969.

GIBALDI, JOSEPH, and WALTER S. ACHTERT. *MLA Handbook for Writers of Research Papers.* 2nd ed. New York: MLA, 1984.

GISH, DUANE T., and RICHARD B. BLISS. "Summary of Scientific Evidence for Creation." *Impact* 95-96 (1981): i–viii.

HODGES, JOHN C., and MARY E. WHITTEN. *Harbrace College Handbook.* 9th ed. San Diego: Harcourt Brace Jovanovich, 1984.

"Improvement Needed in Writing (Righting? Riting?)." Editorial. *Stevens Point [Wisconsin] Journal* 8 Dec. 1986: 4.

KINNEAVY, JAMES L. *A Theory of Discourse.* Englewood Cliffs: Prentice-Hall, 1971.

MINSKY, MARVIN. *The Society of Mind.* New York: Simon & Schuster, 1986.

MIQUELLE, DALE G. "Browse Regrowth and Consumption Following Summer Defoliation by Moose." *Journal of Wildlife Management* 47 (1983): 17–24.

MURPHY, MARY E., and JAMES R. KING. "Dietary Sulfur Amino Acid Availability and Molt Dynamics in White-crowned Sparrows." *Auk* 101 (1984): 164–167.

MURRAY, DONALD M. "Internal Revision: A Process of Discovery." *Research on Composing: Points of Departure.* Ed. Charles R. Cooper and Lee Odell. Urbana: National Council of Teachers of English, 1978.

NAISBITT, JOHN. *Megatrends.* New York: Warner Books, 1982.

NELSON, RALPH A., THOMAS D. I. BECK, and DIANNE L. STEIGER. "Ratio of Serum Urea to Serum Creatinine in Wild Black Bears." *Science* 226 (1984): 841–842.

OLSON, DAVID R. "Culture, Technology, and Intellect." *The Nature of Intelligence.* Ed. Lauren Resnick. Hillsdale: Lawrence Earlbaum Associates, 1976.

*Publication Manual of the American Psychological Association.* 3rd ed. Washington: American Psychological Association, 1983.

REISS, ALBERT J., JR. "Crime Control and the Quality of Life." *American Behavioral Scientist* 27 (Sept./Oct. 1983): 43–58.

RODRIGUES, DAWN, and RAYMOND RODRIGUES. "Computer-Based Creative Problem Solving." *The Computer in Composition Instruction: A Writer's Tool.* Ed. William Wresch. Urbana: National Council of Teachers of English, 1984.

SANDERS, NORRIS M. *Classroom Questions: What Kinds?* New York: Harper & Row, 1966.

SCHNEPF, MAX. Letter to J. Baird Callicott. 1 Apr. 1983.

SMITH, KIM A. "Perceived Influence of Media on What Goes on in a Community." *Journalism Quarterly* 61 (1984): 260–264.

TEMPLE, STANLEY A. "Plant-Animal Mutualism: Coevolution with Dodo Leads to Near Extinction of Plant." *Science* 197 (1977): 885–886.

TUFTE, EDWARD. *The Visual Display of Quantitative Information.* Cheshire: Graphics Press, 1983.

United States Department of Education. The National Commission on Excellence. *A Nation At Risk: The Imperative for Educational Reform.* S. Doc. ED 1.2:N21. Washington: GPO, 1983.

WILLIAMS, DENNIS A., and PATRICIA KING. "Do Males Have a Math Gene?" *Newsweek* 15 Dec. 1980: 73.

# INDEX